MORE BOOKS FROM THE SAGER GROUP

The Swamp: Deceit and Corruption in the CIA
An Elizabeth Petrov Thriller (Book 1)
by Jeff Grant

Chains of Nobility: Brotherhood of the Mamluks (Book 1)
by Brad Graft

Meeting Mozart: A Novel Drawn from the Secret Diaries of Lorenzo Da Ponte
by Howard Jay Smith

Labyrinth of the Wind: A Novel of Love and Nuclear Secrets in Tehran
by Madhav Misra

A Boy and His Dog in Hell: And Other Stories
by Mike Sager

Miss Havilland: A Novel
by Gay Daly

The Orphan's Daughter: A Novel
by Jan Cherubin

Lifeboat No. 8: Surviving the Titanic
by Elizabeth Kaye

Shaman: The Mysterious Life and Impeccable Death of Carlos Castaneda
by Mike Sager

See our entire library at TheSagerGroup.net

A DIARY OF THE DISILLUSIONED
BIG NOISE
FROM
LAPORTE

BY **HOLLY SCHROEDER LINK**

Cover and Interior Designed by Siori Kitajima, SF AppWorks LLC

Cataloging-in-Publication data for this book is available from the Library of Congress
ISBN-13:
eBook: 978-1-950154-76-0
Paperback: 978-1-950154-77-7

Published by The Sager Group LLC
TheSagerGroup.net

A DIARY OF THE DISILLUSIONED

BIG NOISE
— FROM —
LAPORTE

BY HOLLY SCHROEDER LINK

THE SAGER GROUP

Artifex Te Adiuva

This book is dedicated to my brother Danny, my dear friend Paige Claire, and my hero Jeanne Louise Fowerbaugh Chandler.

CONTENTS

AUTHOR'S NOTE

Without my parents Robert and Mae Schroeder, I wouldn't have half the good material I do. They may not have always understood me, but we loved each other and that is worth everything. If you find yourself in these pages, thank you for being part of my journey to awareness. I put this book out into the world in the hopes it would comfort those suffering from loss, depression, dysfunction and bad luck. In the words of Ram Dass, "We're all just walking each other home."

December 10, 1975

Dear Diary,

I can't possibly belong to these people. When are my real parents coming for me? Tonight, at the dinner table, I tried to tell a story about my teacher Mr. Gangwer, and Mom sent me to my room for talking too much. No freedom of speech in this house. So, I wrote a suicide note, folded it into a paper airplane and flew it into the kitchen.

Dear Family,

By the time you read this, I will be gone. Please don't put my first name of Karen on my tombstone. It never suited me.

Goodbye.
Holly Schroeder

"Keepers of private notebooks are a different breed altogether, lonely and resistant rearrangers of things, anxious malcontents, children afflicted apparently at birth with some presentment of loss."
—Joan Didion

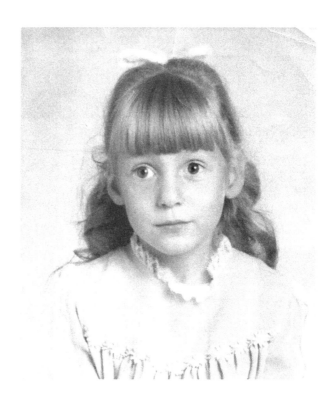

MY MOTHER'S KEEPER

The only thing that separated my mother from her Hoover was childbirth. Vacuuming our modest red-brick house on Country Club Drive in LaPorte, Indiana, is exactly what she was doing when her water broke.

"Dr. Feine, the baby's coming. I'll see you at the hospital." Two hours later, at 10:17 p.m., on New Years Day, 1966, I made my entrance, just in time for Johnny Carson. I won a rattle and a one-year supply of Pampers.

If you were to ask my mother about my birth, she'd tell you with total sincerity, "I didn't have to have any anesthetic," and my father would say, "We missed the tax deduction."

Above all, my parents were pragmatic. They were old-school: Children should respect their elders, do their chores, and be "seen and not heard."

Well, that didn't work for me. I had a lot to say. Expressing myself on paper, at school, at the kitchen table, was as natural as breathing. Held hostage by my inner muse, I had a burning light

inside of me, and I wanted to shine it in everyone's face. I was the oddball. My sister Susan and brother Danny, only two years apart, were like twins, and I was the black sheep who didn't fit.

My mother, unable to show vulnerability, skirted feelings, while I felt too much. I was dramatic, outspoken, and prone to ennui. My mother was often *insensitive*, while I was *over*-sensitive. Like most performers, I wanted everyone to like me, a recipe for disaster. I set myself up for a lifetime of hurt.

As the baby of the family, I was fated to be my mother's keeper. It was as if an unspoken contract existed and we were in cahoots, partners in crime attached at the hip, running errands to the bank, jewelers, church bazaars, Barbara Link's Boutique, Woolworths, and Juanita's Beauty Shop. I loved her more than anyone on the planet, and her approval meant everything to me.

My father taught my mother to drive so that she used both feet and worked the pedals of our yellow and brown Plymouth Reliant station wagon. We didn't bother with seat belts, so I went flying across the front seat a lot, slamming into the door whenever she made a left-hand turn.

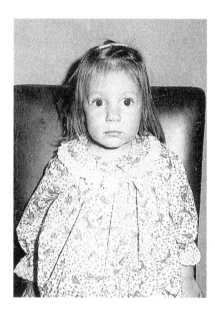
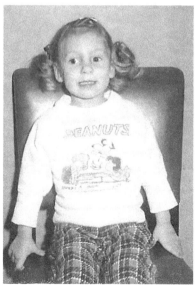

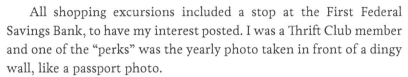

All shopping excursions included a stop at the First Federal Savings Bank, to have my interest posted. I was a Thrift Club member and one of the "perks" was the yearly photo taken in front of a dingy wall, like a passport photo.

Our second errand was a twirl of the racks at Barbara Links Boutique, where my mother found her stylish wardrobe. When I wasn't hiding in the center of the rack startling customers, I was sitting in the corner of the dressing room giving my opinion.

"That color looks good on you. Brings out your eyes. Well, of course, you should get it, Mother! It's on sale!"

Then came the most important errand—a wash and set at Juanita's Beauty Shop. Some kids went to daycare. I went to Juanita's, where my mother was a regular.

Foggy with cigarette smoke and a din of female discussion, Juanita's smelled like a men's club. But this was no place for men. Juanita's was a refuge for women needing escape from their husbands and children. LaPorte housewives gathered here to smoke Virginia Slims, get their hair "done," and discuss the business of living.

Juanita was a busty woman built like a line-backer, who wore exotic, Hawaiian muumuus. A Virginia Slim dangled permanently from her lower lip like it was glued there. She scuffed from one foggy room to another in a pair of pink slippers. Trailing her was a wisp of smoke and Jock, her devoted, black French poodle, his nails matching hers with a sheen of "Cherry Jubilee."

Juanita milled about the shop smoking, ringing up people at the register, and fetching Aqua Net. Finally, she'd sit in her chair, and Jock would bury himself in her crotch as she scratched his head. Sometimes, her cigarette ashes fell into the frizzy pouf on top of his head. One day, I looked at Jock and his afro was smoking.

A lot of prominent women went to Juanita's, including the mayor's wife, Frances Rumely, the only customer who used the front door, where Jock left his calling card. In 1982, on Memorial Day, Frances and her husband, A.J. Rumely Jr. would be murdered in their own bed by a disgruntled employee named Harold Lange. LaPorte, Indiana, would make national news, and my high school sweetheart Daniel Edwards would be the court room artist.

At Juanita's, I did research. I studied piles of cigarette butts in ash trays, flipped through *Cosmopolitan* and eavesdropped on everyone, making mental notes. None of these women seemed all that jazzed about marriage or their husbands. My mother would complain about my dad, and Phyllis Roach, my mother's best friend and hairdresser, would complain about her husband.

"Phyllis, I'm telling you, that man is making me crazy. Yesterday, he accidentally locked his keys in his car because he was picking up tin cans alongside the road. Then, he left his wallet at the bait shop. He talks so much, sometimes I just want to stuff a rag in his mouth!"

"Oh, Mae, I know what you mean. So often I just have to leave the room and go smoke a cigarette."

Marriage didn't sound like much fun to me. I decided right then and there that I would be a Renaissance woman, and instead of being saddled with a husband, I'd live a life of madcap adventures with friends like Phyllis Diller, Carol Burnett, and Jane Goodall.

Every week, Phyllis worked magic and defied gravity with Aqua Net and a tease comb. My mother's hairstyle was a cross between a beehive and a bouffant, which required lots of back-combing at the crown and a pile of bobby pins. During the metamorphosis, my mother's hair took on a Bozo the Clown quality. I'd comment on the likeness and she'd give me *that* look. To preserve the masterpiece, Phyllis circled the hive, spraying a noxious cloud of hairspray. With its stiff lacquer shield and some evening tending, the hive would hold its shape for a week. At night, my mother swathed her masterpiece in toilet paper and bobby pins and slept on a silk pillow, like a queen.

For my mother, appearance was paramount. Her hair was her signature. It didn't matter if your organs were shutting down. What was most important was that your hair looked wonderful and that you were dressed fashionably, with coordinated shoes, purse, gloves, and hat.

My parents were both born and raised in Tolleston, Indiana, my father raised Lutheran, my mother Catholic. My father's side of the family might bicker over who got the glass doorknob when Cousin Leona passed, but my mother's side was so serious about Catholicism that they disowned my mother for marrying my Father, a Lutheran.

Not a Jew or a Buddhist or a Communist, but a Lutheran. So, as a child, I assumed Catholics worshipped a different God than Lutherans. Sure, Lutherans got a wafer and a swig of wine, but Catholics had a birdbath in church and a phone booth with an operator.

At St. John's Lutheran Church, I asked God what was wrong with us. My father's parents George and Lydia Schroeder were wonderful, simple people, but Dad was an only child, so he had few relatives. Sadly, my kind, gentle grandmother Lydia Schroeder died when I was eight. My mother had two sisters and a brother who also had children. We knew our mother's brother Tom and his wife Roberta and their three children, Jeffrey, Lori, and Janice. But the aunts and cousins who lived forty minutes away were, sadly, not a part of our lives. The injustice was categorized as, "just one of those things you're too young to understand."

My mother wouldn't express the pain of it, so she pretended it didn't bother her. But even as a child, I could see that at her very core was the pain of being shut out. And she took it out on all of us. She could be charming and funny one moment and hostile and combative the next. My father, sister, brother, and I were the walking wounded. If our mother had gotten praise growing up, we never heard about it. As she told it, her childhood was grim, a Cinderella story of her scrubbing floors and standing on a stool to wash dishes. The story that makes me the saddest was of the day when she came home and her parents had given away all her pets. No wonder then, that our menagerie grew so fast. Animals were her comfort.

When I was seven, she squared my shoulders, looked me in the eye, and said with conviction,

"My dogs will always come first." And they did. For a time, I tried to grow fur. As it turned out, the dogs were a blessing. Their pure love was much less complicated, and I would inherit my mother's love for animals.

The doghouse became my playpen. The first time I played doctor was in the doghouse with Stephen Tobar, my next-door neighbor. We crawled in there, showed each other our parts, and then stuffed leaves in our underpants. To this day, nothing brings me more comfort than the musky smell of dog.

THE RELIGION OF DOG

In the 1960s, my mother found her tribe with the American Kennel Club and the Basset Hound breed. My parents came up with a kennel name—Dusan, (Susan and Dan combined), and the dog world became our universe.

Jason became my mother's first champion. Most weekends we drove to dog shows so my mother could compete with her prized hounds, and every summer my parents helped organize the LaPorte County Dog Show. My sister and I showed our dogs in junior showmanship, and within a few years, my mother took it to a whole new level and became a breeder. My sister Susie and I helped with every aspect of raising puppies.

In 1972, to accommodate my mother's growing kennel of dogs, we left Country Club Drive to move to the country, where my father designed and built a four-bedroom, three-bath, ranch style home on four acres. The basement and backyard were meant for the basset hounds, and the yard and chicken house he built was home to our poultry.

Ringing the doorbell signaled a cacophony of dogs, cats, ducks, geese, chickens, rabbits, guinea pigs, and exotic birds. Even wild animals were drawn to our house. After 4H meetings, I'd arrive home to five wild rabbits sitting on our front porch. At holidays, strays and injured creatures showed up at our door. One Christmas Eve I looked out the window to see an injured dove sitting patiently on our front steps. Of course, I picked it up and brought it in. We bought it a cage and a mate and Grace lived with us until she died. And the next year, a tiger cat showed up and became ours.

With six basset hounds bellowing in the backyard and our flocks of poultry pooping all over kingdom come, there were always tasks. I used to climb onto the roof of the house and position myself against the chimney so I could read library books uninterrupted. Getting my homework done was always a challenge because my mother wouldn't leave me alone long enough to finish it.

My Mother the Task Master was demanding, controlling, and critical. Dad (who talked out of the side of his mouth) nicknamed her "the Warden." The animals would sound the alarm the second she pulled into the driveway and Dad would alert the troops.

"Battle stations! Battle stations! The Warden's pulling in!" My sister, brother, and I tore through the house to turn off the Zenith Hi-Fi, straighten the kitchen, and make sure there were no dog piddles in the basement.

A mechanical and chemical engineer licensed in four states, my father made the money, but my mother wore the pants, and they were always in style. My mother spoke her truth loudly when possible, often at others' expense. She had no filter or "off" button. An apology was rare. It was her way, or the highway. Two minutes after offending you, she could say something hilarious. Most people held the phone four inches from their ear when in conversation with her. A narcissistic Gemini, she was two people and could change right in front of you. She was equal parts funny and aggressive, with a personality the size of Texas.

Everyone had a story about how she had to have her way. One of my favorites is about our African American cleaning lady Dorothy Delarosa, who worked for us for ten years. We ate lunch together, and I thought she was wise. We regularly gave her clothes and food to take home. Dorothy didn't drive, so my mother picked her up and took her home. When Dorothy's husband Earl died, my parents went to the funeral and stood with Dorothy at the casket.

"Earl looks real nice," said my mother.

"He certainly does," agreed Dorothy.

They lingered there, studying Earl's stiff face and the smooth brown suit he wore. Some other family filed in and Dorothy went to greet them. Dad squinted at Earl's suit.

"That brown suit Earl's wearing sure looks like my favorite suit." My mother was smug.

"I always hated that suit."

THE FORMATIVE YEARS

My parents were constantly at war with one another, especially at the dinner table. I wanted more than anything for them to get along. Then I learned that if I said or did something funny, it alleviated the tension. Suddenly, I had power, and that's how my need to be funny began.

Nothing made me happier than expressing myself. I wrote funny stories and articulated my life experience by drawing. I drew pictures and at age six, started writing in a diary. Early diaries, scrawled in pencil and now faded, resemble a German U-boat war diary.

Being diminutive, I was the kid who was stuffed into laundry baskets and pummeled with the giant canvas ball in crab soccer. Teased by other kids and worse by my teachers, bullying was an everyday occurrence, so I negotiated my way through grade school, developing a big personality to make up for what I lacked in size.

I conformed to the conventions of the day and joined Camp Fire Girls to become a good homemaker and citizen and earn wooden beads, embroidered patches, and satin ribbons. I made and sold cookies, went to day camp, made crafts, had sleepovers at the chalet, and sang for the elderly.

Then I joined 4H so I could exhibit our ducks, geese, and chickens at the fair as well as cookies I'd made for Baking Division I, a drawing of Diana Ross for my arts and crafts Division 2, an insect collection for Insects We See Division I, and photos for Photography Division I. It was a great outlet for Miss Over-Achiever, who was desperate for her parents' approval.

My favorite part of 4H was the yearly Share the Fun competition, which was my humble beginning into the world of entertainment. Carol Cobat, our wildly inventive leader, came up with charming sketches and "numbers" for the yearly Share the Fun competition. Our Center Township Nimble Fingers group usually made it to the finals, which may as well have been the Oscars. I took it very seriously.

December 11, 1975

Today, our Bluebirds troop had to sing Christmas carols for the sick and dying at Sunnyside Nursing Home. I visit our relatives in nursing homes with my mom, so I knew what to expect, but Amy Burris didn't do so well. The smell was so strong, I had to sip the air. These old people are so sad. I feel so sorry for them. Mrs. Bryerly took us into the dining hall, where the old people waited. One woman looked like the apple doll I made last week. She reached out for us, gurgling and weeping. It was sad, like Oliver Twist.

The piano was out of tune, so "Joy to the World" was spooky. Tears streamed down one woman's face as she tried to scoot her wheelchair closer to us. Every time she got a little closer, the front row backed up.

During "Sleigh Ride," we raced through "Come on, it's lovely weather for a sleigh ride together with you," and then we were ahead of the piano. During "Silent Night," a shriveled woman used her walker to come up to Melissa Reisner, our flag bearer. Melissa is very patient, so she let the woman hug her. It was very sweet. Then, this large man shouted and paced. Amy was so upset, she cried on my vest, all over my public service award. She was having a hard time.

"We don't have to touch them, do we?" Then I looked down, and a puddle had formed around Amy's Buster Browns.

May 5, 1976

Marshmallow and Peanuts, my guinea pigs, need cedar shavings, so Mom and I went to Rose's Hatchery in South Bend. The music of tiny peeps overcame us! We forgot about the cedar shavings and bought six goslings.

Dad dragged a shovel behind him in the yard when we got home. He's not happy about our white Embden goslings. I promised I'd take care of them. The goslings are in our kitchen, placed in a box, with food, water, and a light bulb. They peep constantly and huddle together. They even peep in their sleep!

May 15, 1976
My gaggle of geese have chosen me as their leader and follow me everywhere. Today, we found strawberries, poison ivy, and clover. They are so cute. I love it when they hold their tiny wings out and sprint as if they're playing airplane. If I'm out of sight for even a second, they stretch their necks in every direction, peeping for me. I hope they never grow up.

July 1976
My geese are growing like weeds. They're gawky looking, with half fuzz and half feathers. They walk around the yard, plucking grass and flopping down every few minutes to nap. They fall asleep in an instant and their beaks produce a high whistle. I love pressing my nose against their beaks when they sleep. You can feel the air come in and out of their nostrils, and their beaks have a certain smell. Their feet are warm and rubbery. I like to touch their wrinkled, white eyelids and kiss them in the spot where their beaks curl into a smile.

August 1976
The lawn is soggy and squishy so we can't go barefoot. Dad calls the gaggle "the Poop Parade." They wander, waddle, and lounge on every cement surface around the house, so I have to hose everything down once a day.

The geese keep crossing the street to look at the water in the ditch. Then, they stand in the road blocking traffic, and people get mad. I've been herding them back several times a day. Today, this one guy shook his fist at them. So, Dad is going to turn our mud hole in the front yard into a pond. He's an engineer, so I'm sure he knows how to do that.

January 10, 1977
Beth Gebhardt and I went sledding on the toboggan. I went over a very big bump and landed really hard. It hurts when I sit down and when I stand up, so I went to see Dr. Feine, who said I broke my tailbone. I have to wear a girdle to make it heal. How will I get through gym class? Those girls, the scums who wear chains on their pockets, are going to rip me apart. I'll have to change into my gym clothes in the bathroom stall. I hate junior high.

April 16, 1977
Today we drove to Merrillville for the 4H Share the Fun finals. We had to perform first and did just fine. There were so many good acts, and so many crummy ones too. Rinder-cella and Romeo & Juliet were good. Would you believe the crummy acts won? The judges lied on the score sheets. But I got some Show Biz in my blood. Got home at 11:30 p.m.! It was worth all that smiling on stage. I'm a true entertainer!

May 6, 1977
Today I went and saw Grandpa at the nursing home. He sure was alive and chipper! This afternoon Michelle came fishing with me and Dad. The waves were so high, they turned the boat the wrong way. Dad yelled to turn the boat—and we turned it the wrong way. Everything was wound up in the propeller and the equipment sank! Dad was really mad. Michelle couldn't stop laughing, and when Mom heard about it, she was so glad.

May 10, 1977
Poshy, our champion basset hound, had to have emergency surgery after eating six pounds of gravel. None of us can understand why she would eat gravel. She really is a dumb dog.

May 12, 1977

Today, Mom and I went to Kokomo for the dog show. We lost, which made her crabby. Dad went fishing with some Indian guy from work. When we got home, Susie and Danny were dressed for the Prom! Sue and Mike looked great. We all had Frango Mint Wine. Danny went to pick up April and then came back home because he forgot the flowers. Danny and April came back about 10 p.m. April had ripped her dress, and Danny fell off his platform shoes. He may have sprained his ankle at the prom.

May 15, 1978

Today Jim and Brent were trying to get fresh with me. I'm glad. I've had it with these dullsville immature boys. Today math went to English. English to math. They're starting to rebuild the whole school. Today was the big "Spring Concert!" I hardly made any mistakes! Michelle came with me, and at first, I was afraid, I was petrified. I kept thinking she'd get home too late. But everything went perfect. I am so happy, I'm crying.

January 5, 1978

Today, me and Amy Burris got in trouble in the library for talking while watching a film. I got put in the hall because of what I said. Mr. Trafflet said I shouldn't be talking in the library. I said, "Well, you know, it is a free country." He got angry and ordered me to the hall, and then Principal Howes walked by, shook his head, and went "tsk tsk tsk." Amy and I have to write a one-page S.A. on how we should behave in class and have our parents sign it. I'm just going to scribble my mom's name. No one will know the difference.

February 6, 1978

Today, me and Mary got done with Art Club and waited for Mom and she never picked us up! We waited up to 6:00 p.m., and finally she came. She was so mad she said she'd kill me! I had called Dad three times to say come get us. Then, we had to wait for him to arrive. He took me and Mary home. And I ignored Mom the rest of the night. I did make honor roll mention today, but no one cared.

February 22, 1978

Today, we talked about abortions in Health class. It was gross! I plugged my ears and wouldn't listen. Then, in Geography, I answered every question wrong and everyone laughed at me, especially Mr. Kiff and Mr. Zeisig.

February 28, 1978

Today, I got moved in the back in Math and was makin lots of racket! What a blast! Second hour some girls set the waste basket on fire in the girls bathroom and set the fire alarm off! The teachers weren't in the room and me and Dutch made animals with our fingers on the screen of the projector. Sixth hour we saw a play, and the dumb kids didn't know their lines & were too quiet!!

February 29, 1978

Today, me and Michelle went to the library and then to Sages after school. The guy that owns Sages said chocolate prices are going up. He said, "It's all because of Mr. Peanut Picker!" I felt sad. It's like a depression.

March 20, 1978

Mom and Dad have been fighting like cats and dogs.

First Dad said, "Just quit putting me down. You're the one that spends all the money in this house. I don't own a thing. I don't own my bank account or my father's money. You take everything."

Then Mother said, "Oh, shut up. All I want is a divorce and to get away from this house." Then Dad said, "You bitch and just keep buying more shit." I sat in my room praying for them to stop arguing. Why must she take her anger out on him? Doesn't she ever listen to herself? Whenever she buys new clothes (which is very often) she whispers to me that I could wear them too. She says not to tell Dad. She really must think I'm stupid if she expects me not to notice how much money she spends.

May 2, 1978

Today, Mr. Strieter teased me about my size. Dutch kept making these funny noises in Geography. In gym, the band members had to practice so we had eight kids in class. We rode to Kiwanis Field in Tuerff's Lincoln Continental. I sat on Aaron's lap. We played singles. I beat everyone except Tuerff. She's tough and scary. Then, Mike and Susie picked me up in his Cordoba!

May 5, 1978
Mom and I went to Rose's Hatchery for some laying mesh and returned with six mallard ducks. Mom told Dad they're my 4H project and that they're less work than the geese. Dad got angry and said we already have enough shit to fertilize the county. He tried to walk away and slipped in a pile of goose poop.

June 10, 1978
Today, I played a game of scrabble with Danny. I won! Then Beth came over and we played that our dolls John and Fatty were twins, and John was stricken with pneumonia and died, so we had a funeral for him. Through all this my new sunglasses that I was wearing busted. I don't know when or how but now I've got to get to TG&Y to buy another pair before the sale ends. No one wanted to go see a movie with Mom, and Dad said the P.G. movie was trash and rated R. Mom's eyes swelled up with tears, and so I went with her. The movie was about two lovers. He was a hustler and a tennis pro. There was lots of nasty stuff but good tennis games. Afterward, we both got a junior whopper!

July 15, 1978
Mom made Susie and I climb through the dumpsters behind Bernacchi's Farm Market. They have so much lettuce they throw out, which they let us have for our geese and ducks. So, we climb into the dumpster and sort through vegetables and fruit, filling produce boxes with stuff that's still good.

April 6, 1979

Today, I went to Mary's house for her slumber party. We had a beauty contest. The categories were: bathing suit, talent, evening gown & funniest costume competition. I won the talent competition. I did gymnastics to "What Would They Say" by Helen Reddy. We played keep-away, ate & drank pizza, cake, sherbet & pop & did trances. We went to bed at about 3:00 a.m. & Mary started acting snotty. By the way, the only people in the beauty contest were me, D'Jenel, Mary, and Teresa. The rest judged.

May 7, 1979

I'm excited about 4H this summer. Mom and I talked about the Lillovich family, who are undefeated in the poultry division. Every year they win Grand Champion Duck and Grand Champion Goose. The only class they haven't won is the Chicken class. So, we went to Rose's Hatchery for some laying mesh and came home with twelve chickens. Aracanas, Bantam Dwarfs, and Polish chickens. The Aracana chickens will lay a bluish-green egg. Bantams are really cute, and the Polish chickens have feather wigs!

Dad is angry, but we don't care. I named the Polish chickens Horace Vandergelder and Dolly Levi from "Hello Dolly."

May 16, 1979

Today, Mom called in sick for me, and then we were on our way. We stopped at Marshall Fields and I got a new bathing suit. Annie was terrific! Mrs. Hannigan was so evil to those orphans. I taped the songs I liked best with my tape recorder.

May 21, 1979

Today, I wore my blue sun dress to school. I got a couple whistles & you know what Brian McMann said? "Holly thinks she's hot stuff 'cause she isn't wearin' a bra." I was so mad! I'm not wearing a bra. I have nothing to put in it.

Yesterday I said "extra cwedit" accidentally in front of Mr. Gangwer, so now he calls me Elmer Fudd and told Brent Phillips & Lori Harner to call me that. Second and fourth hour we had to move classes. I think Dutch Smith sort of likes me. When I said I was cold, he felt my arm. When I did my oral book report, Casey Rodgers kept staring at my legs. What a day!

May 29, 1979

I didn't make it. I didn't make it. I blew it. My hopes of popularity are all down the drain. My hopes for 8th grade are all gone. I'm finished. I'll be a nothing next year. Just like I was this year. All I can do is cry.

8th grade cheerleaders

1. Carla Burtner
2. Julie Weisner
3. Kelley Kegebein
4. Julie Bales

How I wish I was in one of their shoes.

May 30, 1979

Today, Mom kept calling me Miss Gripe & first hour I broke out crying; all the girls crowded around me, especially Jody Cloutier. I just can't hack volleyball. I'm too short for basketball & I don't know about track. "Annie" from New York was on the Bob Hope special tonight. She sang "Tomorrow." It made me see the light. The sun'll come out, tomorrow, so ya gotta hang on till tomorrow.

June 22, 1979

Today, I had to play golf with Linda Manning. I was so mad! She cheats like anything. On the first hole she said she had an eight when she had a nine! She beat me by two strokes. She can cheat all she wants now. But not at tournament!

July 1, 1979

In Camp Fire Girls, I have become a Trail Seeker, Wood Gatherer, and Fire Maker! At Day Camp, lunch was really good! Mary Chastain brought Julie Wallschlager along and those two were so bored. Then, we had a talent show, which stunk. Me and Jenny and Kathy Hager read the acts to the people watching. Boy, I'm glad Day Camp is almost over.

July 17, 1979
Our Polish chickens are accident-prone and keep bumping into things. Today, they flew into the dog pen. I told Mom I don't think these birds are very smart, and she said,

"Well, they ARE Polish chickens."

The problem is their feather wigs! They can't see where they're flying, so I trimmed the feathers around Horace and Dolly's eyes and they are no longer flying into the dog pen.

July 25, 1979
We have a mean rooster. I named him after King Arthur. He's an Aracana chicken. I love collecting the eggs! They're a blue-green color and taste better than store-bought eggs.

August 1, 1979
Arthur has something against me. He targets me over everyone else in the family. And every time he attacks me in the yard, my mom tells me not to hurt him because he's good to his hens.

My knees are all scraped up from his spurs. He's like a bolt of lightning; he's so fast, I can't get away from him!

August 10, 1979
If the poultry world had a Nazi party, Arthur would be Hitler. I have to be on guard at all times. I feel like he's plotting his next attack. I can't make eye contact with him. He tears across the lawn at breakneck speed, leaving a trail of dust and smoke behind him, like a cartoon!

The only place of safety is my trampoline. When I lie out in the sun on my trampoline, Arthur stands perfectly still under the canvas, head cocked and staring at my butt. Then, he pecks at it. His evil eye peers through the veil of canvas at me. What if he is possessed by the devil? If a doll like the one in Trilogy of Terror can kill people, then I'm sure a rooster can too.

August 13, 1979

Red Pepper is slowly dying. He's blind and crippled and his body is falling apart. He's a very old hamster and it is time to go. I will have a funeral for him.

September 9, 1979

We have about sixty mallard ducks now. The mothers each had a litter of twelve, which, over two summers, adds up to a lot of ducks. I stood on our back deck, hurling loaves of bread at them.

Dad is taking some to a place that will kill them and dress them. I don't like this at all. He left the house with quacking, confused ducks. He returned hours later from that horrible place carrying boxes of naked, headless ducks. A couple of small feathers trailed behind him. I don't want any more ducks. I can't go through this again. My heart can't take it.

October 7, 1979

It's hard to feed the chickens these days because of Arthur. If he sees me in the yard, I have to make a run for it. He's ready to spar in less than five seconds. I don't know how much longer I can live like this. He constantly stabs at my ankles. My legs look terrible, they're so scraped up.

He puffs out his chest out and struts. He throws himself into the air and punches with his feet. Today, we trampled the garden during one of his attacks. Dad will not be happy when he sees his tomatoes.

October 10, 1979

On my way to ceramics class today, I grabbed one of the gallon jugs on the kitchen counter. Mom always has gallons of water on the counter for the fish tank because the fish need it "oxygenated." Halfway through firing my Holly Hobbie coffee mug, the room turned upside down. The pain in my stomach was indescribable. I've never felt anything like it. I broke out in a sweat and went to the bathroom to throw up. I laid on the cold tile and couldn't stand up. Then, I turned colors. I didn't know what to say to the teacher, I was so embarrassed. I thought about that jug of water. Then, I remembered that our basset Jamie had just been to the vet. We are supposed to soak her ankle in a certain solution every night. It was then I realized I'd drunk the vet's prescription. I'm not going to tell Mom. She'll just yell at me.

July 26, 1982

Today was the LaPorte County Dog Show. Mom and Dad had judges and members of the Kennel Club over to the house. Dad talked about his dandelion wine to Richard, who shows terriers. Then, he offered Richard a sample, in a toothpick holder. Richard studied the toothpick holder for a moment, shrugged, and drank it. My Dad was excited to hear what he thought. When I told Mom that Dad served Richard the wine in a toothpick holder she rolled her eyes.

"Oh, for God's sake! I always have to keep an eye on him."

May 1982

We've taken in a police dog named Major who was on the police force for eight years. When his officer retired, he didn't want Major anymore. What a selfish person to abandon his "partner." Major is a German Shepherd whose teeth are like nubs because he chewed on the bars of his cage. He used to jump over six-foot tall fences and now won't even step over a short board that's been placed across the basement steps to keep the bassets from getting upstairs to whiz on the shag. Dad says it's because Major knows he's retired.

Major knows how to open doors and lets himself in and out at will, so all our doorknobs are mangled. The vet called us after his first checkup and said, "Get over here and pick him up, he's opening all the doors and letting the other dogs out!"

June 1982

I can't believe what happened on my first date with Dan Edwards. The doorbell rang, which is always a mistake at our house because hounds are loud barkers. I opened the door, and there was Dan, red-faced and twitchy, with Major attached to his crotch. Dan waved and smiled.

"Hi! I'm here." I was horrified. I couldn't believe Major had gripped Dan's package with his mouth. He was doing what he was trained to do—hold the perpetrator still and wait for the officer.

Not even thinking, I unclamped Majors' jaw, wiped away the spit, and then tried to fix a snag with my index finger on Dan's pants.

"That's okay," Dan said nervously as he scooted away. "They're old anyway."

October 22, 1982

I haven't written in ages! SO much has happened since my last writing, I won't be able to catch up. Teresa Sosinski is dating a boy named Alex who gives us rides home from school, and Dan Edwards comes with. He is so funny and talented! I met him in Mr. Yarno's Television Production class. One day, Mr. Yarno was teaching and Dan was in the control room. Dan attracted my attention by blowing up a balloon and then letting it go so it flew all over the control room. Then he smiled at me. He is so cute and funny.

Teresa and I did our "Enough is Enough" dance in the variety show. The first night, Dan brought me roses and candy and a drawing of himself. He's a great artist and everybody knows it. He has been wonderful! He writes me letters every day and each one has a drawing. I save them in a metal tin.

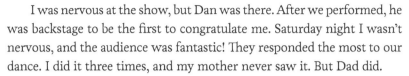

I was nervous at the show, but Dan was there. After we performed, he was backstage to be the first to congratulate me. Saturday night I wasn't nervous, and the audience was fantastic! They responded the most to our dance. I did it three times, and my mother never saw it. But Dad did.

Sometimes, I eat dinner at Dan's house, and he comes over every weekend to my house. Dan's family is so nice. Dan draws, sculpts, and makes masks, and his mother is cool with it. He is the assistant to the art teacher at school!

April 28, 1983

Richard Nixon was in town and Dan talked to the LaPorte *Herald Argus* about drawing Nixon's portrait, so they let him into the event for free. Then, he showed his drawings of Nixon to the Secret Service men, who showed them to Nixon, who said, "So, you drew this picture! You've got a great career ahead of you!" Dan got me an autographed picture that Nixon signed. It says, "Dear Holly, love Richard Nixon."

February 1984

I'm writing my term paper on Barbra Streisand. We have so much in common. She used to hide from her parents too, on the roof of their Brooklyn apartment building. Barbra was also funny looking, with skinny legs and a big nose. Her mother, like mine, wanted her to become a secretary. So, Barbra grew her nails extra-long so she couldn't type! People called her names too. My nicknames include Knobby Knees, Bones, Nose, and Boy Herman.

Purdue University, Owen Hall, Autumn 1984

It took me a while to adjust to living in a dormitory. But now I love it! And I've met some neat people here in Owen Hall. For example, I was in the hallway doing my Katharine Hepburn impersonation for the girls next door, and this statuesque woman in a blue satin robe pirouetted down the hallway, squealing with laughter. My eyes lit up. Talk about dramatic! She is six-one in her bare feet and dresses like Madonna.

Jeanne Louise Fowerbaugh is a civil engineering student, actress, singer, trumpet player, and member of Purdue's All American Marching

Band. She is uninhibited, talented, witty, and the smartest girl I've ever met. How many women can talk about cement **and** Tennessee Williams? Every day we lounge on her pink sofa in her dorm room to discuss men, theater, and how to get into the best parties.

Jeanne likes to introduce us to people with, "Hi, I'm Jeanne, and this is my Cabbage Patch doll Holly."

When we go through the lunch line, we say things like, "I'll have a hard-boiled egg and a Swiss man please." Then, we hold court in the dining room with engineering nerds, who admire how free we are.

Sept. 15, 1985

Yesterday, Jeanne and I went to the Lafayette Square downtown and took four rolls of pictures. It was glorious! Around the fountain on the Courthouse steps, we flaunted and danced. Cars stopped to watch us, convinced we were models or actresses. I wore my red skirt that has suspenders and is perfect for twirling, and Jeanne wore a vintage ensemble. All the while, these guys across the street at a bakery watched us. Then, the boss came out and said he was interrupted in his office and had to come see what the excitement was about. He invited us for free Cokes.

Oct. 23, 1985

Jeanne and I have made a pact to throw caution to the wind and "live life till it hurts."

Today Jeanne, Tammy, and I walked to the middle of the golf course and camped out on a big blanket. We smoked clove cigarettes and listened to the "Cotton Club" as golfers teed off and balls soared over our heads. Men in their plaid pants walked by us, some of them chuckling at our devil-may-care attitude. We plucked autumn leaves up off the ground and studied them. It was glorious. At one point, a nurse walked by and Jeanne said, "What is this? A Monty Python sketch?"

Owen Hall, December 1985

Someone stole Jeanne's lingerie out of an Owen Hall dryer. She had to report every item, bras and panties included, to the campus police.

"Can you describe the items?" the conservative officer asked.

"Well, there was a pricey Victoria's Secret bra I got on sale," Jeanne said.

"What size?" he asked, embarrassed.

"Size 38DD," she said with a smile. He blushed, and Jeanne let out one of her ear-splitting shrieks.

She and I have been discussing the fact that Purdue's Greek system is the third biggest in the country. If I want to go to all the best parties and invite Jeanne along, I'll have to join a sorority. Some people hate the Greek system. I'm now writing for the *Purdue*

Exponent, and most of the students on staff are anti-Greek, but I don't care what they think. I thirst for excitement.

Winter 1985
Jeanne ran in the nude Olympics at Cary Quad this winter, and now she's played the Statue of Liberty in Bandarama during the half-time performance. Over the loudspeaker, she was introduced. "And here she is, Ladies and Gentlemen, the majestic Lady of New York's harbor, The Statue of Liberty." Dignified and composed, Jeanne rose slowly on a platform, dry ice rising around her size-ten feet. She is officially now a national treasure.

Office of the *Purdue Exponent*
Pat Kuhnle, Managing Editor at the *Exponent*, requested I resurrect the 1960s column called "Cuttin' Tape." My job will be to "cut through the red tape" and find the answers to life's most important questions. I'm thrilled at the chance, AND I'm getting paid!

This will appear in each column:

> *Cuttin' Tape is an invaluable service that has been revived for the benefit of the bewitched, bothered, and bewildered. Letters of inquiry regarding University policies and other concerns will be printed, depending on their applicable content. The majority of these letters will be responded to within two weeks of being received. Letters written in poor taste and of no informative value will not be printed.*
>
> *Please write to Cuttin' Tape, in care of the* Exponent. *Room B-50, Purdue Memorial Union, W. Lafayette, 47906, or drop your written questions off at the business office in Room B-58.*

Pi Beta Phi House, Winter 1985
After months of rushing, the final rush parties are happening. It had snowed, and I was a little late getting to the Pi Beta Phi house, where everyone had just gone inside. I sprinted across the lawn in my vintage Deliso Debs. Waiting for me at the door was Active Maureen Drake, who chuckled to herself.

"Get in here, Schroeder," she said as she took my coat and pushed me towards the "Slipper Salon," where I left my shoes.

The first floor had been transformed into "Pi Phi Heaven," and it was magical. The floor was covered in white sheets and pillows, and we had to stoop down as we entered the living room, where millions of tin-foil stars on string hung from the ceiling. Rumor is that the Farmhouse fraternity comes over to "drop the ceiling' and then the Pi Phis hang thousands of stars, one at a time, from the ceiling on the main and second floors. The shimmering stars tinkled in my ears. I'll never forget it. The sisters sang to us under candlelight about Pi Phi heaven.

At the end of the ceremony, all of us aspiring Pi Phi angels left in silence and stood at the end of the sidewalk in a clump. Snow sprinkled down on us as the Actives sang, "Remember the Arrow."

> *Remember the Pi Phi arrow, the wine and the silver blue.*
> *The loyalty and the friendship that you'll find waiting here for you.*
> *Forget all the other's pleadings, the arrow's gleam is bright.*
> *When you choose the Pi Phi arrow, you'll know you've chosen right.*

I was transfixed. The only thing I've ever wanted more than a bid from this house is a chimpanzee.

Purdue University, Pi Beta Phi, September 21, 1986

> *Sweet as the rose's fragrance*
> *As true as the arrow's flight*
> *As fine as the silvers gleaming*
> *May your dreams be tonight.*
>
> *Tomorrow you'll be wearing*
> *The golden shaft we wear*
> *Tomorrow you'll be sharing*
> *The friendship that we share.*

As the bird awakens
Perhaps you'll see just why
We've waited and wished lovingly
To welcome you to Pi Phi.

I cannot believe it. How did I manage to pull this off? I have been initiated into the Indiana Delta Chapter of Pi Beta Phi! My brother is thrilled, and I'm over the moon. Inspiration Week (part of initiation) was a challenge. Every night for eight days, we had to be in bed by 7 or 9 p.m. The dragging and pounding of the senior canes hindered our sleep, and we were awakened in the night to be led, single file, eyes closed, right hand on the shoulder of the girl in front of us, down the wooden banister to the formal living room. The Actives wore black and sang to us about friendship and loyalty, and a second later, they intimidated us, listing rules for the week. For example, we had to carry our paddles with us at all times, even in the shower, as well as a dollar in change and stamps. I wasn't careful enough and Active Heidi Miller took my paddle. And at every landing on the stairs, we must recite the Greek alphabet, which has taken me forever to learn. At the end of Hell week, we had a dinner where all of us pledges had to "work together" to eat because our utensils were tied together with twine and silver-blue yarn. While one girl cut her food, the other girl had to wait.

I'm one of the more boisterous of my pledge class. One night I got really annoyed with all the rules and snuck out the side door with a bag of clothes and books. I made sure no one was watching as I high-tailed it out of there and walked across campus to Mark Sabbe's apartment, where he gave me the new Cyndi Lauper tape! That night I had a nightmare that our president, Monique Ponsot, was standing outside dressed in black, jabbing her cane into the cement. It was so real, I made Mark go outside and look to see if she was there. In the morning, she called Mark, looking for me! He lied about my whereabouts.

When I came back to the house everyone wanted to know where I'd been. Since Mark is the editor of the *Purdue Exponent* and I'm a reporter/advice columnist, the actives are concerned we'll publish a story about hazing. As if! I mean, come on. Some of my pledge sisters are tickled that I gave everyone a scare. Apparently, no one has ever done that, but I'm a rebel. Because I ran away, my sisters nicknamed me "Awol." And I like it.

Autumn, 1986

Letters have been pouring in for Ms. Cuttin' Tape—scribbled, typed, and sometimes covered in grease. From the innocuous to the absurd, I have a steady supply of good material. The research takes as long as the writing. With my trusty *Exponent* badge, I have the authority to call anywhere in the country, which I love! I wonder if this is how advice columnist Ann Landers feels. I try to put some humor into each answer:

Dear Cuttin' Tape,

What is the difference between skim milk, two percent milk, and whole milk? Do certain cows produce different kinds of milk, or does man change the milk to how he wants it? What are the differences in calories, too?

—Milk and Cookies

Dear Milk and Cookies,

Cuttin' Tape talked to Elsie the Cow and Elsie says that skim milk comes from the same place that minute steaks come from—really thin cows. All kidding aside, William Evers, assistant professor of foods and nutrition, says, "Man has been skimming milk for years."

According to Evers, to make skim milk, the milk is allowed to sit until the fat rises to the top, where it is "skimmed" off. This fat is then used to make other dairy products, such as butter.

Evers says whole milk is about four to five percent fat. Infants need extra calories, which is why they should be fed whole milk. "Two percent milk is less fattening," Evers says. "However, it depends on how much milk you drink."

Dear Cuttin' Tape,

We are three females who feel very naïve . . . we were wondering how many nocturnal emissions are average for college-aged males. This is a serious question, and we really need to know.

—High and Dry in Meredith

Dear High and Dry in Meredith,

What are you doing? My mother reads this column. Having discussed explicit questions before with Dana Mason, assistant professor of nursing, I asked her to give me the details. A "wet dream" is a nocturnal emission. Mason says a college-aged male who is not sexually active may have one or two per week. Otherwise, she says, they rarely occur.

Erections, however, arise ten to twelve times a night. In case this is one of those "Everything you wanted to know about sex but were afraid to ask" questions, Mason says the act of having sex expends 154

calories and semen contains 36 calories per ejaculation. You probably
wanted to know that, too.

Spring 1986

Jeanne and I were invited to a performance by the Wabash College
Glee Club. She knows one of the guys, and the other one is a friend
of his. The whole night was like a movie. From the moment our
dates picked us up in a camper (stocked with booze) and drove us to
Wabash College, it was non-stop revelry.

By the time we arrived at Wabash College and staggered out of
the camper, we were both inebriated. Our dates were performing in
a Glee Club concert. We were careful to enter the bucolic Wabash
chapel, as quietly as we could, but we were so drunk we walked
sideways.

From our pews, we flirted with our dates, who averted their eyes
to avoid laughing. They maintained their dignity and dulcet intona-
tions as we blew kisses to them. As an older gentleman sang "The
Ol' Wabash," Jeanne leaned over to me and said, "Oh my God, Holly.
We're witnessing heritage."

Unfortunately, I had to go to the bathroom, which was bad
timing. My heels echoed on the chapel floor, so I walked in slow
motion. After the concert, we went to a restaurant in town which
was in a house. I couldn't tell you what we ate. I just remember the
wine. After dinner we walked to the Kappa Sigma house because
they were having a dance. It was there that Jeanne's date dumped
her for a game of double bid euchre with four fellas. (Jeanne tends
to attract bi-sexuals.) I said, "Screw him" and dumped my date
so we could wander the streets till we found the Fiji house. We
couldn't find the entrance, so we climbed in through a window.
Two gentlemen helped us down to the dance floor, where we
grabbed two fraternity boys, kicked off our shoes, and danced as
hard as we could.

My date eventually found us, asking people in the street if they'd
seen Jeanne and I, which they had. We all had a tour of the Fiji house
and then left, back home to Purdue in the camper. We got back to
Purdue, our feet on fire, at 3 a.m. I will never forget this night!

U-Sing, 1987

What a week. I'm the song chairman for U-Sing. We've rehearsed intensely for the past ten days. We sounded wonderful at St. Tom's! I've grown very fond of Theta Chi's U-Sing director Paul Remde. He directed both songs for U-Sing because I wanted to be able to relax and watch him direct, as he knows more about directing than I. Friday night, we had a TG with the Theta Chi house and rehearsed half-drunk for visiting parents. Mine weren't there, thank God.

Saturday, Mom and Dad came up for the weekend festivities. Brunch was lovely. Our group performed well at the Union, and at five o'clock, Paul and I found out we had made Night Sing! At 9:38 p.m., we stood on the Elliott Hall of Music stage and had a glorious time belting out "The Virgin Mary had a Baby Boy." Later, me, Paul, and Becky Wray stood backstage with all the other directors and waited for the winners to be announced. The houses that won 5th, 4th, and 3rd were announced. Then I heard, "For 2nd place, the winners are, Pi Beta Phi and Theta Chi!" I jumped three feet off the risers! Becky Wray grabbed and clutched the trophy as if she herself had earned it! Father Phil was perhaps the happiest because he can now get the addition he wants.

I celebrated at Theta Chi's till 1:30 a.m. and then went to Phi Delts to see Bob Connors, whom I've been dating. He was pissed I'd been at Theta Chis all that time. Good Lord. John Daly and Bob Schap were at Phi Delts and congratulated me. It was epic!

Grand Prix Weekend, 1987

I think my time here is meant to be just the way it is. I've had a perfectly spontaneous Grand Prix weekend! Prior to the race, I had the flu, but one night, it just disappeared. Thursday, Friday, and Saturday night run together into a blur. Wednesday night was the lip sync contest, and I sang Cindy Lauper's "Change of Heart," which was a hit with the crowd. Thursday night we had a skating party with Beta Theta Pi, and I've decided my obsession with Dave Woods is silly. Bob, whom I now call "Beau," walked into the Beta house at 12 p.m. to invite me to the Phi Delt's toga party. Then, he and I left and went back to Phi Delts, where we danced until 4:30 a.m. It was the best time with him ever. It was hard to get up the next day.

Friday night I went to Betas. The Robert Redford look-alike that everyone thinks is gorgeous kept watching me dance with his fraternity brothers and accused me of "blowing him off" several times. Every time I dance with him, he asks me if he is that bad a dancer and if I would teach him to dance. At one point, he whisked me away in his arms and up the stairs to order a pizza. He's a romantic.

Shannon Conley and Mary Walters strolled in my room, and I was running around the third floor in my underwear, trying to prepare for the race. We all left for Beta Theta Pi and were drinking beer out of plastic cups on the way. A cop driving behind Mary turned on his lights. Shannon and I were so busy talking we didn't notice until Mary calmly said, "Shannon, here, hold my beer." (She's so dry and funny.) The cop pulled over someone else, thankfully.

After the race, I went back to Beta Theta Pi and played catch in the front yard, jumping for fly balls in my long dress. Rob Baldwin took me for a ride up and down Littleton on the handlebars of his bike. My dress flew up. I went home with Sophie Schauer but stopped at Phi Delts on the way to get my purse from Mary. I saw Beau, who was supposed to be studying. We scavenged for pig in the kitchen. I went home and slept until 9 p.m.

10 p.m. at Betas, I danced with a gorgeous Beta named Brian, whom I've always admired. I can still hear the band and see Brian's perfect profile.

Sadly, I really drank a lot and couldn't tell I was intoxicated. Sophie informed me later that I put my head in her arm pit and moaned with exhaustion.

At 2 a.m. Joanna Banana and I walked to Sigma Chis, and just as we got there, I heard a voice that lit me up, and there was Schappy about to leave in a van. Oh, went the strings of my heart!

Sigma Chis was glorious fun. Andy from my Spanish class was there, and we went for a ride in some wooden cart on wheels. Several Fijis were riding kegs across the beer splattered floor, and Schappy was a non-stop social light. Andy kept telling me to go talk to him. I said, "I can't. I'm so used to being pursued." And then I said, "Screw that."

I did chat with Bob and we went into his room. Mary tagged along and sat like a zombie next to me. Jeff George ran in at one point and wrote all over Bob's face with a marker. At 4 a.m. I drove Mary and Joanna home, and Bob came with. We ended up talking till 6:30 a.m. We discussed parents, D.C., and his jacket.

He said, "That guy last night (the other Bob) looked at me as if he was going to cry. I don't like to get in the way." Then he asked me if I was going back to my boyfriend. Do I really have to pick just one?

He kissed me for a time and I just loved having my face next to his. I played with his hair and looked into his eyes. He dresses like a bum, but his character is so lovable, and that hair!

We talked about Winnie the Pooh, and I did an impersonation of Pooh as my voice had been scratchy for two days. He was delighted. I drove home with the sun in my heart. Love is so light. I like both Bobs, but I really find Schappy more of a man. Got to bed at 6:30 a.m. I really have to stop this late-night partying.

BACK HOME AGAIN IN INDIANA

PURDUE UNIVERSITY, May 20, 1988

I've been sent out into the world by Orville Redenbacher, the King of Corn. Yes, Purdue is known as an agricultural and engineering school, but couldn't they have done better than Orville? I only get *one* commencement ceremony, and somehow, I feel a bit let down. This is to be the final celebration of four years of tremendous growth, unbridled joy, and friendship. You know who would have been perfect? Carol Burnett. Phyllis Diller. Bob Hope!

I became my own person here. I wouldn't know where to start with how much I've learned getting my Bachelor of Arts. These have been the best four years of my life! Can a corn magnate infuse and energize me with hope and passion to pursue the real world? Because right now, I'd really like to stay here.

My Pi Phi sorority sister Jodi Scutchfield and I arrived late, having stopped to talk to every Phi Delt, Beta, and Sig Ep on the way to our respective lines. And then there was the traditional taping of arrows onto our graduation caps so our Pi Phi sisters can spot us. As trumpets resounded on the steps of Hovde Hall and the fountain sparkled, "Back Home in Indiana" chimed on the clock tower. Tears rolled down my face. It was solemn and stately, like a funeral. MY funeral.

> *Back home again in Indiana*
> *And it seems that I can see*
> *The gleaming candlelight, still burning bright*
> *Through the sycamores for me.*
> *The new-mown hay sends all its fragrance*
> *Through the fields I used to roam,*
> *When I dream about the moonlight on the Wabash*

Then I long for my Indiana home.
When I dream about the moonlight on the Wabash,
Back home again in Indiana.

Prayers and speeches followed inside Elliott. Mark Sabbe, my boyfriend of two years, sat a few rows in front of me. He turned around and spit his tongue out at me and laughed. Why couldn't it have worked out with him? I love his sense of humor, intelligence, writing talent, and handsome looks. What was I thinking when I broke up with him? The questions continued. What now? How am I going to adjust? Where do I go next?

My stomach was tight, my head swollen. Why did we all insist on going out in grand style last night? Such was the way. Well, that's all gone now. No more fun and freedom for me. No more late-night shenanigans, mixers with the best fraternities in town, and best of all, doing the secret handshake and secret knock before chapter meetings.

The guy next to me (graduating with high academic achievement) looked down at the wadded tissue in my hand. College was a different experience for him. He doesn't understand where and what I came from and how I blossomed here in a way I never could in LaPorte Indiana.

"May you go out on the wings of eagles," said the dean as the orchestra broke into "Hail Purdue." This was too much. People around me are happy, but me? I'm **weeping.** I've been living in one of the top sororities on campus, with waiters, access to all the best parties, and Monday night formal dinners. I have fallen in love with learning and never missed a class. College is freedom, education, parties, booze, and hot guys all in one place. Why would I celebrate the end of that?

Mom and Dad arrived in separate cars. Dad and Danny came in one so they could have a piece of peach pie at the Corner Café in Monon, Indiana. My mother and sister arrived in the other so they can leave quickly after the ceremony. Josephine, our mother's English toy spaniel is due with puppies. I'm graduating from college, and once again, a dog is more important.

After the ceremony, I exited somber Hovde Hall into pande-monium. Squinting in the bright sunlight, I deflected a champagne cork, which hit me square on the head. Graduates embraced and posed for pictures with family members. There was no one waiting for me, however. My parents were up the street at the armory, a meeting place of sentimental significance to my father because that's where the WWII tanks were stored.

Blotchy from crying, I made my way to the armory, where my father positioned me in front of an M12 Abrams. My sister wore her green graduation gown from Michigan State University. My mother scolded me for crying and snapped a few pictures of us with her antiquated 1972 Kodak Instamatic. It was a real Norman Rockwell moment.

At dinner, my mother gave me a present, a dress for job inter-views. The pattern features stalks of yellow wheat. One of my sorority sisters bounced into the dining room. Her parents had sprung for a boob job. But me, I got a grain-inspired dress from Carson's.

"Is this because I graduated from an agricultural school?" I asked.

"No. It was on sale."

Mom can't possibly understand how I feel. This has been the most extraordinary time of my life. I've only JUST begun to discover who I am. After my family left, Jodi and I went to the cold air dorm and sobbed on our beds. So many nights, I lay in my bed, listening to Farmhouse men serenade us and Delt pledges sing, "I know a pretty Pi Phi." How will I keep track of time without the bell tower on campus and our grandfather clock in the living room as they strike on the hour? How can I leave this womb where I'm allowed to be who I am? It's taken me 22 years to feel like I really belong and am accepted and appreciated. I don't want to leave. This is home. My heart is here.

How will I get by without my friends and freedom? Now, me and my ulcer are going back to prison at my parents' house, regressing back to LaPorte, Indiana, to live with my controlling mother and eccentric father, where my every move will be scrutinized and nothing I do will be enough. I can't believe my college days and life as a sorority girl are past me. I don't know how I will survive living in the real world.

O Sisters in the wine and blue, sing soft, sing sweet, sing clear
The while we pass our Pi Phi cup, the cup of love and cheer.
Drink deep the joys of college days, embrace the bond so true.
And pledge eternal loyalty to the wine and silver-blue.

LaPorte Indiana, June 19, 1988

Cold reality indeed. I feel like I'm serving time. Maybe it's because I'm unemployed, but my mother thinks I'm working for her. How many trips to Bernacchi's Farm Market and the Jewel supermarket does one woman need? My dad defended me.

"Mae, the kid is doing the best she can."

Mom doesn't understand why I would send resumes to a company that isn't actively looking to hire someone. I tried to explain that setting up an "informational interview" allows one to connect with a company so that when they are hiring, we've already become acquainted! But she doesn't think I know what I'm doing. She never does.

"Oh ye of little faith," I muttered.

Hinsdale, Illinois, October 15, 1988

I can't endure my mother's scrutiny. So, I've moved in with my big brother Danny. He's a biochemist now. Mom drove with me in my car, with Dad in the other car, to Danny's apartment in Burr Ridge.

She got choked up in the car and said she was going to miss me. That meant a lot to me since she rarely shows that kind of emotion.

Danny understands the real world and doesn't put me down when he has reason to. I'll never forget how clueless I was when I waitressed at the Rusty Pelican. I saw how much the girls made and failed to realize the Rusty Pelican wasn't their first waitressing job.

We had to order drinks in a certain order and garnish them appropriately. Just because I'm good at *consuming* drinks doesn't mean I have any idea how to *garnish* them. Plus, I couldn't carry all those dinners on a tray. I can't perch a tray on my shoulder bones. I was in over my head. I'm a terrible waitress.

The "uniform," a skimpy wrap-around skirt, kept moving around. Every time I looked down, the slit in the skirt had slid around and exposed my crotch. I was a disaster. On my fourth day, I spilled a margarita on a customer. The manager apologized to the guest and took me to the side.

"I think maybe it's time to call it a day," he said.

"So, come back tomorrow?" I asked.

"No need to come back."

I was horrified, yet relieved. It wasn't a good fit. Then, I turned in my wrap-around skirt and bow tie and left the Rusty Pelican, in my leotard, never to return. I got home to Danny's apartment.

"Awfully early to be home, isn't it? Did you get canned?" The look on my face said it all.

"Well, getting fired builds character," Danny said. We watched *The Simpsons* together, and all was right with the world.

November 15, 1988

I got the job at Park & Montgomery Advertising as a receptionist and writer! The creative director, a beautiful and stylish woman named Paige Claire, loved my portfolio. The owner, Sue, previously an airline stewardess, started this small ad agency three years ago.

Every day, Sue enthusiastically claps her hands and rubs them together like she's up to no good.

"Good morning! Good morning," she always says. "You look great, and you smell good too!" Then she brushes the dandruff of her shoulders and we get to work.

Paige often calls me into her office for an assignment. I play the over-eager underling without a clue, and Paige plays the boss. She uses phrases like, "Lord High Poo Bah of Upper Butt Crack," and "cluster fuck." She told me the other day that if I'm ever going to kill myself to do it right the first time.

"Otherwise, you'll end up in the hospital wearing mittens," she said. I promised I'd always remember that.

Paige's office is decorated with antiques and pigs. I love her sense of humor AND style. Sometimes she flops into her impressive big leather chair like Lily Tomlin's Edith Ann and props her shapely legs in high heels on her desk. Then, she speaks with a lisp, and we cackle and wheeze with laughter. At night, we review the days horrors over the phone. Then Danny gets on the phone too.

"He is SO sweet, Holly," Paige always says.

December 5, 1988

I'm going to stay in Paige's River North loft in Chicago for a week when she's on vacation. Every day there is a note for me with clues that lead me to a present. She has given me some amazing jewelry and clothes! To be in her home is to be surrounded by charm and whimsy. She is such a decorator and artiste. She was married to an RCA record producer and lived in Los Angeles for 15 years, hobnobbing with Elton John, Olivia Newton John, Neil Sedaka, and the like. She's had a fascinating life.

Paige cut an album which became very popular in Japan. In the United States, it didn't get the response she wanted, so she rarely speaks of it. I asked to hear it and she wouldn't oblige. So, I took the liberty to find it in the record cabinet and play it. Honestly, she and Olivia Newton John were on the same playing field, only Olivia made it. Timing is everything. I'd love to hear the whole story, but Paige can be secretive about things. She is insecure about stuff and I don't know why. She's beautiful, creative, brilliant, hilarious, and an impeccable dresser.

When my parents came to see Danny and me, they stopped by the office to see where I work. After they met everyone and left, Paige pulled me aside and said,

"Are those **really** your parents? Are you sure you didn't just find them wandering around the parking lot?"

December 25, 1988
We followed our regular tradition of opening presents on Christmas Eve and church on Christmas Day. Dad, always the jokester, wrapped up a new phone cord as a Christmas gift for Mom—since she pulled the last one out of the wall.

January 10, 1989
I'm just an entry level peon, so I don't know what happened, but Sue fired Paige and had the police escort her out of the building. Did it have to come to THAT?

March 6, 1989
I finally got freelance writing work for Spiegel, which is in Oakbrook. I write product descriptions for clothing, shoes, and bedding, so I'm learning about style sheets and writing into layouts. Working at an advertising agency like Leo Burnett or J. Walter Thompson is what I *really* want, but this will do for now.

Danny's Moluccan cockatoo Porsche is so loud, when she shrieks, the whole apartment complex hears her. One day she was going off and a neighbor thought I was being attacked.

"Nope," I said. "It's just Porsche vocalizing."

April 10, 1990

I've been looking for an apartment in the city. I'll know it when I find it. The other night, I came out of my bedroom, and Danny was lying down on the couch, his pant legs soaking wet. He had gone for a walk and fell in a swamp. Then he told me about the bad dreams he's been having. I feel bad now I'm moving out. But I have to spread my wings and fly. I want to so badly to live in Chicago, Chicago, that toddling town!

A LEAP OF FAITH

Growing up 70 minutes from the Chicago Loop, our family took the South Shore Train into the city to see musicals and plays, see the Marshall Field's windows at Christmas, and eat German food at The Berghoff, which has been a beloved establishment since 1898.

My Aunty Anna, who became a United States citizen in 1937, often ate there with us. If there was a dill pickle on my plate, she took it and waved it at me. "Pickles aren't good for children," she'd say as she devoured it. Born in Germany, she moved to the United States to become a nurse and nanny. She never married and lived at the Margaret Manor Home at 1121 Orleans Street. She was a wonderful nanny to many children. When kids got antsy, she'd say with her thick German accent, "Pinch your glove."

Living in the melting pot that is Chicago was instrumental in developing my identity. The diverse population, history, culture, and energy of that city buoyed me up. I practically floated down the sidewalk. It took a summer to find a great apartment just a few blocks away from Wrigley Field, with a mailbox like Holly Golightly's in *Breakfast at Tiffany's*. When I finally saw the movie in my 20's, I recognized myself in Holly Golightly, a skinny farm kid intent on escaping her past by moving to the big city and living with her cat. My telephone wasn't kept in a valise, but I had the cat and a Japanese neighbor who lived upstairs. And yes, he often let me in when I forgot my key.

Boys Town at that time was a bit seedy, but I embraced the grit. I lived blocks from edgy thrift stores like Flashy Trash, Beatnix, and the Brown Elephant, and around the corner from Thai restaurants and mod bars. I wanted to share these hip, edgy stores and dining establishments with my mother. She had no interest in any of that.

"It's just so dirty here," she'd say. I lived smack dab in the middle of a diverse city, and where does she want to go? To Jewel, the supermarket.

"I want to see if it's like my Jewel!"

We walked down Addison Avenue, and she advised me, "Now listen. If you ever think you're going to be robbed, swallow your jewelry. That's what the gypsies always did."

Chicago Illinois, August 10, 1990

It took me a few months to find my first apartment, but I knew it the second I walked in. The building is called "The Florence." It has a claw foot tub, and the previous tenant, a Frenchman, did some whimsical painting. The building is 100 years old! Parking is a pain in the ass, but I try not to dwell on it. Instead, I learned the Chicago bump, which is gently touching the car in front of you and giving it a little push forward so you can squeeze into a too tight space. Driving around during a Cubs game, I can hear Harry Carey sing "Take Me Out to the Ballgame," which makes me feel warm and fuzzy inside. The warm glow of night games lights up my living room. Mia and I do the tango and listen to the crowd cheer.

My job as a copywriter at Evans Furs is going well. My favorite person there is the layout artist Dee Dosé, who looks like Snow White. She has impeccable fashion sense, jet black hair, and a wicked good sense of humor. She has taught me so much about men, and most importantly, that my ideas of marriage and "happily ever after" are unrealistic. She told me all about her husbands and the animals she's rescued. I was sure from her stories that she'd led a glamorous life, but she set me straight.

"My first husband was gorgeous. Unfortunately for me, he was also gay, which ended badly. Nothing is as it appears. I got married because I got asked, a good reason to go to the prom but not good enough to get married. When my second husband and I got married, we did so on my lunch hour at the Skokie Courthouse. We had to borrow a judge who was in the middle of a murder trial. Then my mother's pacemaker set off the security alarm. *Sigh*. What you need, Holly, is a husband like my Freddy."

Her Freddy was a gangly, tall man with a sweet disposition who was devoted to her. The day he delivered a chair for her office, Dee and I stood on the corner of State and Monroe waiting for him.

"Look for the long sedan with an arm hanging out the window dragging on the ground," she told me. I guffawed—until I saw a long sedan with an arm hanging out the window dragging on the ground. Freddy was almost as tall as the Sears Tower. He effortlessly piled Dee's Louis VX chairs into his trunk. Then, he bent down like Lurch from *The Adams Family* and shook my hand.

August 19, 1990

I'm getting two kittens from my mom. Oreo, the tiny black and white cat my mother found in a parking lot, gave birth in my father's closet. She had a one-night stand with a big white tom cat who came to visit her any chance he could. I wanted just the runt, the only black kitten, but mom said I couldn't take just one. So, I named the black kitten Blue (after Bob Dylan's "Tangled Up in Blue") and the white male kitten Mia, which I nicknamed Mary Walters in college one night at a stoplight because she looked like

Mia Farrow, and because "Mia" means "mine" in Italian. Mia is very androgynous and likes to wear a crochet bonnet and pink doll sweater. I told Dee all about Mia and Blue. She told me about Roosevelt, a cat she adored that made quite a splash during a dinner party. Roosevelt's perch was the top of the refrigerator. One night during a dinner party, he fell asleep, slipped off his perch and landed in the soup du jour.

September 17, 1990

I'm learning how to become an improviser through Player's Workshop. At first, I questioned the value of playing games like kitty in the corner, but I've already noticed a difference in my awareness of space. It **is** wonderful exploring ways to be in a room full of show folk willing to look ridiculous. Improvisation is wildly popular here in Chicago.

Regardless of how I feel before the class, I'm energized and tested for three hours, which does wonders for my spirit. The fundamentals of improvisation are great training for life. Having grown up in a household full of "no," it is life changing to change that approach to "Yes, and..." There's no following a script. It's all about going with the flow and being in the moment. Don't plan on what you're going to say, listen to others, and let it *happen*. For that reason, improvisation has become a spiritual practice for me.

Josephine Forsberg introduced herself last week and encouraged us to discover ourselves through Players Workshop. She said she had a student who she always had to treat to dinner because he never had any money—and now he's worth millions. He couldn't afford class, so he painted her kitchen. That student is Bill Murray, who promised her a white Rolls-Royce once he made it big. I'm disappointed to know that he never delivered on the Rolls.

I absolutely adore the people in my class, and our teacher David Murphy. We trust each other in our pursuit of comedy and have become a family of misfits.

Most of our troupe. Left to right: David Murphy, Debbie Bickford, Susan Sheldon, Steve Lipshutz, Ron Moon, Eric Farone, Roy Sanchez, Sue Wright, Holly Schroeder, Jon Findley, Margaret Mitchell

September 25, 1990

I met a guy on the roof! He's a model and photographer with two names, one for each persona. I call him Ken, his professional, model name. He comes over and rifles through my closet, pulling out what I should wear, and then we go dance at NEO. He also cooks. He'll just show up and pull out my pots and pans and start cooking. He makes great spaghetti. He hangs out with Mia and me on my 1930s couch that feels like Astro Turf. I still can't believe I got that couch for $40.

Ken is gay which is good because I don't have time for shenanigans. He has wonderful fashion sense, wit, and moves like a leopard.

October 15, 1990

My teacher David in improv class said last week, "Holly, you're a funny woman." I'll take a compliment where I can get it. For years, I've felt hindered by my ability to see the humor when others can't.

Oscar Wilde did say nothing ruins a romance as much as a sense of humor in the woman.

October 31, 1990

I had an awesome Halloween party with my improvisation friends and a few folks from the *Spirit of Chicago*. One guy, Miles Stroth, showed up dressed as a woman, with black fishnets over his bowed legs. He told me he's bow-legged because he was hit by a car and left for dead. Miles studies improvisation with the infamous Del Close. He's the perfect party guest, as he always has a brilliant comeback.

Miles drank too much, so I said he could stay over. When I woke up, he was in bed next to me, still dressed as a woman in black fishnets, short black skirt, and bustier. He had mascara smeared on his cheek. My sweet, black cat Blue was between us, sleeping on his back. Miles opened his eyes looked at me (now out of my black wig) and said,

"You duped me. I thought you were a brunette."

I hope he calls me. He's hilarious.

November 28, 1990

The cats and I have met our upstairs neighbor, Hero Yamagucchi, an elderly Japanese man missing some teeth, who always wears a trench coat and smokes cigars. Mia and Blue had squeezed between the air conditioner and the screen to reach the windowsill and fell two stories to the sidewalk below. Hero witnessed my panic as I tore out of the Florence in my nightshirt. He stood there like Colombo, sucking on his cigar and giggling.

"They're okay! Don't you know? Cats bounce!"

Hero's mother was an Olympic skater. They all lived in a Japanese internment camp, so Hero gets checks from the government. Hero and his brother lived with her in the apartment above mine for many years. The mailbox still featured a blurry tag with his brother's name on it. I assumed Hero was Bill because Hero wasn't on the mailbox, just Bill. Finally, he set me straight.

"Hero's my name, not Bill. Bill's my brother. Been dead 20 years!"

Hero eats at the diner down the street and puffs on his cigar while he ambles down the sidewalk. He talks to Mia and Blue through the window and giggles.

Mia has Hero and me trained. This is how it always goes: Mia will throw himself against the apartment door to be released into the wilds of The Florence, whose carpeting is dingy and stained. Mia rolls all over it and rubs against the walls, making eyes at me. He does this for a while, and when I go to the bathroom or turn my back, he ventures off.

Then the yowling starts from the dark, dirty hole in the wall on the second floor. This is how Mia calls attention to himself. What a showman. Hero, in his taped Woody Allen glasses, will emerge from his dusty, dark apartment with a flashlight and meet me at the hole. We stand outside it and call to Mia to come out of the wall. Mia will stay just out of reach, close enough to be seen, but not close enough to be grabbed. He is a royal pain in my ass. After ten minutes of this, he finally caves and lets me pull him out.

Hero will chuckle and waddle back to his apartment. I'll go back to mine with a filthy cat. And this is how THAT goes: I wash Mia in my white, claw foot tub, like a purification ritual. His grey fur, the color of soot, becoming snowball white again. He'll be all tickled with himself, and I'll have more laundry to do.

December 27, 1990

Went home to Indiana for Christmas with my parents and brother. We stayed true to our tradition and opened presents on Christmas Eve. As a joke, Dad, forever the prankster, gave Mom a doorknob. "Merry Christmas!" he said. She gave him *that* look. Danny and I each received a box of assorted nails and screws, complete with K-mart price tag.

My mom gave me a book, her bookmark in the middle.

"Don't lose my place," she said. She burnt the rolls like usual and Dad said,

"It wouldn't be dinner at home without burnt offerings." There was the usual bickering and occasional eruption because Mother had to have her way as always about everything. But then there was a stirring moment as we drove to midnight mass at St. John's. On WLS, there was this almost spooky, eerily gorgeous instrumental version of *Silent night*. Danny said, "Wow, that was beautiful." The music was breathtaking. I wish they'd play that sort of music at St. John's Lutheran Church. It would be so much easier to stay awake. Instead, all four of us, under the spell of a lackluster sermon, fell asleep in the pew, our eyes fluttering open when the pastor said,

"Is midnight service on Christmas Eve an opportunity to wear our new clothes or a chance to rejoice? Or is it a test to see who can stay awake?" If there was more hope in his sermons and less fear, I wouldn't go into a coma.

When the holiday was over, Danny and I drove back to Chicago in his truck with Porsche his cockatoo and my cats. We stuffed ourselves in the cab with all our gifts and laundry. Porsche, on Danny's shoulder, nibbled on his ear and tried to pull his glasses off as he drove down I94.

Mia climbed all over our gifts and through the steering wheel, and Blue yowled from under the seat. Porsche tried to nibble on Mia's fur and Mia swatted at her. Danny dropped me off at my apartment on Reta Street, and I stood in my living room window and watched him walk through the snow to his truck. A sadness came over me as I watched his labored, patient lumber, which is distinctly his own.

I know he's lonely. Shy and nerdish, he hasn't had good luck with girls. I'll never forget a story he told me about a girl he had a date with. When Danny arrived at the house, her brother had no idea where she was. They sat and talked a while, and when the brother went to get something out of the closet, he discovered his sister hiding in it. She didn't want to go on the date with Danny.

When Danny and I decided to throw a party at the apartment, he invited everyone from work, and I invited my friend Julie. Danny went out and bought cold cuts and beer and set it all up. No one showed up but his Chinese friend from work and my friend Julie. Heartbreaking. And then he wondered if Julie would be interested in going out with him and I had to tell him she's a lesbian.

I hope he has an amazing vacation in Mexico with his buddy Sergio. He deserves so much. Mom isn't thrilled that he's going, but she is a professional worry wart.

UNSPEAKABLE LOSS

All it takes is one day to change the course of an entire life. January 11, 1991, changed the course of mine. As for my parents? They would never fully recover. I don't know how anyone could be so insensitive and thoughtless to leave the following on my parents answering machine:

"I'm sorry to inform you, but your son drowned in Mexico on January 11."

My brother Danny was dead at 31. We'd never see him again. Life is precarious at best. God is not always merciful and God is not there when you need him. Bad things happen to good people, and once you're in that camp, there's no unlearning the truth. All those years my mother endured of Catholic school and all my father's devotion to the Lutheran church couldn't save them from losing their only son. For me, God and religion looked like a big hoax.

The details were murky. The guys went swimming near a waterfall in Guatemala called "The Blue Waters." One-minute Danny was there, the next he was gone. He fell in a waterfall, and another guy, whom Danny had only just met, drowned trying to save him.

January 13, 1991
Everything is a blur. It's unreal and gathering the self-control and thought to continue takes all my energy. Danny is a movie in my mind, now. I see him laughing and flaring his nostrils to make me laugh. I see him driving his blue Cordoba with the 8-track tape playing The Grateful Dead. I remember how proud he was of his job at the mushroom farm in our hometown. I think about how he used to let me ride on the back of his bike when we lived on Country Club Drive. When he went through puberty and grew hair all over his body, I called him "the hairy monster." I can't imagine life without my big brother. He was always there. And now he's gone.

WhyDanny? He was the gentlest of souls, smart, kind, and he deserved a full life. He didn't have a mean bone in his body. He was an Eagle Scout and played the violin.

I wasn't fit to drive. My ex-boyfriend Bob, aka Beau, drove me to my parents. He was there at my parents' house when the official telegram arrived. Seeing a woman get out of a truck and walk a tragedy to the front door was all too much.

January 14, 1991

We have learned that Danny's friend Sergio had to get Danny's body from Guatemala to Mexico City. Sergio had to have the undertakers in each town sign legal papers to deliver Danny to Mexico City and then to the United States.

Then we learned that the mother of John Clay, the other fella who died, had flown to Mexico to the exact place of the tragedy. Her son was missing for four days before they found him. She told my mother that Danny lay under a lean-to for two days before being embalmed. They had kept him in the water for a while to keep him cold.

Sergio drove Danny in a Mexican funeral casket in the back of a pick-up truck to Ville Hermosa and then to Mexico. It took four days for the casket and Danny to arrive from Mexico, during which time funeral arrangements had to be made. Should we cremate him there, or should we fly him home in a casket bought by his friend Sergio? My parents were discussing options, and my father broke down. He reached out for my mother, who wouldn't even put her arms around him. I wanted to shake her for being so cold.

To get his son back, my father had to pay the American Embassy in Mexico City five thousand dollars. A lot of tourists die in Mexico—it's a source of income. We are at the mercy of the Mexican government.

January 15, 1991
We were told that once the casket arrived from Mexico, it was leaking at O'Hare Airport, and the officials there needed it transported immediately. As soon as the hearse arrived in LaPorte to the funeral home, Dad drove his own car to the funeral home and Mom drove hers.

Once Mom and I got to the Haverstock's parking lot, we saw that the hearse had arrived. The garage was open and there was Dad sneaking around. Mother shouted across the parking lot.

"Bob, get out of there!" It was awful. I knew he just wanted to confirm that it really was Danny in the casket, but honestly. We all agreed that since he wasn't embalmed in Mexico, that wouldn't be a good idea. It's all morbid and tragic. Just remember him as he was before death.

Inside Larry's office we were told, "We have to bury him as soon as possible. And we'll have the memorial on Monday." There are no words to describe how I felt watching my father process the reality that his only son and first child was decomposing. Dad was in full-blown denial.

"Is he wearing a gold band with a diamond and blue and white tennis shoes?" he asked. Larry's helpless expression mirrored my own. My mother abruptly ended the conversation, as she so often did, with a horrifying comment.

She turned to my father and said, "He's Jell-O, Bob. Go home."

It was the worst moment of my life, and even the undertaker flinched as this grotesque comment hung in the air. I wanted to crawl in a hole and die. My poor father got up and left the room. At that moment, I would have given anything, including my own life, to turn back the clock and rewrite the chain of events that led us there.

January 16, 1991

We buried Danny today in Pine Lake Cemetery. It was so bitterly cold every breath stung my lungs. I don't know how my father will survive this. People have odd reactions when a loved one dies, and my dad is a little odd to begin with. He wanted to leave a note attached to the casket, but my mother had to discourage this small gesture of desperation.

As they read the Lord's Prayer, I noticed that 50 feet away, three grave diggers leaned against their shovels. One of them flicked his cigarette butt on the ground. Business as usual. I can't get that image out of my head.

Danny was an overgrown little boy. His quiet nature stabilized the chaos in our house. With him gone, what will happen now? I am devastated. My brother deserved a full life and didn't get one.

"It was just his time. God swooped down and picked him up," said Mom. I don't buy it. I need answers, and I need them now.

I didn't want to leave Danny in that cemetery. I felt as if we betrayed him by leaving him in the frozen ground and driving away. What a horrible custom, burying people in the ground. So many monstrous people in the world—murderers, thieves—who are still here on the planet. Yet my kind, decent brother doing cancer research is gone. I feel betrayed.

January 17, 1991

Danny was in the house, I'm sure of it. I was in my bed, listening to Elton John's "Daniel" on my Walkman and it kept turning off. I'd turn it on, it would turn off. The batteries were new. I swear to God Danny was there, trying to tell me it's okay. I cannot explain it. A feeling of peace washed over me.

Odd things have happened in my parent's house. One of the cats got spooked in the basement and ran up the wall, causing one of the tiles in the ceiling of Danny's bedroom to fall down. On top of it was a deck of girly playing cards and Alice Cooper's record "Life in Hell," which was broken in half. Danny hid these things in the ceiling when he was in high school, years ago.

January 26, 1991

I drove to Danny's apartment today to empty his dresser drawers and remove every issue of *High Times Magazine*, a tiny bit of marijuana, and anything else incriminating. The second I walked in, the smell of the place—metal, gun powder, and newspapers was a punch to the gut. The comment I made before he went on vacation played in a loop in my head.

"You'll have a wonderful time in Mexico, Danny. You'll think you died and went to heaven! In which case, I get Aunt Penny's 1930s table." Then we laughed because we both love that table. It was a *joke*.

I put Aunt Penny's table and boxes of things in my car, plopped Danny's pith helmet on my head, and his Grateful Dead tape into my deck and drove back to the city, crying the whole way. Next week, my parents and I will empty his apartment.

February 1, 1991

I can't sleep, the depression about Danny has crippled me. It is hard for me to be in public, so it's nearly impossible to write sales copy about fur coats. I'm struggling, so I went to Dee for answers. Any chance I can, I go to her cube for a quip and a quibble. Today, I asked her if she thought Danny could see us. Dee put down her pen and looked me square in the eye.

"Holly, who knows? He may be busy. He's probably thin and having an affair."

February 13, 1991

Today my boss scolded me for wearing a Calvin Klein wrap dress to work, claiming it was too sexy. Immediately, I went to Dee, who said, "Oh, please, don't listen to her. Sexy never hurt anyone unless they were in a bad neighborhood."

February 15, 1991

Half the creative department was let go, including Dee. I've never experienced a sudden lay off before, and my emotions were too close to the surface. My boss scolded me, saying "Get a hold of yourself" as I cried at the company meeting. I couldn't pull it together. The president was touched by my concern for my coworkers and slid a box of Kleenex down the table to me. Worried about Dee, I went to her cube after the meeting.

"I feel so bad for you and Bob and everyone else. I know I shouldn't be so emotional, but I can't stop crying." Dee was no stranger to the corporate world and squared my shoulders.

"You can't control your emotions, Holly. You can only leave town." She hugged me, and we hauled four large shopping bags full of office supplies to the elevator. Dee calmly put on her Pendleton coat, black wool beret, leather gloves, and walked out the door. Just like that.

February 21, 1991

Danny's luggage finally arrived at my parents' house. My mom did what she always did and washed and folded his clothes. There was a letter in his luggage addressed to me that described the chain of events leading to his death.

Danny always had the spirit of an adventurer. Every summer he went to Camp ToPeNeBee summer camp sponsored by the Boy Scouts and was a member of the Adventure Club.

I know why he wanted to go, but this trip to Mexico was fraught with peril from day one. He called this trip the Trek of the Gulf Fleet. In his diary, he listed omens. On New Year's Eve, while driving through Lebanon, Missouri, they hit an ice patch and their truck went over a guard rail into a ditch. He wrote:

"The wheels are up in the air like a dead horse, and I'm upside down staring at dirt and rock for a windshield. The sun roof yielded the same damn view. There are few things more exhilirating than walking away from a totalled vehicle without a scratch! We got a hotel room to crash and salvage everything in the morning. My camera is full of crud. But the bottle of rum is NOT broken!"

I wish they'd stopped their trip and come home, but instead, they continued with a different car. They did make it to Mexico

City and had a wonderful time until January 11, when he drowned. The last sentence of the letter was: *Driving in Mexico City takes a lot of testicular fortitude.*

Every day, the first thought upon waking is that my big brother is dead. Why did God take my big brother, the Eagle Scout, the biochemist without a mean bone in his body? Making him laugh was my joy. Will it ever get easier? Will it ever make sense?

I try to find comfort in quotes like this:

> *Be patient toward all that is unsolved in your heart. Try to love the questions themselves like locked rooms or books that are written in a foreign tongue. The point is to live everything. LIVE the questions now. Perhaps you will then gradually without noticing it, live your way some distant day into the answers.*
>
> —R.M. Rilke

February 23, 1991

Standing at a cross walk today it hit me. I could die at any moment. Why wait to pursue what I really want? My mother isn't taking a subway every day to a job that doesn't fulfill her. I'm not sure it matters *what* I do with my life. She will always judge and criticize me because she sees me as an extension of herself, not a separate person with her own identity. I could end up dead before my time, like my big brother.

May 8, 1991

I was sitting on the couch, next to the armrest, thinking about Danny, feeling bereft. Mia, perched on the armrest, placed his paw on top of my hand and looked deep into my eyes. I'll never forget it. He was so deliberate in how he did it, I was struck speechless. He kept his paw there and looked into my eyes. My friend Larry Kaplan was visiting with us. He picked up his camera and took this shot. I call it American Gothic.

June 28, 1991

Evans let me go. I had a flash—a feeling—wash over me before the phone rang. It's like I knew, so I wasn't surprised when a voice said, "Holly will you please come to Human Resources?"

They axed Marta and Dee six months ago, and now it's my turn. That's business. Somehow, I don't feel all that sad. They gave me *one* paid personal day for Danny's funeral. They can shove it. I walked down State Street carrying two shopping bags full of office supplies. I felt light as air and skipped home! Now is my chance to pursue acting. Danny would totally approve.

August 1, 1991

I was in LaPorte at my parents' house recently. Dad and I went to the cemetery to visit Danny's grave.

"I still can't believe he's gone," said Dad. "I miss him so much. It's almost like he was never here at all."

Unbearable. To hear him say that, I just want to smother our pain, bury it, burn it, anything but feel it.

FINDING MY LIGHT

I'd been trying to make sense of my life, which toed a fine line between tragedy and comedy since day one, but Danny's death took me to a different level. At 24, I knew the truth about life, that I could never be safe from tragedy. No wonder I felt so at home in the theater.

The only family member who encouraged my interest in theater was my big brother Danny. In high school, when I played Martha Brewster in *Arsenic and Old Lace*, he came to every show. He paid me twenty bucks to squeeze "Where's the beef?" into the script. My mother had a dog show the weekend of the show, so she came to a dress rehearsal, instead. This was the first of many times she would do this. I looked out at her in the audience, and she was asleep.

> *It is not childish to live with uncertainty, to devote oneself to a craft rather than an institution. It's courageous and requires a courage of the order that the institutionally co-opted are ill equipped to perceive. They are so unequipped to perceive it that they can only call it childish and so excuse their exploitation of you.*
>
> —David Mamet

My parents didn't understand my attraction to the arts, so they tried to shut it down. They refused to encourage a career in theatre let alone pay for an acting degree, so I did something practical and got a B.A. in Communication. Without a theatre degree, I decided to get educated in any way I could. I was all in and looked at every job as a stepping-stone. I wasn't driven by money, only artistic exploration. It never dawned on me that investing in such a career is a huge risk.

July 17, 1991

I've taken a job on the *Spirit of Chicago* cruise ship as a singing, dancing waitress. My sorority sister Jodi Scutchfield encouraged me to take singing lessons and audition. I took a slew of lessons with a recommended teacher, learned "The Lullaby of Broadway," auditioned, and got the job.

Then, a gal I work with on the boat gave me the name of a voice teacher, Kathryn Hartgrove. I've been going to her once a week when I can afford it. She's helping me develop my head voice since my chest voice is already developed. Like Ethel Merman and Patty LuPone, I'm a "belter." That's my type.

Perhaps it will all pay off. The other day on the Spirit of Chicago, I dedicated my solo to one of my tables and they gave me a $100 tip!

Our improv show *A Taste of Chicago* was a success. It's a big thrill to get applause on the Second City stage, where so many greats got their start, like John Belushi, Dan Aykroyd, Alan Arkin, Bill Murray, and Joan Rivers. Our teacher and director, David Murphy, was proud of us, as was family that attended. My Uncle Tom and Aunt Bobbi and my Mom were there. Debbie Bickford, Eric Farone, Jon Findley, Steve Lipshutz, Margaret Mitchell, Ron Moon, Ron Packowitz, Roy Sanchez, Susan Sheldon, Sue Wright, and Chad Wright pulled it off. We each brought our own physicality and humor. A whole year to prepare for this show and Chad lost his voice, which meant he had to bellow a lot of his lines. In the words of Gilda Radner, "It's always something."

October 20, 1991

Great news! A fellow thespian hooked me up with a promotional company that's hiring actors for a Miller Lite promotion. It's an easy $25 an hour gig for about three months. All I have to do is pass out beer coupons in the liquor departments of Jewel Food stores, dressed as an alien! How hard can it be?

The costume consists of a skin-tight, white spandex jumpsuit, gloves, and a bulbous alien head. The gloves have six-inch long fingers and the nylon and foam head is surprisingly realistic!

Because I'm an alternate alien, I have to share my head with other actors. This is the first job I've ever had that requires me to meet people at random street corners to hand off my head. Today, some dude named Zachary called me and said,

"I need the head. What time can you bring it to the corner of Clark and Belmont?"

October 25, 1991

I have a system. I put on my spandex costume at home, drive to the liquor store, put my alien head on in the car, and casually walk into the store. Once I find the Miller Lite display and pull out my coupons, I put on my fingers. Handing out coupons with six-inch long fingers is challenging, but I'm making it work.

I have no peripheral vision so the world bobs in front of me. It's kind of surreal. What I do is stand still and wait for shoppers to walk by. Many of them think I'm a cardboard cutout. As they pass by, I do a sharp alien move and say "Greetings" waving my elongated phalanges. They jump and laugh, embarrassed. Then I hand them a $2.00 coupon for Miller Lite.

November 10, 1991

Children don't like aliens appearing suddenly out of nowhere. Today, three kids shrieked and covered their faces to hide from me, the hideous alien. When parents force them to shake my hand of spindly fingers? Awkward.

Three hours into my shift today, some teenage kids snuck up behind me, smacked the back of my head and ran. I thought about chasing them, but I'd hate to get fired. Being an alien is my big gig right now.

I have to admit, the head of my costume is getting to me. The screen by my mouth is too small to breathe through and the head is stuffy. I started thinking about all the germs festering in the foam next to my mouth. I thought I was going to suffocate. What if I get a head cold/runny nose during this gig?

December 3, 1991

I caught a cold. I had to stuff a Kleenex up my nostrils or snot runs down onto my upper lip.

Today, a dusty, toothless man told me his entire life story, beginning with his birth on a potato farm. I felt so sorry for him. Some people just don't have good luck or lineage.

Then, my mom called to express her disappointment in me.

"Four years of college and you're not a secretary, you're an alien."

"Actually, Mom, I'm an *alternate* alien," I corrected. "I have to share my head with other actors. There just aren't enough heads to go around." I had to cover my mouth from laughing out loud as she expelled one of her long sighs.

January 22, 1992

I let my neighbor, Christian Langworthy, move in from down the hall. He's always here anyway and his brother irritates him. Since he's an Amerasian poet, it can't hurt having him to share stories and the rent. My second bedroom is small, but he says it's big enough for a bed and his saxophone. He's a romantic.

Christian was born in Vietnam. His mother was a prostitute, and his father an American soldier. He has foggy memories of his mother with other men. He was adopted at the age of four by an American family. He and his brother arrived in America on a winters' day wearing shorts and sandals. It's been good having him around, and he's so delighted by Mia's antics. The other day he left me this note:

> *Holly,*
>
> *Mia and I had an enjoyable evening. We listened to Tchaikovsky, read a little Hemingway (though we grew bored of it), and discussed the philosophy of Al Farabi in relation to the Islamic religion. Mia is the coolest, most intelligent feline to live in this century.*
>
> *Christian*

February 15, 1992

Mia has become my muse, my best friend, and my little man. This month, he is going through a rebellious phase. I bought an albino frog (white with pink eyes) at the pet store on Valentine's Day, which I named Alfie. Since I don't have a boyfriend, I felt I deserved a frog. Mia keeps reaching into the tank to touch him with his paw.

Mia doesn't like the sound of the saxophone. Christian was practicing the other day, and after he finished, he placed the sax in the stand and walked away. Mia, peeking around the corner, ran into the room, jumped up in the air like a kung fu cat, whacked the mouthpiece and ran.

June 10, 1992

I have a paying role in a Second City show! I am playing a cow in an improvisational show called *Dreams, Detectives & Mermaids* written by an improv alum. Halfway through the show I sing:

"Milk me, milk me, give my udder a squeeze. Do it quickly before it all turns to cheese."

It's all up from here.

September 15, 1992

Because our graduation show was such a big hit, our improvisation group got a gig at a comedy club called Who's On First. Jon Findley picked me up and we drove out to Elmhurst with Debbie and Susan.

As we pulled up to the club, our faces fell. It looked like Bob's country hole in the wall. We didn't even know where the front door was. Jon tried to pull open an orange door and it was locked.

He's always so positive, and said, "Oh, I don't think this is it!"

We finally found it, and when we opened it, the stench of beer and stale cigarettes nearly knocked us over.

Emo Phillips, Rosanne Barr, Howie Mandell, and other greats have performed at this joint. Most of the comics were dreadful, but there was a juggler/fire eater who was funny. We did okay. We adjusted to the small width of the stage and the absence of musical accompaniment. On our way home, a hooker on North Avenue ran in front of the car with her dress up, exposing herself. Debbie, Susan, and I shrieked and pointed. Jon didn't even blink.

March 18, 1993

I'm doing an improvisational show called *Menu Mania* at the Candlelight Forum Theater in Summit Illinois, with a cast of five, including Jim Blanchette, whom I adore. There are menus for breakfast, lunch, and dinner posted onstage, and we perform sketches on demand like Beatnik Rap, Mystery of the Ninja Turtles, Moe and Joe's Yuk Yuk Show, and Midday Horror Theater.

Today, we forfeited our pay to perform for the children of Cabrini Green. I'm SO glad we did. They were the most appreciative audience yet. Some of these poor kids weren't even wearing shoes.

When we finished, the kids presented us with a basket of fruit and goodies. I had to stifle tears as these five children proudly carried it onstage and gave it to us. I will never forget it.

Timberlake Playhouse, Mt. Carroll, Illinois, June 30, 1993

I'm sick over the fact that Danny can't see any of these productions. He would love this theater and all its quirks. He would feel safe to be himself here. After seeing *Smoke on the Mountain*, Mom said,

"Can you imagine how much Danny would have loved visiting you here?"

I want to share Blue Grass Gospel music with Danny and this wonderful show. I don't think I've ever had such an amazing time as these past few months. This experience has changed me. The collective joy of doing theater is healing and being a catalyst for the audience to transcend their own struggles is such a gift. Celebrating the human condition is life affirming. Danny would have gone ape over these shows. I'm so proud of my reviews.

> *I have saved the best for last, and that is Holly Schroeder in the part of another sister, June. June admits right up front that she doesn't sing. But what she does is steal the show as the sound effects person and "signer" (even though she is told there are no deaf people in the congregation). She plays everything from a scrub board to cowbells and some odd objects in between. If you've never seen a "singer" improvise and ad lib, you will here.*
>
> —Grace Whitten, Herald Wire Editor

> *Worthy of special mention is the straight-faced performance of Holly Schroeder as June Sanders, one of Burl's daughters. According to June, she doesn't sing, she signs. Throughout the show, Schroeder*

furnishes the rhythm for the music on at least 10 different instruments. In addition to "normal" percussion instruments such as a triangle, cymbal, and a homemade looking tiny bass drum, she plays spoons, a washboard, cow bells, and salad bowls. At one point, the audience burst into spontaneous laughter and applause at her appearance with a new sound effect of sand-paper between her knees.

—Sarah Thornkike, Whiteside News Sentinel

August 1993

What an incredible summer! From the time I drove down that gravel path to cabin #5 until I sadly pulled away, it was momentous. I am not the same. This summer has been the best of my life.

My cabin mate, Elvira Ponticelli, became one of my closest friends. There was a mother bird that built her nest in the eaves of our cabin, so we were awakened at all hours by her feeding her babies. We told the fellas building sets and they nailed a board over the hole which was not the solution we were hoping for. We ordered them to take it off and just dealt with the noise. We lay in bed at night talking about life, love, and the theater serenaded by baby birds.

Smoke on the Mountain changed my life. It took me some time before I found the balance I needed for the character of June Sanders. I learned some sign language and made up some of my own, thanks to Elvira's sister Ermalinda, who actually *is* a signer. She taught me a lot. I also played 15 different percussion instruments. I was fearful I couldn't pull it off, but I managed to do better than I thought. I really loved doing sign language. I wonder if should consider becoming a signer?

By the time opening night arrived, I was filled with so much love, it poured out of me. No one could know what this show meant to me. It was such a joy to tell this story and sing Blue Grass Gospel music with a fantastic cast.

What is comical about this theater is that it has a tin roof, so if it's raining hard, we stop the show. During the final performance, a storm rolled in. When I stretched out my arms and said,

"God's power is loud like thunder," thunder rolled over the theater, rattling the tin roof. The hair on my arms stood on end.

Yaakov Sullivan, who once lived on a kibbutz, is hilarious. We were inseparable at times. I call him The King of Kvetch. When it rained for four days straight, he dramatically whined,

"This rain is insufferable. Here I am, stuck in this mud hole, with nothing but my dream of being a celebrity chef." Then, he'd go into the Timberlake kitchen and whip up something divine.

I never dreamed it would be such a productive and emotionally healing summer. I loved sitting on the swing at the front of the theater watching the storms roll in, being surrounded by endless fields of corn, stars at night that seem close enough to touch, campfires where everyone relaxes and talks. Sheer heaven. This is my tribe.

Randy Rogers directed us in *Anything Goes*. We told ghost stories some nights and drank pitchers of Bloody Mary's. One night, Randy said to me with such conviction,

"Your success will be in playing yourself onstage, instead of other characters." Patty Choate suggested I do a one-woman show. No one in my family ever encouraged me like this. In fact, during a recent conversation with my dad, when he started thinking of other careers for me, he said,

"You know what you'd be great at? Sales. You should consider a career selling pipe couplings."

While playing Erma in *Anything Goes* and singing Cole Porter's "Buddie Beware," I learned that there's nothing more fun than dancing with sailors. Forest, an actor who joined us for this show, became so dear to me. We created an ingenious movement piece for the variety show. I also sang "Sweet Dreams," and Kathy the cook said,

"Just when I thought I'd seen you do it all, you sang Patsy Cline beautifully."

Her husband Jim Warfield owns Raven's Grin Inn, the haunted house in Mt. Carroll, Illinois. He lives in this old house that he's got rigged with all sorts of curiosities and frights. The front door is a draw bridge, there's a refrigerator door that opens to a staircase, and he built a "bed slide" that travels through the house from the second floor to the wine cellar, which is haunted by the "lady in white."

I am thankful my parents saw some of the shows at Timberlake Playhouse. Mom told me during the run of *Smoke on the Mountain* that during the intermission, Dad went into the men's room and the guys were chuckling about my performance, comparing me to Lucille Ball. To be discussed in the men's john and likened to Lucille Ball is a compliment if there ever was one.

TIMING IS EVERYTHING

"To get to the fruit of the tree, one must go out on a limb." Thanks to Shirley MacLaine, that phrase became my mantra. Throwing caution to the wind, I went at life with wild abandon. I'm lucky I didn't end up dead in a gutter.

After Timberlake Playhouse, I flew out to Los Angeles to visit my dear friend Scott Carter, who lives there now.

September 1, 1993

I believe in magic. I'm only just learning how to create it. I flew out to L.A. on August 26. John Miranda, Scott's roommate, picked me up at LAX. Within an hour, I was lolling on a couch in the office of Norman Jewison, in my Betsy Johnson floral number. John is a script editor for Norman, a director I've admired since *Moonstruck*.

On Friday, when John took me to his office, I studied Steven Spielberg's awards. There were reminders of all his films throughout the bungalow, which has a Jacuzzi, game room, kitchen with chef, herb garden, on-staff trainer, and security staff. On the wall was a framed letter from a fan who, while seeing E.T., lost her contact lens in the movie theater. "You pushed my cry button," she claimed as she requested payment to replace the lost contact lens. Spielberg sent her a check for the contact lens and the movie, since she missed some of it searching for the contact lens. Spielberg is gifted and kind.

The same day, we went to Universal City and got in free due to John's connections with Amblin. We rode the "Back to the Future" ride twice. It was a blast! The tribute to Lucille Ball sent shivers through me. John and I quote movie lines constantly. *Postcards from the Edge* is one of our favorite sources.

This summer, Richard Choate told me about a dear writer friend of his whom he met in Iowa. They'd both been screenwriters in Los Angeles and had acted together at Timberlake Playhouse. David almost came to TLP this summer but couldn't because he is a co-producer/writer of *The Adventures of Brisco County* on FOX.

Richard thought David and I would hit it off and I'd get a tour of the lot, so I reached out to David. I met David at Lana Thai Restaurant in Sherman Oaks. The Pad Thai was to die for. Would you believe David grew up in South Bend, Indiana, a half hour from me?

When he asked me what I want from life, I said, "A kiss to build a dream on." His eyes lit up.

David offered me a tour of FOX and picked me up on Wednesday. I watched filming, chatted with crew members, and then sat in David's office, where he asked for suggestions for a cliff hanger. I was flattered and felt useful. Our eyes met for an uncomfortable suspension of time. Our desperate search for an exciting conflict for the hero was intermittently interrupted with phone calls.

"Is there enough money in the budget for a herd of cattle?" David asked.

"No, we've already used snakes. I can't let go of the dynamite idea either. Jim likes the cattle stampede. Let's call the cattle expert!"

Then, he took me on a tour of the FOX sound stages and sets. Later, we went to Santa Monica for dinner, where I said, "I wish I lived here. If I did, I'd want to date you."

My honesty took him by surprise, and he choked on his ahi tuna. "Me too," he said.

At the crosswalk, he put his arm around me and bumped my hip with his. I bumped back. The days that followed were glorious. With our mutual interest in films, fresh dialogue, and story, we were never at a loss for words. Later, we watched the pilot episode of *The Adventures of Brisco County*, and when David's name appeared on the screen, I got so excited I jumped into his lap. We were intertwined within minutes. When he dropped me back off at John and Scott's apartment, he invited me to hang out with him at his house in Minneapolis.

After visiting the Museum of Intolerance with Yaakov Sullivan, who was in town, I came back to find an impressive tropical flower arrangement. John Miranda called it "bucks deluxe." It was stunning

. . . and from David . . . with a note that said: "Let's enjoy this one step at a time." My God, roses from the right man!

That evening, he came by at 9:30 p.m. One look at him grinning at me through the screen door and I lost all my manners. I ran out the door and into his arms.

"What do you want to do?" I asked him.

"Breathe the air you breathe," he answered. I wondered if he'd heard that in a movie or if it was his own.

At Mel's Diner we sat on the same side of the booth and stared into each other's eyes. We were destined to meet.

"This is the most pleasant surprise," he said. "God, I'm glad you called me!"

I'm over the moon!

September 7, 1993

I am 30,000 feet up in the air flying to Minneapolis to spend time with David. This has happened so fast. I can't believe it! He makes my heart race.

When I was at the Abbey Coffee Shop with John, Scott, and Gannon, we met a numerologist who read our cards and told me, "Your future includes travel, new beginnings, and a love that will last. You're going to travel around the globe."

September 14, 1993

I can only say that David is everything I've ever wished for: talented, generous, funny, witty, strong, passionate, masculine, and his house is spectacular. We rode bikes, cooked together, watched movies, made love, and went to the Mall of America. Every time our eyes met I fell a few feet.

We talk about movies, plays, books, writing, and shop for home décor. And now he wants me to move in with him! For the longest time, I've felt I wasn't going to meet my man in Chicago. Considering how we met, this seems meant to be. I cannot believe the sequence of events. I feel ALIVE! The only route is to take the biggest risk of my life. He has asked me to move to Minneapolis to be with him.

February 1, 1994

Shit. Jane Ryan Productions offered me a six-month contract to be the lead singer of an 8-person cast aboard the Queen Elizabeth II for their Transatlantic World Cruise. THIS is the type of opportunity I've been waiting for, but why does it have to come exactly when I've agreed to move to Minneapolis to be with David? WHY? Talk about bad timing.

The QE2 will begin its voyage from Cape Town, South Africa, and travel to Portugal, Morocco, and then Southampton. Then we fly to Los Angeles, where we board a second ship and travel through the Panama Canal, to Cabo San Lucas, Aruba, and conclude in Florida. Then we fly to Los Angles, where we board the Sagafjord for the second phase of the contract, which entails sailing all over Alaska for three months.

This is it! My ticket to stardom, international travel, and exotic ports of call! How can I turn this down? They auditioned in 17 cities and picked me! Such an opportunity may never come again. And guess what? There's a Fanny Brice medley. This is my chance to do *Funny Girl* material!

The contract calls for a month of rehearsal in Florida, for which the pay is $300 a week, plus room and board. At sea, the salary is $500 a week, plus room and board. I will have my own room and no cruise ship duties. The dancers have duties and live two to a cabin. The 50-minute reviews include a 1940's radio show, a Las Vegas-style review, a musical "whodunit" mystery show, and a holiday review.

What a great opportunity to see the world and get paid for it!

February 12, 1994

I had a "going away" bash in my Chicago apartment. My closest friends met David and wished me the best on my move to Minneapolis and my journey as a performer on the QE2. Crying most of the way to Minnesota, I kept wondering if I was doing the right thing. I left behind so many friends for someone I met this past summer. I've been waiting for David all my life, right? And my dreams, too. Why did they have to happen at the same time? Oy vey gevalt.

February 14, 1994

I arrived in Minneapolis with David today. I can't wait to cook him my signature dishes, romp like kids, and be who I am with someone who appreciates me. I kind of wish I hadn't accepted the contract. I just fear it will never come again. I don't want to blow it with David, but we aren't engaged yet. Maybe he'll respect and appreciate me more if I contribute something financially to the relationship? I've never been in this situation before. I wish someone would just tell me what to do.

February 20, 1994

I'll be doing my own cabaret onboard, which is exciting, except that I must have musical charts made for the band's guitarist and piano player. I've never worked on a cruise ship, so I'm trusting that Jane Ryan Productions is a top-notch operation, as Jane hires a lot of performers for the various ships she has contracts with. And this is for Cunard.

IN THE BELLY OF THE WHALE

February 24, 1994, Fort Lauderdale, Florida

It was torturous saying goodbye to David, but I didn't have time to wallow. Our cast started rehearsals immediately in a warehouse five miles from the hotel. None of us realized there would be this much material to learn in one month. There are four fifty-minute reviews and four five-minute openers, all featuring different choreography and costume changes. We'll be memorizing music at the hotel at night. I'll be a better sight reader after this.

Brian, a singer/dancer originally from the Midwest, volunteered to be our manager and van driver. He and I are so on the same page. He's a good egg and my new favorite person.

February 26, 1994

Pierre and I giggled today over the errors in our sheet music. Kander & Ebb's "How Lucky Can You Get?" is incorrect. This is what's printed in our score:

"Suddenly my shoulder and the smell on my lips."

It's supposed to read: *"Satin on my shoulder and a smile on my lips."*

Today our music director didn't show up for rehearsal, and Pierre and I just sat in the van listening to our Walkmans and memorizing lyrics. Pierre misses Migel, so he drinks at night at the hotel. I certainly can't drink while memorizing lyrics. There are so many songs looping in my brain, I can't sleep. Two of the dancers, David and Maria, are engaged. Missy, our ballerina from the South, is allergic to feathers and bees. How unfortunate, considering there are feathers sewn into most of her costumes, and there's an angry hive of bees outside the warehouse entrance.

February 29, 1994

The cast is not ready for an audience. Two of the shows aren't completely written and we've barely rehearsed "Hooray for

Hollywood." We're all stressed out and had to run what we could in the warehouse in front of an audience, complete with costume changes.

There was nothing provided for us to change behind, so the audience got to see us perform and change into our costumes, which is shabby. Missy was really peeved. And I wasn't wearing my best underwear.

March 21, 1994

We just left New York and are on our way to South Africa. South African Airlines is an elegant airline. Free drinks.

As I listen to "Stardust" by Nat King Cole, I'm in heaven, remembering the week I met David. Jogging into the sunsets in Sherman Oaks and flying through the clouds to Minneapolis to fall head over heels. It's almost like everything in my life is too good to be true. Everything has been leading to this. While I was packing, I realized that what the psychic I met at the Abbey in West Hollowood predicted is coming true. Change, love, travel. It's happening, just like he said it would.

March 22, 1994, Cape Town, South Africa

We flew from Fort Lauderdale to New York to Johannesburg Africa to Cape Town. Then, spent the night in a hotel, boarded the ship early in the morning, and began rehearsing. No time to catch our breaths.

When we boarded, the staff took our passports and locked them away, claiming it was "policy" that they hold onto them. Many of the passengers are English, privileged, and at death's door.

March 23, off the coast of Africa, 8 p.m.

Don't have a lot of time to write because of rehearsals. Did I mention how long it takes to walk to the dining room? It's a commute.

FYI, I have 36 costumes, which means I change nine times in each review. Thank God we have dressers. It's in the contract! I swear, my Oleg Cassini sequined gown for the finale weighs ten pounds. Good thing I only wear it for one number.

11 p.m.

There are no dressers and there are no dressing rooms. The assistant cruise director will hang a curtain between us and our audience. So, we change in the hallway—the same one used by passengers on their way in and out of the show. Clearly, this isn't as sophisticated a gig as I'd thought. I'm trying to take it in my stride, but I guess I expected more from Cunard, a classy operation.

March 24, 3 a.m., Walvis Bay

Is there such a thing as guerilla theater? Tonight, we ran the show all the way through, which was excruciating enough, but then we had to do it all over again at 2 a.m. because they put a new person on lights. Wouldn't want to make time and energy efficient decisions or anything. I'm out of sorts and my human clock is off, which makes it hard for me to remember choreography and lyrics. And my stomach churns.

March 25, 1994

I think I've been sold into white slavery by my agent. And she's getting 20%. The QE2 is stuffy, and there is a definite class system. Being lowly performers, we eat in the Mauritania room, the dining room for serfs. They just keep reheating old food for us. I prefer porridge to what they feed us. I am literally surviving on Saltines and wilted lettuce. I have no appetite and am dropping weight. I've gone from a size 4 to a size 2 in one month, withering away like a dried husk. What will David say when he sees I've lost my tits and ass somewhere between Minneapolis and the coast of Africa?

March 27, 1994

What I've noticed is that Maria, who is Hispanic, and Kristine, who is Chinese, are lovely women and both brunettes, so the producers naturally put them in **blonde** wigs. As for Missy, the fair, redheaded Texan, they put her in a **brunette** wig. My wig is my worst color—ash blonde. So now, instead of looking pretty, we all look **cheap**.

Here's the blow-by-blow account of the day's misfires.

10 a.m.

In the "Hooray for Hollywood" number I hold a parasol, Pierre's arm, and a microphone as I shimmy across the stage in a skin-tight gown. On my head is a Mae West wig, glued and sewn into a massive hat full of teal and white feathers that I have to balance on my head, while I sing enthusiastically,

"Hooray for Hollywood! Where you're terrific if you're even good!"

2 p.m.

The "Monster Mash" number for the Halloween show requires one of the dancers to wear an enormous pumpkin costume. The topper? A toilet bowl plunger held on with yet another giant chin strap.

4 p.m.

Belting out "Big Noise from Winnetka" is a bit of a thrill, I must admit.

> *I am the one they call the Big Noise.*
> *I'm looking fine and feeling sharp.*
> *I just flew in from Winnetka, don't you know?*
> *I'm gonna blow this joint apart!*
>
> *Big Noise flew in from Winnetka,*
> *Stole each fellow's heart and then. . .*
> *Big Noise flew in from Winnetka, don't you know?*
> *And Big Noise flew right out again.*

Harmonizing with Pierre on numbers like "Night and Day" is delightful. Pierre's voice is velvety, and we blend together well. If it was just us and the music all would be fine, but it's the nonsensical decisions our producer has made that weigh the show and cast down.

The producer spent thousands on the costumes for the Latin opener, but we didn't have time to learn all of it because it wasn't written by the time we sailed, so we have to wear the Latin costumes for the Fanny Brice medley. Hilarious.

I don't think I'm getting paid enough to look this cheap. I'll be singing, "How Lucky Can You Get?" and "More Than You Know" wearing gold scrolls, green feathers, sequins, and spandex. When we walked out in costume, the band played a few bad notes, and a cymbal fell on the floor, spinning and clattering. I look like a Fabergé egg.

March 27, 1994
I had one morning to sightsee, and because Table Mountain was closed, Brian and I went to the flea market in town. The dollar is

strong, so I bought a mirror made of camel bone and a bronze African bust to begin my African art collection.

Learned today that the Grand Lounge, our "stage," can't be used during the day because of Bingo. So, we have to rehearse from midnight till 3 or 4 a.m. Our shows are second fiddle to Bingo.

March 30, 1994

What a snafu! Some Hungarian waiters informed us that our passports were confiscated when we boarded to discourage us from jumping ship. Apparently, that happens a lot. I remember having this odd feeling when they asked for my passport and put it in a box.

March 31, 9 p.m., The Bay of Biscay

This is the roughest passage of the voyage. The 963-foot long, 70,300-ton ship is rolling and swaying. Of all the nights for Radio City Rockettes to perform, this shouldn't have been the one. They are all about precision.

It is amazing to think that I'm living on this gigantic, historic vessel and can see the Radio City Rockettes tonight! Filled with enthusiasm, I went to the Grand Lounge. Oh, to have legs like a Rockette! They tried valiantly to stay in unison, but when the ship pitched, two of them fell forward, their smiles strained. Linked by their arms, the rest of the Rockettes followed suit. Wild applause.

I had to serpentine back to my room and saw a guy holding onto a railing puke into a bird of paradise. All night long, my body rolled back and forth in bed, bumping into the wall. I was lucky to sleep 2 hours.

April 1, 1994

Happy April Fool's Day! Who's the fool? I am!

April 2, 1994

I heard over the intercom tonight, "Starlight, starlight, Mauritania room." This is ship code for "Get the doctor, quick!" A passenger had had a heart attack and keeled over in the breakfast nook.

April 3, 1994

I love running into Albert and Finn. They're a dapper, gay couple who have been together a long time. God, how I love the gays. What Albert said today was quite profound:

"Through the years, my companion and I have traveled the world. Next year, we're going somewhere else." And then we all laughed in a very British way.

During the show tonight, male passengers strolled through our "dressing room" during our quick changes. Missy, who is really a Southern Belle, chased them out in her thong. She said she didn't study ballet her whole life to be humiliated like this. I feel the same. My left boob popped out of my Morticia dress during the Halloween number and the senior citizen whose lap I sat on didn't even notice. We all went to the bar after the show and drank. I'm so glad Brian is here. I don't know what I'd do without him.

April 4, 1994, Agadir, Morocco

I was so excited to get off the ship, since we'd been at sea for ten days straight! We weren't permitted off the boat in Walvis Bay or St. Helena. We did stop at a port whose main export is pigeon poop. We couldn't get off there, which was probably just as well, since there isn't much to see except poop.

By the time we got to Morocco, I practically clawed my way off the boat. There was a man bleeding in the street and people just stepped over him. Brian, Paul, (costumer), and I walked to the *Souk*, a market just like in the movies. Arabic, French, Tachelhit, and Moroccan are the spoken languages. It is rare that Americans visit Agadir, so we stuck out like nuns at an AC/DC concert. We walked through aisles of stalls selling fruit, herbs, vibrant spices in bags, curly-toed shoes, leather goods, brass, bronze, jewelry, swords, rugs, and blankets. It was overwhelming. I looked at some leather purses for a few minutes and when I started to walk away, the swarthy vendor hit me with a leather satchel and said, "FUCK!"

No doubt they think that because we're Americans we have money. However, we are young American *performers*, which means we do not. I felt anxious. Then, some grizzled, stooped man approached Paul and me. After some struggling to understand him because of how prepos-terous it all was, this Moroccan man in a diaper tried to buy me for 4,000 camels. Paul and I thought he was kidding but then took stock of where we were—at a Souk in Agadir, Morocco, where anything can happen. Dorothy, we're not in Kansas anymore. There's nothing scarier to me than Third World poverty. This man is wearing a dirty diaper.

Paul turned beet red, Brian took a step back to gather his compo-sure, and I said,

"Don't you think I'm worth a lot more?" The man held up four fingers again. It was awkward. We just sort of stumbled away and then high-tailed it out of there.

The beach, lined by luxury hotels, is beautiful and what Agadir is known for. I rode a camel down the beach for a small fee. I felt tall for a change. Brian, Steve, and I ate at Daffy, a Moroccan restaurant. I ordered chicken tagine—meat prepared in an earthen casserole bowl with prunes, lemons, and olives.

Before we boarded the ship, I called my father from a greasy pay phone and told him about the Moroccan man who wanted to buy me for 4,000 camels. His response?

"Four thousand camels? That's a very good price."

April 5, 1994

Today, we were in Lisbon, Portugal, a beautiful city. Brian, Steve, and I shopped in the *Baixa* and wandered up and down cobble-stone streets. We saw the monastery of Jeronimo and the Museum of Coaches. Oh, to ride around Lisbon in one of those gold-plated, gem-encrusted coaches!

April 6, 1994

My mental state is improving because David is going to take a cruise aboard the Sagafjord! He decided this after calling me the other morning at sea. I didn't know who it was at first because of the hour and the buzz on the line. I thought it was Pierre calling me about rehearsal and said,

"Pierre? What time is it?"

So, David left for Los Angeles a week early to be with friends, and we will be on board the ship together for a whole week!

April 7, 1994

We survived the ordeal of flying from England to Los Angeles and switching ships. I'm now on the Sagafjord, a much smaller ship. When David saw me, he was taken aback. I've lost enough weight that I look sickly. It is so good to have him by my side.

His room is lovely. My "accommodations" are pitiful. My room is two doors down from the engine room and smells like gas fumes. There is no way I can sleep on the grotesque mattress. It's about three inches thick and on a bed of rusty springs—like something you'd sleep on at Rikers Island.

The "dresser" has three small drawers and one long one only three inches wide. For socks? Belts? Lipstick? You pull it out two inches and it falls on the floor. Because my closet is 12 inches wide, all those gowns for my cabaret and my two bulging suitcases will have to be stored in the shower. I'm supposed to "live" like this for 4 months? Seriously? I can guarantee the woman making millions off her performers has never lived in a room so pitiful. I asked Brian if he thought there might be a rat in my room.

"No," he said. "A rat would never live in anything this small."

Thank God I can stay in David's room with him while he's onboard, but after he leaves, I'm back to this shameful closet called a "room." Not sure I can hang on for the whole contract.

April 8, 1994, Cabo, San Lucas
The cast has worked 19 days straight without a day off, which is a breach of contract. David called a lawyer, who said the contract is "onerous," meaning I have no protection and that I should just run as fast I can and don't tell anyone where I'm going. I should have had a lawyer look at the contract in the first place, but it wasn't sent to me until two days before I left home. Hmmm, it's all starting to make sense now.

One contract clause says that each performer will pay a $1,000 fine for quitting before the end of the contract. It is in very small print. The clause that states each performer will not receive the first paycheck until having performed on the ship for one month was in even smaller print. My lawyer suggested I get my hands on my first check, which should have been sent to David's house by now, cash it, and bolt.

April 9, 1994
There's a trio onboard. Our cast swapped gripes in the Mauretania room. The flautist (from Arkansas) said every time they perform during high tea, the maid fires up the Hoover and vacuums through three pieces. We saw this today exactly as described. I don't get how someone (in this case, the maid) can be that oblivious. So, I set an example and stole flowers from the bathrooms of The Lido Room and gave the musicians flowers at the end of their set yelling, "Bravo! Bravo!"

April 10, 1994
Wealthy older people don't make the best audiences. After one of our *Hooray for Hollywood* numbers, Pierre reacted to the smattering of applause.

"I don't get it!" he said, throwing up his hands. "I'm a sucker for a kick line."

David has gotten to know the cast and says he'd love to just shell out $1,000 per cast member to get us OFF this ship. He feels bad for us, as he's been at rehearsals and performances. I'm so glad he's filmed some of them.

David and I laughed so hard over "Summertime," this evening. I was singing my heart out (all the while poked by pins, as the dress hasn't been altered yet), and the male dancer Tim had Christine up in the air above his head. He couldn't keep her balanced, and she rocked back and forth four times on his strained arm, then tumbled like a sack of potatoes down his body and onto the floor. Tim paused and looked awkward, and then he went with it graciously, holding her hand and spinning out to pose as if it were planned that way. Then he picked her up off the floor, and she sprung up. Pose. David and I howled with laughter.

April 11, 1994, Costa Rica

When we arrived in Costa Rica, David and I caught a cab from the ship to the rain forest for a hike. The cab driver stopped on a bridge and mentioned there were white alligators below and told us to take a peek. When we were craning our necks over the railing, a shady character walked by the cab, reached in the window and stole my camera and purse.

"David!" I screamed, pointing at the thief. "Get him!" It was like an episode of *Hawaii 5-0*. The brigand dropped my possessions in the weeds and ran away. One more shock to my system and I'm going to have a stroke.

April 14, 1994

Last night, David proposed! We had just heard the opera trio and Elliott Finkel perform. Standing at the stern, under the stars of the balmy night sky, David got serious.

"Remember in L.A. before we met, how you said, 'You'll know me?' I realized my mind didn't, but my heart did. I've been waiting for you all my life. Will you be my wife?"

I was completely caught off guard. Turns out, he's been planning this for a while! I. Am. Stunned. For a second, I thought I should make him wait for my answer, but I couldn't.

"YES, I will marry you!"

We called my parents from a pay phone.

David said to my mother, "I just want to thank you for bringing such a wonderful woman into the world!"

You know what my mother said?

"I didn't have to have any anesthetic!"

April 17, 1994, In the Panama Canal

During the closing number tonight, Kristine's fishnet stockings got snagged on Armand's sequined jacket, and as he flipped her off his shoulder, her ankle twisted. We took our bows, and as we exited the ballroom, the cruise director stood in the hallway, our dressing room, kicked our costumes and yelled, "Get these off the floor, damn you, guests are coming through!"

The handsome ship's doctor wrapped Kristine's ankle afterward and said, "It's a good thing the next show is three days away. She may have to be replaced."

That's brilliant! I thought. If we get fired, we don't have to pay the $1,000 fine. I wish I'd thought of that.

Chicago Illinois, April 22, 1994

I've jumped ship! David and I plotted for several days. Two of the dancers—David and Maria—are leaving as well. David paid for a return flight home for me and it wasn't cheap. I feel bad about that.

I had to lie to the purser, saying I needed my passport out of the safe and that I'd return it at the end of the day. He was hesitant, but I explained that I'd lost my driver's license and needed a form of identification to cash a check. He gave it to me.

David's suitcases were handled for him, and we exited the ship carefully because our cast was supposed to rehearse at 10 a.m.

We flagged down a cab and took it to the hotel in Fort Lauderdale. Our neighbor had forwarded the mail. We ripped it open, frantically hoping the check would be there. Instead, there was an invitation from a dating service, and free return address labels from St. Jude's.

At his house, a message on my answering machine said there was a warrant out for my arrest. The producer claimed I signed off the ship "improperly." You can't get arrested for jumping ship in Florida—it's an American port. Then, they called my mother and told her there was a warrant out for my arrest. Thanks for THAT.

My mother then called, let out one of her long sighs and said, "I knew you shouldn't have taken this job. **Where** are you, and how much is the bail?" I'm so exhausted, I feel like I could sleep for weeks.

May 10, 1994

My agent, after forging my name on my check, deposited it in her account. She claimed that the bank had issued a "stop payment" and she was never paid. She lied. I called the bank and a teller confirmed there never was a stop payment issued. The check had cleared *before* my escape and my agent pocketed the money.

I then called the labor department and talked to a woman named Joyce Markham, who informed me that I was one of many actors who'd been "screwed" by this agent. The agency was presently under investigation for stealing from its talent. Most of the small, non-union bond has been claimed. I most likely won't see a dime for a month of work. I don't know who to kill first. Jane Ryan Productions or Allied Artists, my agent.

I racked up my credit cards, got an ulcer, and didn't make a dime doing it. My agent has no idea what I've been through, and then to take what little money I made? I'm so mad I can't see anything but red. I want to send them roadkill in a box.

June 2, 1994

I'm playing Sister Robert Anne at Timberlake Playhouse and its opening night. We're doing splits and round offs in our habits, and I'm singing the top line in all the group numbers. I'm getting a work-out playing a nun.

I told a Chicagoan the story about my agent cashing my check and keeping the cash and he said, "Are they pulling that crap again?"

July 10, 1994

Talked to Joyce Markham today at the Department of Labor. My agent just filed for bankruptcy. She has been banned from the acting community and is now representing writers. Seriously.

NO GUTS NO GLORY

"The actor is the bravest soul I know. My god, it's hard to be an actor. I know of no greater act of courage than to walk out on an empty stage, seeing the silhouettes of four ominous figures sitting in the darkened theater, with your mouth drying and your fingers trembling, trying to keep the pages in hand from rattling and your eyes on the lines so you don't automatically skip the two most important speeches in the scene, and all the while trying to give a performance worthy of an opening night . . . and then to finally get through it, only to hear from the voice in the darkened theater, "Thank you." And to do it time after time, year after year, even after you've proven yourself in show after show, requires more than courage and fearlessness. It requires such dedication to your craft and to the work you've chosen for your life."

—Neil Simon in 1983, upon accepting an award from Equity

December 10, 1994

Sometimes I hate auditioning and leave feeling hollow. Other times, I connect with people at the other side of the table and it's a rush. The latest show I got cast in is a new musical staged by The Refreshment Committee, in St. Paul, Minnesota. Jeff and Mary Miller started this theater, and they have big, beautiful hearts. I'm playing a Scottish scrub woman named Sadie McKibben. My big numbers are "Search for a Sign" and "Why do I see God?" which I sing to Opal, an orphan. We all join hands and say a prayer before every show. It brings the cast together and gives the show some sparkle.

I've learned how to vocally balance the emotional and technical in this show. I worked with Emma Small, the voice teacher, because, as a mezzo soprano, the songs were challenging for my range. She saved me. Carol McCormick from Eleanor Moore came to see me, and I've signed with them. Hooray!

Christmas Day, 1994

Opal closed Dec. 23 to a full house. It was the critic's choice in both papers. On December 22, the author Robert Nassif Lindsey came with his family to see our production. What an exhilarating moment during the curtain call when Jeff Miller, the director, came on stage and thanked Robert for his rich script. I cried.

I've never had the honor of meeting the writer of a show I've performed in, so I feel lucky for this experience. Jeff and Mary Miller are generous, warm-hearted people. It was worth moving to Minnesota just to work with them. Their little girl, Mandy Miller, who played Opal, was a delight.

Summer, 1994

David is irritated with the packages my mother keeps mailing me. Instead of throwing things out, she pays the United States Post Office to mail them to me. The last package had a *Reader's Digest* article on "Ticks, The Enemy," an old Buff Puff from under the bathroom sink, sock hangers for David, and a half-eaten candy bar.

"I got your package, Mom."

"Did David like the sock hangers?"

"Um, I appreciate the thought Mom, but David doesn't hang up his clothes let alone his socks, so I don't see him using them. I didn't even know sock hangers existed!

"Oh, yes. What about the Buff Puff? You can use that can't you?"

"Is this the same Buff Puff from the 1980's that's been under the sink all these years?"

"I saw you using it once so I thought you might want it," she answered.

"Mom, why would I use a 14-year-old Buff Puff? It's full of bacteria."

"Did you try the chocolate bar? It's good, isn't it!"

"Yes, I ate what was left of the chocolate bar. Thank you for thinking of me." She really is a character out of a novel.

March 9, 1995

I can hardly believe this, but the wedding is off. I moved to Minneapolis to be with David and now he's taking back his proposal.

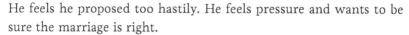

He feels he proposed too hastily. He feels pressure and wants to be sure the marriage is right.

I'm watching the sunset wondering where to go from here. Did I relax too much? Did I make a mistake by trusting him? David assured me it's not me, but how do I *not* take David's fear of commitment personally? The very thing that attracted him to me is now pushing him away. My ambitions get in the way of me being the woman he wants ultimately. He wants a mouse.

David says he needs time to work out his feelings, except that he doesn't seem to have feelings, unless he's watching a movie. I believed in him, in us. I didn't doubt our level of commitment, and less than a year later, he's taking back his promise. He does that a lot actually.

My emotions run the gamut from sadness to anger. I don't trust him anymore and take long walks around Lake of the Isles running it all through my head. A couple of close friends have said he's killing my spirit. Why is he trying to kill the light in me? He was so gung-ho and determined to have me, and now that he does, he wants to change me.

> *Men*
> *They hail you as their morning star*
> *Because you are the way you are.*
> *If you return the sentiment,*
> *They'll try to make you different;*
> *And once they have you, safe and sound,*
> *They want to change you all around.*
> *Your moods and ways they put a curse on;*
> *They'd make of you another person.*
> *They cannot let you go your gait;*
> *They influence and educate.*
> *They'd alter all that they admired.*
> *They make me sick, they make me tired.*
> —Dorothy Parker

April 13, 1995

Mother called me today to tell me about the bleeding icon at the Holy Trinity Orthodox Church on Johnson Road in Michigan City,

Indiana. The press and locals are calling the crucifixion of Christ a "miracle" and a "sign from God" because it is oozing oil.

"Holly, I finally saw the bleeding icon. I didn't want to wait in line with a bunch of Indiana rednecks, so I waited until a slow day. The church has put plastic around the icon to protect it. It's not flowing like a faucet or anything. It is just oozing balsam. It's like . . . a slow leak."

May 1, 1995
Heidi Chronicles opened this weekend at the New Tradition Theater. The role of Susan Johnston has been hard to focus on with my personal life unravelling. It seems I can never have a good personal life and professional one at the same time.

Timberlake Playhouse, Mount Carroll, Illinois
June 15, 1995
I'm back at Timberlake. Would you believe David and I are doing a farce, "Taking Steps," together? Artistic Director Jim Zvanut offered David a role too, since David performed at Timberlake years ago. I'm hoping it will help "us", as we're currently in a holding pattern.

July 3, 1995
Rehearsing *Annie Get your Gun* all day and doing the farce at night has been vocally draining. My body has been pushed to the absolute limit. But what a gift to sing this music and work with the cast. Of all the songs I sing, I think my favorite is "Moonshine Lullaby," which I sing to the children in the train car.

July 4, 1995
Our first dress rehearsal and we're belting out,
"There's no people like show people, they smile when they are low. Even with a turkey that you know will fold, you may be stranded out in the cold. . ."
And the lights went out. A transformer blew outside the theatre, so there we were in the dark. We continued rehearsing but with

flashlights. Then the fire department arrived. We did what we could until we had power again.

In the evening, we ran the show again. Honestly, the costumer has managed to make the chorus look better than the leads. She put me in a heavy woollen full-length skirt clasped with a giant safety pin for the "Anything You Can Do" number. I'm supposed to sing, "Yes, I—" then quickly crawl between Frank's legs, stand up, arms out, and sing— "Caaaaaannn!" Well, it didn't go that way at all.

As I crawled between Frank's legs, the safety pin gave way, and when I stood and held out my arms, precisely on the downbeat, my skirt fell to my ankles. I kept singing.

". . .caaaan!" The cast members howled with laughter, and the expression on Director Jim Zvanut's face is forever etched in my memory. He looked like Monster from the Muppets. Thank God I was wearing underwear.

NOTE TO SELF: *Always wear underwear onstage.*

August 1, 1995

We had a heat wave of record temperatures that lasted five days! 786 people died in Chicago, and chickens exploded in Iowa. Poor chickens.

Annie Get Your Gun had standing ovations every night and was a good experience, except for several misfires. The prop mistress had a lot on her plate and didn't always load my rifle. Sharp-shooter Annie Oakley pulls the trigger and a faint "click" is heard.

During the last show, I was in the middle of "Lost in His Arms," when one of the techies dropped a rubber chicken from the catwalk onto my lap. Sadly, David did not see the show. He's working in L.A. For now, I will continue to live in the house.

July 2, 1996

I am absolutely lost. I just couldn't bear the loneliness and living in limbo. David came back from ten months in L.A. and immediately committed to playing a role in *I Hate Hamlet* in Des Moines, Iowa, at a community theater. I distinctly remember *him* saying to *me* two years ago that he was afraid I would leave town for theater gigs, since I'm a performer. Here we are two years later, and he's the one leaving town, again.

He will pay to live in an icky hotel (while his mansion on a lake is being cared for by me), to act in a show our friend Richard Choate is directing. Here's the headline:

Hollywood Screenwriter Leaves Fiancée in the Lurch to Play Womanizer John Barrymore.

Actions speak louder than words. I believed him when he said we'd pick up where we left off. Clearly, I'm nothing more than his house-sitter. It hurts.

I asked him if I should move out and he said I could stay until I move to Los Angeles. That is a huge relief because I can't imagine moving twice right now. Just can't handle that emotionally or physically.

The other day, one of David's old girlfriends (Jewish) called. He had likened me to her on several occasions. She called to find out when the wedding is and when I said the wedding *isn't*, she said,

"Oh, I'm not surprised."

It didn't take long for details to surface.

"I had to go into therapy after dating him," she said. "My therapist said he's a sociopath. He has no conscience and won't take responsibility for what he does and says." I felt the blood drain out of my face, down my neck, and all the way to my feet. This explains so much. I'm relieved to know it's not ALL me. I thought I knew "love," but I don't. Not sure I will ever trust myself again to choose a good man.

July 7, 1996

Speaking of not taking responsibility, David invited a couple he met over for brunch on Sunday. They are both actors, and the guy offered to coach David in stage combat and fencing for his upcoming lead role as John Barrymore.

So, I'm supposed to put on a happy face and prepare for brunch with strangers. Two hours before they were to arrive, he's watching

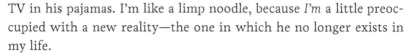

TV in his pajamas. I'm like a limp noodle, because *I'm* a little preoccupied with a new reality—the one in which he no longer exists in my life.

I bring up the fact that company is coming over in two hours and there's been no mention of how that "brunch" is going to appear on the kitchen table. This man doesn't even fold his own laundry after someone has washed it for him. He'll *say* he will do it, but he won't.

I went to Lund's to buy breakfast for this couple. When the two guys were horsing around in the backyard with shields and swords, I turned to the wife and said,

"You seem like a lovely person, so I'm sorry I'm not very upbeat. David and I broke up for good and I have to move out so, I guess I'm not feeling up for company." The look on her face said it all. She couldn't believe he wanted to have brunch and learn how to fence in the middle of all this.

Other people have been kind. A woman at the bookstore in Calhoun Square suggested I read *Life's Companion, Journal Writing as a Spiritual Quest* by Christina Baldwin. I find comfort in excerpts like this:

> *We look for whatever can help us make sense of the moment. We write. Life has taught me that it knows better plans than we can imagine, so that I try to submerge my own desires into a calm willingness to accept what comes and to make the most of it, then wait again.*

I long for normalcy and routine. I struggle with making decisions. I doubt my every move. Sometimes, when I walk into a coffee shop or restaurant I can't decide where to sit. Then I change my mind and move. I'm not right in the head. I don't sleep and have considered suicide. Lake of the Isles is my comfort. Sometimes, I take a pillow and sleep on one of the benches there, like a homeless person.

August 10, 1996

I'm at Theater L'Homme Dieu in Alexandria, Minnesota, playing Gladys Hotchkiss in *The Pajama Game*. This theater has been open since 1961. Mia hangs out in the wardrobe department during the day with the seamstresses. They told me he's been very helpful, rolling on patterns and sitting in the box labelled "whites." He sets an example of how to go with the flow and manages to make the best of our circumstances. Before I left Minneapolis with Mia, Mother said, "That poor cat, the way you drag him around the country like a gypsy. I feel sorry for him."

"He LOVES every minute of it," I told her. Because he does.

Tonight is opening night, and David just called to tell me I need to be out of his house in two weeks. How thoughtful, on opening day. Problem is, I'm not *near* Minneapolis to look for an apartment and we're rehearsing by day and performing by night. I bring up the fact that I'm several hours from Minneapolis, but he doesn't care. There is no emotion on his part. I know what happened. SHE told him she wants me out of the house she's about to move into. And I've got to be onstage in four hours dancing like Carol Haney, singing:

> *"I've got (clang clang,) fs-s-s-s-s-s-s steam heat. I've got (clang clang), fs-s-s-s-s-s-s steam heat. I. I've got (clang clang), fs-s-s-s-s-s-s steam heat. And I need your love to keep away the cold."*

"Steam Heat" is a great percussive song and I'd really like to enjoy doing it. "Hernandos Hideaway" is equally cool but, I won't have a home when this is done, so I'm too fearful and anxious to enjoy starring in the *Pajama Game*, for which I'm getting paid a pittance, as per normal.

August 27, 1996

The choreographer from *Opal* introduced me to her friend Steve Anderson, and I'll be living in his basement until I find an apartment. Steve has been a Godsend, but it's a little awkward. I wish I could be more jovial but there's always a swirling in my guts. I'm trying to put thoughts of David out of my head, but I'm consumed by them. They loop and loop in my brain.

I went over to David's house, as he's back in Des Moines, to get a few more of my things and discovered, quite by accident, that he has been lying to me for months. I pulled a book off the shelf that I had started reading six months ago and a letter fell out. A letter from the woman he's been *courting* while I take care of his house. It's very clear they are intimately involved. Honestly, she sounds like she's 12-years-old.

Turns out, he moved on while in Des Moines and replaced me with a younger girl. So, I was living in his house while he was dallying with someone else. I think there may have been a period of time when he was sleeping with both of us at the same time. Ugh. I remember him telling me about her, describing her as "plain and a mediocre actress."

"Are you involved with someone else?" I asked. "Why would you keep returning to Des Moines? The show is over."

He assured me he wasn't foolish enough to get involved in another relationship. I know he's lying to my face. I had our therapist Dr. Fowler write a healthy, non-accusatory letter to him in which I suggest I move out or we go back to therapy.

When I walked into the house after he'd read it, he was stunned.

He said, "That is the most to-the-point letter I've ever gotten. I have to say I'm *relieved!* Do you want to go see the movie *Twister?*" Honest to God, my knees gave way. I'm an after-thought for him. WHAT happened? I just want to understand what I did or didn't do. If I start to cry, he'll say,

"Are you really going to cry again? I won't discuss it again."

I feel betrayed, confused and terrified. Do I deserve this? When I told my mother how devastated I am, she said,

"Just so you know, they'll get married, and then she's going to get pregnant. And **she** won't leave him."

I am at an all-time low, and instead of helping me, she kicks me further down the stairs. I recall when my parents came to visit David and I and my mother showed up with two basset hounds. She never asked if she could bring them. David was angry and I don't blame him.

I said to her, "Mom, you can't just show up with dogs to some-one's house. You need to ask if it's okay."

"I don't need to ask," she said. "I'm the mother."

My parents ended their visit early, which really bothered me. I can't seem to make them happy and David at the same time. I laid down on the floor and cried out of frustration. David's response?

"I don't think I want to marry someone who ends up on the floor in a fetal position when her parents leave." Nice.

September 14, 1996

I've been living in a dusty one-bedroom apartment, about the size of David's mud room. Today, I tried to scrub out dark stains from the linoleum floor in the kitchen as Mia reached under the stove to fish out an old greasy cat toy. He's trying to amuse me because I'm so low. I can't believe where I am both physically and emotionally. I left Chicago for David and now I'm alone, surrounded by passive aggressive Norwegians, although I am very fond of Garrison Keillor and *A Prairie Home Companion*. And I **have** met some marvelous people.

When my dear friend Scott Carter was in town, he knocked on the door and asked if he could just move my stuff. David knows Scott and has spent quality time with him. David told Scott he'd rather just put my things in the garage. Scott tried to get me to see that this will save me the headache of moving things out of the house.

Richard Choate called and apologized for David's bad behavior. He wondered why David was involved with this other girl when I was waiting for him at home, and he mentioned it to David. So, David moved *on* and this girl moved *in*.

October 2, 1996

I started therapy again with a more affordable therapist through my insurance. I talked mostly about my mother and how cruel she can be and that nothing I ever do is enough. The therapist showed me a page in the medical dictionary on narcissism. It's an awful feeling to recognize my mother in a medical dictionary. My mother was my hero when I was a child. For a second, I see her photo next to this description. The photo comes to life and she waves at me.

She wants to control you.
Her love is conditional.
She can't or won't validate your feelings.
She belittles you.
She tries to manipulate you.
She thinks she's above the rules.
She is unpredictable.
It's all about how things look.
She cannot see your point of view.
She is emotionally volatile.

I'm now on Zoloft for depression. My former cleaning lady connected me with a woman in St. Paul who needs a tenant on her third floor. This apartment I've been in is not a good fit.

October 15, 1996

Jean Manuel Denis has been a Godsend. Each of us is struggling with our own demons. She has two lovely daughters and a huge house with equally big bills. She furnished the third floor—a charming space which has become my port in the storm. If I could erase David from my mind, I would. It hurts. A person always has a choice in how to treat someone else. The fact that he chose to be cruel makes me so very sad. And now I've met this kind family.

Jean invites me downstairs to dinner with her girls, which is SO wonderful. They love it when I sing upstairs and often request songs. Her dog Vinny is terrified of Mia, who taunts him. They have a huge orange tabby cat, Charlie, who respects Mia, and her other cat, Menoux (he's French), is always waiting for me when I get home. I feel so safe in her house. I will never forget the kindness they've shown me.

October 20, 1996

I really wish I could harness my psychic abilities. I went to dinner with my neighbor Susan and said, "My plan is to move to Los Angeles in a few months. Now watch, someone will try and change my plans!" An hour later, leaving the restaurant, she and I ran into Bob Alwine, the artistic director from the Ordway Music Theater.

"I'm so glad I ran into you," he said. "I want to talk to you about a musical we're doing at the Ordway. We need a woman to understudy the entire female cast, three women, who range in ages from mid-20's to mid-40's. And you're the only woman in town I know who can handle such a range of ages."

I auditioned for *I Love a Piano*, which will be directed by Ray Roderick from New York. The producer is Kevin McCollum. To my surprise, I was cast.

Bob told me the director asked him why all the Chanhassen Dinner Theater performers are members of Actors Equity and I wasn't. I am repeatedly overlooked in this town because I'm not from Minneapolis. It took a New York director to cast me at the Ordway.

So, after months of gut-wrenching despair over David, I decided I had two choices. Walk into Lake of the Isles and drown myself or do an Irving Berlin Review called *I Love A Piano*. I chose Irving. He is an American treasure, after all. With 65 songs to learn in three different harmonies, I don't have time to cry. Plus, I'm doing a one-woman show at the Bryant Lake Bowl for the Fringe Festival on Monday. It will be my therapy.

November 10, 1996

After weeks of never going on, it has happened! Karen who played Ginger, though stubborn, succumbed to the flu. She fought tooth and nail to keep it together, but her voice gave out. Keep in mind, Terry and I, the other understudy, haven't run the whole show onstage. We watch it on a monitor in a rehearsal space. We've had one walk through without costumes.

I have a one-woman show going up at the Bryant Lake Bowl in three days, so I got to the theatre late, and the techies, who always teased me by saying "You're on today," finally meant it.

"Where've you been?" they asked. "You're going on!"

Fuck! The one day I'm late.

I scrambled to slather on makeup, pull on my tights, dance pants and character shoes, and clip my mic to my bra. Lou, one of the sound guys, threaded my mic through my hair and fastened the pack around my waist. I slipped into my dress held open by the wardrobe lady and the announcement came:

"Good afternoon, ladies and gentlemen, in today's performance of *I Love A Piano*, the role of Ginger will be played by Holly Schroeder." There was a finality to it that, oddly enough, put me at ease. There was no getting out of this challenge. I'd have to meet it head on.

The other actors assured me I'd be okay and that they would push and pull me through the blocking. Thank God the backstage people know the show better than anyone. The dressers grabbed me when I got offstage, saying "Put this on." They zipped me up, turned me around, and pushed me back on stage through 12 changes. They saved me.

It was an out of body experience. When I stepped onstage for the opening number, I physically felt like I was two feet above my shoes. Three different harmonies for 65 different Irving Berlin songs were swimming in my head, not to mention choreography. Once my smile relaxed and I could feel my limbs, I brought more of myself to the part. My voice felt fluid and the challenge of hitting the harmonies was a ride. I'll never forget what went through my head as I marched in place, singing "Alexanders Ragtime Band." I thought, holy shit. If I can pull this off, with minimal rehearsal, I can do *anything*.

A defining moment in the show for me was the final number, "I Love A Piano." There really is nothing like that feeling of knowing you have the entire audience in the palm of your hand. As I stood next to the piano in a full-length black gown, the spotlight hit. Silence. And there it was! That scene in *Funny Girl* when Barbra Streisand sings "My Man." The black full-length gown, the spotlight, and three chords. You could hear a pin drop. I had an out of body experience.

As a child I went wild when the band played.
How I ran to the man as his hand swayed.
Clarinets were my pets and a slide trombone I thought was simply
divine. . .
But today when they play I can hiss them. Every bar is a jar to my
system,
But there's one musical instrument that I call mine.

I was so in the moment, the back of my head lifted off.

After the show, the stage manager told me she couldn't get over how well I did.

"I just wish someone other than me could have seen it," she said. "Kevin McCullom the producer is out of town, as is Bob Alwine. You were astonishing!"

It was a rite of passage playing an understudy. Thank God for Irving and his music. Imagine if I'd drowned myself in Lake of the Isles over a man who doesn't value me.

January 10, 1997

I'm putting together a demo reel of my commercial spots before I move to Los Angeles. One of my favorites is a spot I did for Gabbert's. At the audition, I pretended to be a wealthy Gabbert's customer, pointed at the imaginary piece of furniture and mouthed "love it." I think that's why I got the spot.

The shoot was something. They had a giant armoire rigged up with chains, ropes, and a pully because I had to physically pick up the armoire and run off with it. I was in a suit and high heels and directed to make a sound as I lifted the armoire so as to cue the fellas on either side, who hoisted it up with the ropes. Then, I balanced it against my body to keep it from turning. That was the challenge, so we had to do a lot of takes. My bum knee popped in and out of the socket, but I didn't say anything. Once the armoire was hoisted, the crew helped pull it across a track as I appeared to be running away with it. By the end of the shoot, I was bruised up and down my thighs.

March 15, 1997

Apparently, there are posters of me and the armoire all over Gabbert's. Several people called me. I wasn't paid for that, so I called my agent, who informed me that no one told her they were making a poster. I remember a photo being taken during the shoot. She negotiated (after the fact) an extra $100 for my "image." Wow. Am I only worth $100 here? In Morocco, I was worth 4,000 camels.

May 2, 1997

I booked a commercial for the Iowa Safety Bureau. Because I'm playing a scientist in a white lab coat, I impersonated my father's speaking pattern. It is so far, the funniest commercial I've done. There's a part where I'm walking down a hallway saying, "Experiments teach us that the best remedy for injury is. . ." and a banana peel hits the glass window. It took about seven takes to get it right. I wish it was running in more states than Iowa.

August 2006

I just did a commercial with a little person. Jim Cunningham and I played a married couple in a 30-second spot with our "children." We were on set in a holiday scene—decorating the Christmas tree with a string of lights. The angry elf is supposed to burst in the front door, spill a wooden wagon full of coal on our living room floor, and say angrily, "This is all you're gettin' for Christmas," and exit. And then Jim gets a shock from the lights because there's a short.

Speaking of short, in walks a little person dressed up as an elf in a green costume, with white and red striped tights on his muscular, compact legs. On his feet were green curly-toed shoes with a bell on the tip of each toe. Pretty severe curl on the shoes. And then, he had on a matching hat with a bell on the tip, so everywhere he went, he jingled. Talk about a stereotype. It was over the top.

Unfortunately, the wooden floor was slick from fake snow. So, when he entered, his stout legs went right out from under him. All of us, cast and crew gasped and watched him go up into the air, curly toes and all and come back down hard, on his back. Safe to say, we were all horrified.

The heat of embarrassment flooded his face. Everyone was concerned he was hurt, but he got right up, brushed himself off, and said he was okay. An assistant roughed up the floor, they checked his slippers, and we did another take. He was more than a trooper. I was so impressed by him I can't even remember the product.

I CRIED IN THE TUB TO SAVE MONEY ON KLEENEX

I've always suffered from "the grass is always greener" syndrome. Even as a child, I thought life would be better in California. I fantasized about Los Angeles the way other girls dreamt of their wedding day. It was just a matter of time before I lived in the land of fruit and nuts.

After some acting and commercial success in Minneapolis and Chicago, I decided I was ready for lurid Los Angeles. At 31, I was practically "over the hill." If not now, when? I knew the film industry was the most competitive, merciless, cut-throat business in the world (second only to the Medellin drug cartel), but I refused to live in fear of failing. I wanted to inhabit my days and risk my significance. I had my sights set on a sitcom. What I didn't realize is that no matter how much talent you have, without the right connections, luck, and discipline you will be tested to your limits.

Sept. 17, 1997, Minneapolis, MN.
Scott Carter helped me pack all my possessions, including Mia, into a Ryder truck. Together, we began the 2,000-mile trek on September 18. My actor/singer/dancer friend Doug Anderson, who let me store a bunch of my things in his attic, gave me a magnificent sendoff when he did a school cheer in the driveway and cartwheels all the way down the lane.

September 19, 1997, Nebraska
God that cat tests me. Mia was lost for two hours this morning inside a box spring at a Budget Inn. I was in such a panic running up and down the halls, my heart beating so fast. It was Scott's idea to look in the box spring, and there was Mia, yawning and squinting at us. I nearly choked him.

September 20, 1997, Las Vegas

I'm three hours outside of Los Angeles. Scott is driving and I'm hiding in the back of the Ryder truck with my diary, Mia, and all my belongings. This the craziest, riskiest thing I've ever done in my life.

Mother just said on the phone, "You don't have roots anywhere. Are you ever going to get married and have a home? You're like a tumbleweed blowing from town to town." Her support still means more to me than anyone else's. I wish she could see me as a separate person from herself, but I think she views me as an extension of her, so when I do something she would never consider, it makes her crazy.

Lately, I've been experimenting with visualization and powerful thoughts. I decided I would get the Nordic Track commercial before I left the house and when I got called back for the second audition, I wondered why there were other actors there. It is my commercial, I said to myself. And I got it! It was a fun spot. Jim Cunningham is such a joy to work with. The wardrobe gal said the director was worried I was too thin.

"Whatever you do, put the lead in something baggy," he'd said. Perhaps this means I'm thin enough for Los Angeles.

I saw a shooting star in Utah and wished on it. Everyone believes I'll do well in L.A., so why can't I believe it? I didn't even believe director David Moe was being sincere when he said,

"You are the cat's meow."

I didn't expect my crush on David Moe to be met with equal affection. I took him to a wine tasting at Ivory's. I was anxious, frenetic, and giddy because I'm consumed with goodbyes, fear, and hope. If he feels emotions for me, why didn't he make an effort? Because he's Norwegian? If I hadn't called him and made a date, who knows if we'd see each other again. Why do people stand there and let a good thing walk out of their lives? Why?

Scott and I decided a great way to begin the L.A. Experiment is to ride the "Space Shot" at the top of the Stratosphere Tower. It dominates the Las Vegas skyline at 1,149 feet. The ride attached to it is the world's third highest thrill ride—a zero gravity simulator consisting of a 192-foot steel tower. Sixteen riders are strapped into it and then catapulted straight up 160 feet in the air, at 45 miles per hour. Then, the riders free fall back to

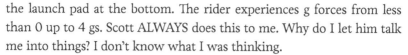

the launch pad at the bottom. The rider experiences g forces from less than 0 up to 4 gs. Scott ALWAYS does this to me. Why do I let him talk me into things? I don't know what I was thinking.

The tower alone is 115 stories high. Riding the Space Shoot sends you up an additional 160 feet into the air. The 1100+ foot tower was originally supposed to be higher. However, the FAA determined that building the Tower higher would put it directly in one of the alternate flight paths for McCarran airport. The Stratosphere Corp decided to keep the height to a mere 135 stories.

When we shot up, I felt like it was mach speed. I nearly soiled my shorts. The only thing between me and the ground 866 feet below us, was a dingy, flimsy canvas "safety belt." We were so high, people looked like ants below. I didn't dare breathe.

Dangling over the Las Vegas strip, I couldn't help imagining how easy it would be to slip out of my plastic swing. White knuckling it, my entire body was so clenched, my anus hurt. I've honestly never been so terrified in my life.

Scott shouted, "Are you okay?" But I couldn't speak. Wide-eyed, I see it unfold in my head. A wind knocks me out of the chair, I float for one second like a Warner Bros. cartoon, then drop like a stone and splat on top of Caesar's Palace. The headline: "Actress Bound for Hollywood Falls Flat in Vegas." My mother is quoted: "I told her she'd never make it there."

September 21, 1997, Los Angeles, 2 a.m.
Our warm welcome from the city of Los Angeles is an $85 ticket for parking a commercial vehicle in a residential area. I had no idea you can't park a moving van on the street. I mean, if there's no driveway what are we supposed to do? Hang it in a tree?

September 25, 1997
Scott and I have looked at a lot of places, and I must say, Los Angeles is nothing like the Midwest. There's a spooky quality to it that I'm struggling with. We looked at one place with such a bad layout and eerie feeling Scott said, "I'd cry myself to sleep every night if we lived here."

Oct. 5, 1997, West Hollywood

I'd rather have a root canal than look for an apartment in L.A. "Charming" means small, "character" means run down, and "prime location" means spitting distance from the freeway. My guts are churning.

Oct. 6, 1997, Santa Monica Blvd.

I seem to move from one trendy neighborhood to another, carting along books I've yet to read, garter belts I've never worn and half-finished photo albums. I should throw it all in the trash, but no! I cart it from city to city, dream to dream.

Oct. 7, 1997

Scott recently came out of the closet, so he wants to live in West Hollywood, gay Mecca. It IS very clean and relatively safe. We saw a great place that's a little pricey at $1400 a month, near a bondage store and the Paper Bag Princess. There's an avocado tree outside and a gorgeous bougainvillea, and it has a back deck! Mia is in love with our apartment and Scott. He likes to come to the window instead of the door and meow to be let in. When I come home, he jumps onto the back deck railing and then onto the small house in front of ours and leans over the gutter, meowing at me as I get out of the car.

I really like Lawrence, the landlord. He's from Chicago and was thrilled when he saw our credit ratings. He asked me what I do, and I said I'm an actress and a writer. His face fell.

"Oh great," he sighed heavily. "Another one. Listen, kid, this ain't Chicago. This is one tough town."

The apartment is conveniently near a Kinko's, which is crawling with actors. The salesperson told me it's best to come around 10:00 a.m. before they wake up.

October 31, 1997

Went to the Halloween parade in West Hollywood. People here pull out ALL the stops. While Scott and I pulled costumes out of our closets, people here work on them for months. We went to the parade with a couple of Scott's friends. I haven't laughed this hard in a long time. A "gay" time was had by all.

Left to right: Tim Smith, Doug Rago, Scott Rutledge, Stephen Arel, and me in front

November 10, 1997

I tried to make phone calls today, but after it rained, the phone went dead. The phone company said it's because the line got wet. I don't even know how to respond to this. In the Midwest, it rains, snows, sleets, and hails—and our phones still work.

November 11, 1997

Coming from Minnesota, Los Angeles is not going to be easy. I must embrace the moments of frustration and loneliness. This journey is about spiritual growth, not fame and fortune. How do I explain this to those with big expectations? This journey will teach me what I need to learn.

November 12, 1997

I was supposed to get my new headshots taken today and El Nino rained on my parade. I woke up to a monsoon! There was nothing I could do. But I learned something important.

Only two things shut down Hollywood: rain and the Jewish holidays.

November 15, 1997

In this land of appearances, you are what you drive. Therefore, I'm an '89 Ford Escort with missing hubcaps. But I do see the beauty here. And my favorite thing about California is the flora and fauna. The bougainvillea we have in our yard is stunning! I do wish we had a lemon tree. I can't imagine having free lemons in my yard.

We do have an avocado tree which drops green grenades on the ground. They're hard and take quite some time to ripen. Most are nicked too because the squirrels take bites out of them. I try to get to them before the squirrels do but I think they gnaw on them when they're still hanging on the tree. The first avocado I snagged from our tree ripened and was so delicious. I just can't get over the fact that something so wonderful grows on a tree in my yard!

November 22, 1997

Clawing for a survival job (waitressing, temping, catering) is much harder here than in the Midwest. The masses are all trying to do the same thing—juggle several part-time gigs to pay the bills but be free enough to still pursue the Biz. Because of this, what typically happens is that life becomes more about the struggle than the dream. I don't have time for that. I got a late start in the business.

November 28, 1997

Today, after having a stare down with one of the squirrels over an avocado on the ground, I asked Scott when we should put in the storm windows. He burst out laughing. It seems SO odd to me that they don't use storm windows. The neighborhoods are surreal. So many homes are one level, boxy, and made of stucco. And where are the children? I don't ever see any children playing. Did the child catcher from *Chitty Chitty Bang Bang* take them all away? I mean, really. Where ARE the children?

December 1, 1997

I was having a wonderful dream this morning about Michael Keaton. I've always liked him. Right when he and I were about to make love, the phone rang and woke me up. It was Mother, who wanted to tell

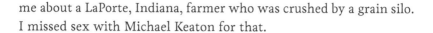

me about a LaPorte, Indiana, farmer who was crushed by a grain silo. I missed sex with Michael Keaton for that.

December 12, 1997

Baba Ram Dass, American spiritual teacher, psychologist and author has been my life support system. I listen to his Spiritual Awakening tape series in the car because it keeps me calm in traffic. I don't leave home without my Thomas Guide and Ram Dass.

December 14, 1997

Had my first colonic today. Nurse Wang filled my colon with saline and said, "You no have rice every day or pasta. And no dairy, Miss. You don't drink alcohol either. It like poison to you!"

Story of my life. I can't eat the fun stuff. I must say it was a tad uncomfortable having a tube up my ass, but I feel like a different person now. They gave me a special juice to energize me, so I floated around Trader Joes looking at orchids.

December 15, 1997

My friend Debby insisted I go to an industry party to make contacts. Asked to list our new year resolutions on a large poster, Debby wrote, "find a Catholic church, find a good man, donate time at a soup kitchen." I wrote, "Get an agent, get a nose job, get a series."

December 25, 1997, Chicago

Merry Christmas. It's the most wonderful time of the year. Flying home for the holiday, my luggage was stolen, including a brand spanking new pair of Dolce & Gabanna pants and all the Christmas presents I bought. This is the first and last time I ever spend $100 on one pair of pants, even if they do make my ass look like you can bounce a quarter off it. I never even got to wear them.

America West will reimburse passengers for $2,000 max, and only after you scream, sob, rend the only clothes you have left, and provide receipts.

January 3, 1998
I am so glad that I live a few blocks from the Bodhi Tree bookstore. I go there frequently to find some balance in my otherwise wonky life. I've always lacked balance.

Calm is what I feel when I read about Taoism and Buddhism. I can't afford to buy a lot of books, so I sit there and read and mingle with other spiritual seekers. The store has an amazing energy and it's not just because they sell over-priced crystals, rocks, candles, and oils.

I've learned that I'm going to have to learn how to control my mind. I've been a prisoner too long. When I'm busy, I'm healthier emotionally because my mind can't wander and get tangled up in negative thoughts. My dharma is to collect stories and experiences. That is my journey. An awakening through experience! I'm a wanderer. My home is in my heart. I have what I'm looking for, I must only look further within. It's not the town I live in that holds the key to my peace. The town I live in must be capable of freeing my spirit without draining my soul. I'm not so sure L.A. is the place for me.

January 10, 1998
I'm taking the Brian Riese on-camera class. It costs $170 per month. There are about 15 people in my class, which meets once a week. We do scenes and then get a critique.

On the first day, I met this gal Susan sitting next to me. We talked about Los Angeles and the industry. She asked me if I was married and I said "no," to which she said,

"Good! That way you can sleep your way to the top."

Our teacher Brian has several classes. I did the math. The guy is a millionaire, making a huge living off of ambitious, starving actors. And he's not the only one. There are all these "workshops' which cost from $50 to $100 for an evening with a casting director. People do them to get seen by casting directors.

NOTE TO SELF: In Los Angeles, you've got to pay to play.

January 15, 1998
After writing an entire catalog for Warner Bros. consumer products division, I've landed a better writing gig with Charles Carney,

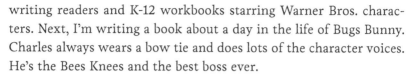

writing readers and K-12 workbooks starring Warner Bros. characters. Next, I'm writing a book about a day in the life of Bugs Bunny. Charles always wears a bow tie and does lots of the character voices. He's the Bees Knees and the best boss ever.

The Warner Bros. workshop? Fascinating. My brother Danny would just LOVE all I'm learning. He never, ever missed Saturday morning cartoons. Here are a couple of cartoon facts:

The Golden Era of animation was 1940-1958.

Bugs Bunny made his debut on July 27, 1940, in "A Wild Hare." He became the number one box office star and was the "personification of the American spirit."

Bugs Bunny IS Groucho Marx. He plays with words and wins.

The kicking of Elmer Fudd's butt was a take-off on Laurel and Hardy.

Carl Stalling was the music brilliance behind the Looney Tunes. He was at Disney for eight years. He had a pencil mustache, always a wore a suit, spats, and wrote 600 cartoon scores (one per week).

In 1939, Tex Avery wrote "Thugs with Dirty Mug's". Many of these cartoons were not created for children and were shown before adult movies.

Porky Pig debuted in 1935 in the cartoon "I Haven't Got a Hat." Joe Daugherty, who did Porky's voice, really did have a stutter.

Leon Schlesinger (a snappy dresser, always with a flower in his lapel), was only interested in making money, had no creativity, and a speech impediment. Daffy Duck is actually Leon Schlesinger's voice. Mel Blanc was the one actor who could do most of the voices. He was the only one to get credit for his voices, which was Leon Schlesinger's arrangement with him instead of a raise. Mel was allergic to carrots, so they recorded the carrot bite at the end of the day.

Jan. 13, 1998

There's good news and bad news. I had to file fraud charges. A crook got his paws on one of my deposit slips and siphoned money out of my checking account. Laqueta at the Bounce of America Bank says it's the work of a professional. This sort of thing doesn't happen very often in the Midwest. In fact, people there often use checking account deposit slips to write out their phone number if they're out of business cards. But here's some good news. I got an agent! I signed with Bobby Ball!

January 15, 1998

Phil, the gay guy who lives in the apartment below us has two gay friends who are always visiting. They call each other "Mary," so Scott and I refer to them as "The Three Mary's."

The Mary's smoke, sashay, and talk "hair". My bedroom closet, situated above their bedroom, smells like the dance floor of The Manhole.

I called Lawrence and said,

"What is this apartment building made of? Popsicle sticks? I can hear everything the Mary's say and SMELL them too! And all that cigarette smoke is getting into my wardrobe!"

"They don't build things in California the way they do in the Midwest. This ain't Chicago kid," said Lawrence.

So, I covered the floor of my closet with masking tape.

January 27, 1998

I got two responses from the 20 part-time job positions I applied for. One is from a company that needs someone to sew slipcovers, and the other from a special events company. I pursued the latter and met with a Jewish couple who have owned their company for 16 years. He was a wearing a yarmulke.

They interviewed me for two hours and then asked me to start work tomorrow.

January 28, 1998

Today was my first day. I brought a small turkey sandwich to work. The woman wouldn't let me put it in their refrigerator because they're "kosher." Sigh. I had to keep the turkey sandwich, with mayo, wrapped in a piece of plastic wrap placed inside a paper bag, in my purse until lunchtime. What the hell do they think is going to happen? They've got chopped liver in their fridge, but I can't put a lousy turkey sandwich in there? Is my turkey going to contaminate their corned beef and babkas?

February 6, 1998

No such thing as normal neighbors in West Hollywood. Lawrence came by to check the plumbing today and said the gay guy in the front house leaves his front door open at night so cruising homosexuals can watch him lounge on his fainting couch and play with himself. Lawrence is fed up.

"How could I have known the guy's a whack job? He came to look at the place with his mother!"

"This ain't Chicago, kid," I said with a smile.

March 1, 1998

After eight months of hunting for a survival job, I've landed a legal assistant position at a small law firm in Los Angeles on Lankershim Blvd. There's a French bakery across the street and a well-stocked beauty supply store next door. I slather on the expensive eye cream I can't afford during my lunch hour.

My boss Tom used to be a pilot and damaged his hearing, so he talks loudly and jiggles his coins in his pants a lot. The secretary, Molly, a classy woman (I have no idea how old she is) tells me stories about boating with Humphrey Bogart.

March 4, 1998

I was at a stoplight on Santa Monica Blvd today, surrounded by tacky mini malls and the infestation of traffic and exhaust. The driver next to me leaned out the window of his pick-up truck and said to me,

"It was the end of the rainbow 20 years ago, but those days are gone."

March 5, 1998

Molly knows Phyllis Diller! LORD! I have GOT to find a way to meet her.

Molly also told me today how to do the proper face-lift.

"It's best not to do something major, but instead, start small with minor tucks. I told everyone I was going to Europe and just walked a couple blocks over to the clinic. Then, I came back home a couple days later with 'souvenirs' from France and a tighter face. My husband didn't notice until he got the bill."

March 11, 1998
I don't think its Tom's *coins* that he's jiggling in his pockets. John took me to lunch in his Mercedes. He really loves his car. He said that when he dies, he wants to be buried in it.

"Can you believe we used to drive around for fun?" he said. "That was when it was safe to drive through any neighborhood. God damn Koreans ruined everything."

March 20, 1998
I do feel in a way like I've found my tribe out here. I've never lived by anyone's rules and that's very California. A lot of people out here are unconventional types chasing unrealistic dreams. And I like that I meet people easily, even if all I'm doing is going to the coffee shop.

March 24, 1998
I've been rehearsing for a show for the Lehman Engel Workshop. Berton Averre, a member of the Knack, who helped write "My Sharona," has written a musical called "Jungle Man." I'll be singing the title song from the show. Some of the lyrics include:

> *"It's like a fantasy from somewhere in my youth. I can't believe that this is happening to me. It's kind of scary, but I've got to face the truth. I want to schtup a guy, whose home is in a tree."*

February 1, 1998
I had three commercial auditions today, all of them inane. Lost for an hour in Culver City with the wrong street name. Yesterday, I met a woman who is a yoga hypno-therapist, motivational speaker, and author, now training to become a minister. She used to be an actress and studied with Stella Adler in NYC. She said, "The healing arts aren't that different from the performing arts." Not sure I agree. THIS I agree with:

When you're aligned with the deeper truth within yourself, then you magnetize people and circumstances that align with your truth—the light within you. The problem is not out there, it's within here. Be an instrument of good. Our job is our ministry.

February 8, 1998

Today I was at the Self Realization Center, in Pacific Palisades. The lecture was so inspiring. This is what church should be like. One of the many points that really stuck with me was: If we can't change ourselves, how can we change the world?

Greed is the source of violent behavior and discontent in the world. Here in La La Land, it runs rampant. If I must encounter financial ruin to learn my purpose and direction, so be it. I'm going for broke.

Here in the garden of the Self Realization Center they honor every religion. I've never understood how people can be so narrow-minded as to believe that there's only one "right" religion. How could there be when God has created so many different people and cultures?

The Mahatma Ghandi World Peace Memorial is here too. 50 years ago, he was assassinated. People don't grasp the intensity of suffering and diligence that comes with enlightenment. After everything Ghandi went through and did for others, someone had to kill him?

When Ghandi passed on, he left behind his glasses, a pair of sandals, a loin cloth, and a pocket watch. And here I am, pursuing a life of illusion, in a soulless city where people are defined by their wealth and fame. When I'm here at the center, I feel better.

February 10, 1998

Everyone in this neighborhood seems to be a little *off*. The girl who moved in below us is bulimic. I knew I should have moved to Toluca Lake.

February 15, 1998

Saw a one man show at Howard Fine Acting Studio. The guy told a story about his first audition with a casting director, who had a huge stack of pictures on her desk. She was calling the agent listed on the photo. Accidentally, the picture slipped off the stack into the trash. The actor sitting there went to retrieve it and hand it to her. She motioned him "no" and just picked up the next picture/resume off the stack and called THAT agent. The entire audience (which was mostly actors) moaned in unison.

February 20, 1998
I've made an acute observation. In this land of "fruits and nuts," the native Californians I've met are grounded and sensible. It's the people that move here from somewhere else that are "nuts."

March 1, 1998
Went hiking with Roger Nygard in Topanga Canyon. He's lived in L.A. for 12 years.

He wants to copy my tape of my parents' phone conversations. He knows funny and really makes me laugh.

He takes me to various restaurants around Los Angeles. We talk about comedy, films, Minnesota, and my past boyfriends. He gets such a kick out of my stories. He'll pick me up in his fancy car and I'll say,

"What shack are you taking me to, tonight?" And then we'll laugh.

March 18, 1998
When it rains, it pours. I'm helping with the Robert McKee Story Seminar, which is taking place for three days near my apartment. I got a reduced rate on the seminar cost for being an assistant.

I have to say, screenwriting seems like the perfect medium for me. I'd so much rather write dialogue and develop characters and stories than write product and marketing copy. The last day of the seminar goes late, and then I have an early morning call time for the Fox Family Channel shoot. Feeling anxious about giving my best to all of the above.

March 19, 1998
Doing a promo for a cable network. Trixie (a standard poodle) and I have matching wardrobes. In one spot, the trainer tried to get Trixie

to steal a hamburger off the table, but Trixie wouldn't obey and walked off the set.

The idea is that these are a series of video phone conversations which will air on Fox Family Channel. The guy behind the camera, or the "video phone," is playing my Aunt Ruth, and I have three children and a spectacular wardrobe! We talk to our Aunt Ruth through the phone. There is a red macaw on a perch and Trixie wears accessories like scarves, jewelry, and shoes that match mine.

I did nine, 15-second spots in one day. If I hadn't been hyperfocused, I couldn't have pulled it off. The director was so pleased and told me so. My agent was shocked that we shot that many in one day and feels they're not paying enough. Well, what else is new? I don't mind though. It was a blast, and they're going to be great for my commercial reel. We'll also be doing voiceovers for Fox Family Channel, which will add up to another $2,000.

Every part of it went well, except for the bozo on walkie-talkie who badgered the makeup artist within ten minutes of me sitting in the makeup chair.

"How many more minutes? They need her on set as **soon** as possible!" I got anxious. Surely this guy knows it takes more than ten minutes to do hair and makeup?

"She just started, and look at this," I said, pointing to the dark circles under my eyes. The Story Seminar took its toll and I looked haggard. I needed makeup.

As we walked to the set, he notified the director of every step, "She's ready, we're approaching, we're rounding the corner, 30 seconds away. . ." Good Lord.

The animals added a lot to the shoot. The poodle was stunning, as was the red macaw. My "kids" consisted of a five-year old, jet-propelled little boy, a sweet sixteen, freckle-faced redhead, and a hungry, teenage boy who sits at the kitchen table and eats in each spot. For example, in one spot, he eats orange cheese puffs, in another, white Hostess Snowballs.

I didn't get the script until the night before, so I was nervous about getting all my lines, but it went swimmingly. The director was thrilled and told me so. I know there is voice over work coming later for this series of Fox Family Channel commercials. Wish I could do this every day!

March 28, 1998
I walked into the laundry room today and the gay guy from the front house was folding his speedo. He told me he'd pierced his penis.

"It's really cool!" he said. "You want to see it?" I declined. Twice.

April 6, 1998
I came close to getting a series of spots for Amana. They auditioned hundreds in New York, Toronto, and here. The gal sleeping with the power person got it. Once again, I'm sleeping with the wrong guy.

April 10, 1998
Today I was hired for an acting job in a non-union industrial film as a grocery store manager. The takes were shot between shopping carts rattling by and people wandering into frame. While delivering the last take, a twig of a woman came into frame, reaching for some Ex-Lax. Leaving the store, a girl of twelve who saw the shoot approached me.

"It's glamorous being an actress, isn't it?!!"

I had been searching my purse for a coupon for toilet paper. I didn't have the heart to tell her the truth.

"It can be! But it's more work than glamour." She had the glint of stardust in her eyes.

April 20, 1998
Last night, I catered at a Temple and a woman said to me, "You speak very well for a caterer!" I almost whacked her over the head with the challah. I am not a caterer. None of us are actual caterers. Being an actor means always having to say, "I have a survival job."

May 1, 1998
The best part of my week was working a catering gig for "Great Presentations," where I served fajitas to 3,000 people on the beach near Will Rogers State Beach. There were so many beautiful orchids as part of the décor!

Two hours into the event, the power went out, leaving all 3,100 of us in darkness. I hadn't eaten dinner and was so hungry, so I inhaled four empanadas in the appetizer tent. Since they are throwing out these orchids after the event, I took the liberty to put four of them in my trunk.

May 10, 1998

I'm doing a non-union commercial tomorrow called the "Loan Arranger." The scenario is my husband and me laboring over a stack of bills. The masked man known as the "Loan Arranger" will come in and save the day. It's cheesy as hell but pays $400.

May 16, 1998

I got coerced into checking out a class at The Church of Scientology. That "church" has some bucks behind it. The film they showed me in a very elegant screening room was so manipulative. I laughed out loud a few times. How do people fall for this? They wanted to know my thoughts on it.

"You may be able to ease the suffering of people like John Travolta, Kirstie Alley, and Juliette Lewis, but I was raised Lutheran and suffering is our life. Don't call me. I'll call you." And I left.

May 18, 1998

Even when you go to a doctor in Los Angeles, you're bound to meet someone who is "in the industry." I've been participating in a study of depression. They put me through the ringer before they accepted me to the study—five hours of questioning, an EKG, urine samples, and a blood test. One of the interviewers asked me, "What do you think is causing your depression? As soon as I said, "My career," he got all excited. Turns out he's an actor too. When the main doctor left the room we commiserated, as actors do.

One of the psychiatrists asked if I'd ever considered killing anyone.

"Just family," I said.

Then he said, "This is probably preparation for a screenplay." The appointment turned into a stand-up routine.

The doctor told me I have a heart murmur.

"It's slight but you need to keep an eye on it," he warned.

"A heart murmur?" I asked. "What is it saying? Get out of the business? Doc, you're not going to kill me with these drugs, are you?" I asked.

"Well, don't take the fun out of it," he said.

I went walking later in Griffith Park, after proofing catalog copy for Service Merchandise, and met an older Israelian who invited me to coffee. Turns out, his wife is Debra Aquila, director of casting at Paramount.

Then, I'm at Priscilla's and the blonde behind the counter points at me and says,

"You lived on my street in Chicago! You and I have the same voice teacher!" It was Heidi Fecht, who lives here now too. She's the gal I met working on the *Spirit of Chicago* who referred me to my voice teacher Kathryn Hartgrove. It is a small world, after all.

May 20, 1998

Today, I was convinced we were having an earthquake and ran outside in my shower cap and bunny slippers. I looked around expecting mass hysteria. Turns out, it was just the washer on spin cycle.

May 27, 1998

Roger Nygard came over to pick me up and take me to a documentary.

"I have conditions," I said. He loved that.

Since we were going to a barbecue at writer/producer Scott Nimerfro's house after the movie, Roger helped me make an artichoke dip for the party. Unfortunately, George showed up at the front door to invite me to another barbecue. Roger waited in the kitchen and watched it transpire in the living room mirror. Damn this small apartment. George didn't know Roger was in the kitchen. After George left, Roger said,

"How many men ARE you dating? And why does George have stop-over privileges?" Roger always has a good comeback.

June 5, 1998

I had an infomercial audition today for Epil Stop hair remover. The guy asked me to lift my skirt a little higher so they could zoom in on my thighs. Then he said, "A little higher, a little higher."

After that, I catered a party at a Bel Air mansion where I accidentally tripped and spilled a pitcher of margaritas into the pool. As I've said before, I am NOT a caterer. I'm an actress, singer, and writer who sometimes *moonlights* in the catering business.

June 7, 1998

Catered a movie premiere party for Columbia Tri-Star Pictures' *Godzilla*. Bob, the over- zealous kindergarten teacher, was there. Everyone knows there's *something* wrong with him. We just don't know *what*. In an effort to be the first to reach some guests at the party, he knocked over a table and some chairs. Last time I worked with him, he knocked over a can of Sterno and set a tablecloth on fire.

Patrick, the Irish comedian I often work with, was there. He used to share an apartment with Drew Carey. Patrick always tries to make me laugh at inappropriate times. As we watched a pretty girl in a skintight skirt walk by he leaned in and said, "These days, girls wear such short skirts, you can see their biscuit whiskers."

June 19, 1998

I got the Epil Stop hair remover infomercial! The shoot was today. I had a proofreading gig at FTD, so I knew I had to nail the script in a few takes. I got it in three.

This nondescript blonde girl was talking herself up at the shoot while we were waiting. She said in that Valley girl voice that gets under my skin,

"Oh, my gawd, I've been soooo busy doing films."

She was such a phony. Film actors don't waste their time doing infomercials. This I know.

I said, "Really? If you're sooo busy doing films, why are you doing an Epil Stop hair remover **infomercial**?" She didn't have an answer for me. Actresses like that give the rest of us a bad name. I was almost relieved to leave the shoot and go proofread copy about mixed floral bouquets.

June 29, 1998

I feel close to getting some stable work. Got another writing project through Warner Bros. I'll be writing educational materials starring the Animaniacs. That excites me.

July 1, 1998

A non-union theater about an hour from here is holding auditions for *Funny Girl*. I went and sang, "I'm the Greatest Star." They had me read from the script, which was a cake walk because, let's face it, I AM Fanny Brice.

They told me at the audition they'd like me to play the understudy! That annoying voice in my head whispered, "Always the understudy, never the lead."

Of course, I'm not going to listen to that voice because the understudy gets to go on at some point, and this is a role I've always wanted. I told them I would think about it and call them the next day.

July 2, 1998

The show doesn't pay much and it's a long drive away. With my funds being what they are, I can't AFFORD to play Fanny Brice at this theatre. People back home were surprised to find out that a lot of performers pay to do theater out here. It isn't about doing it for the joy. People do it to get "seen" by casting directors. That to me is the wrong reason to do theater. But when in Rome.

So, it's not in the cards for me to play Fanny Brice just yet. Gotta find another theater. If I don't get cast in the next ten years though, I'm going to have to settle for playing Mrs. Strakosh.

August 17, 1998

I'm interviewing to be Tracy Ullman's personal assistant! Can you imagine? I adore her. She's one of my heroes. I'm going to perfect my resume and land this job!

August 20, 1998

Got called to reschedule my interview for the personal assistant job. It's now a week away.

August 27, 1998

I took the whole morning to get ready and drive to Santa Monica for the interview. The ditz behind the desk looked at me funny and said, "Who are you?"

"My interview for the personal assistant position was rescheduled to today," I said.

She just twirled her hair, chomped on her gum, shrugged her shoulders, and said,

"Oh, that position was filled already."

They might have called and cancelled my interview, but no. I have found that business etiquette and manners are different out here. I left feeling small. I drove by Fred Segal and saw a Malibu Barbie, all pink with balloon boobs, tottering around on her Manolo Blahniks. Not only did I **not** get to meet Tracy Ullman, but I didn't even get a chance at the job. I feel so helpless out here.

August 29, 1998

Tonight, I worked the 50th Annual Emmy Awards at the Shrine Auditorium. All night, this bald guy barked at us, telling us which door goes to food pickup and which one to "scullery." I should've blacked out a tooth or two and worn my eye patch.

We had to do a photo of all of us standing at three o'clock position next to our main table, with our hands behind our backs. The floor is a sea of round, shimmering gold tables, with a box of Godiva chocolates at each table setting. 2,800 people were expected to attend. Surveying the gigantic room, the gold décor, and elegant tableware, I got a chill. It is a feat to organize such an event and I feel lucky to be part of the wonder and magic of it all, even if I was dressed as a penguin.

When the guests arrived, Whitney Houston entered first. Whispers and pointing from the penguins. I saw Billy Crystal again, but this time didn't run up to him as he was surrounded by suits. Flashbulbs popped as the room got louder. Helena Bonham Carter has amazing cleavage and skin. Fran Drescher looked lovely. When I saw Tracy Ullman, I was tempted to shout, "HEY TRACY! I was supposed to be your personal assistant!" I was invisible among the dewy celebrities sipping Pellegrino.

My tables were a football field away from the kitchen. Carrying a tray full of heavy dinners on my puny shoulders is awkward, so I bent over like a question mark winding in and out of clumps of celebrities. Scuttling like a beetle from one bussing stand to the next, I was a disaster. I have NEVER been a good waitress. Hence the reason I'm not a waitress.

Michael worked the event too, so I set off to find him. I spotted him on the second floor, and we converged.

"I haven't seen one star up here," he said angrily. "I've been stuck among the executives and doing all the work."

"And all for a whopping twelve dollars an hour," I added. "I've never felt so underappreciated," I said. Michael grabbed my shoulders and shook me.

"We've got to break through!" he shouted.

"You break through," I answered. "I'm getting the hell out of this town. This is one tough town!"

When I got into my car at the end of the night, I looked at myself. There were coffee stains on my shirt, my hem was coming out of my pants, my eyes drooped, hair hung limply at my temples, my skin was blotchy, and there was a piece of spinach between my front teeth. I looked like a scullery maid.

August 30, 1998

After working the Emmy Awards Dinner last night, I feel like a limp noodle. I literally sat in a chair at a coffee shop in West Hollywood all afternoon. Didn't have the physical energy to get up and get a second cup. You know what I will have made last night? About $60. Before taxes. She works hard for the money. So hard for the money.

September 2, 1998

I flew to Minneapolis for a visit and went to the Renaissance Festival, the State Fair, Perrin Post's theater opening of *Zombies from the Beyond*, spent a day on the St. Croix with Kurt Law, who is a diamond rep (he wants to sell my diamond for me), and visited Greg Borden and Jim Faust in their new house in North Minneapolis.

At Greg and Jim's house, we drove around Worth Parkway in Jim's '63 Thunderbird with the sliding steering wheel. Jim is a collector of vintage cars, kitchen appliances, and vacuum cleaners.

I'm going to interview him and write a profile on him for a magazine. He is one of the funniest men I know.

My favorite Jim quotes include: "I'm falling apart like a meatloaf sandwich" and "He's hiding in the corner like the Boston Strangler."

We watched part of *The Lady in A Cage*, starring Olivia de Havilland and James Caan, as well as *The Wild, Wild World of Jayne Mansfield*. Over dinner we told funny stories about the mercurial characters we've dated. His partner Greg talked about an old boyfriend who threw a cement block through their picture window because the gravy was too salty.

September 15, 1998

I'm back in Los Angeles, where I had a copywriting interview with Flynt Publications. It was 10 a.m. when I rode the elevator up with a skinhead. He was just getting to work and carried his skateboard under his arm. Turns out, he was the head of the writing department and interviewed me.

I'm so naive. I honestly thought *Leg World* was a hosiery catalog. I'm so used to writing product descriptions, it didn't dawn on me that I'd be writing porn. The skinhead said,

"We're looking for a specific type of writer," as he handed me a copy of *Leg World*. The page I opened it up to showed two women eating each other. I think I may have blanched and blushed. I couldn't hide my shock. He smiled and said,

"I don't think Flynt is the place for you." I felt so out of place and awkward, I didn't try to change his mind.

October 10, 1998

I interviewed at Demi Moore's production company for a personal assistant position.

They corrected me on the pronunciation of Demi. The only way I can remember it is, "It's 'dummy' but with an 'e'."

Demi's business partner has known her for many years. She asked me what I thought of Los Angeles.

I said, "It's all about connections."

She said, "Well you figured it out pretty quick." I didn't get a good vibe from her or the office, but we'll see.

October 13, 1998

I catered a Viagra convention full of Italians. It was so nice to see people with big noses.

So many exotic women. It's no surprise I felt dwarfed by their beauty and prestige. They're all living better lives. It's so hard not to compare oneself to other people here in La La Land.

All that schlepping, serving, and smiling can wear a girl out. I forgot to remove my bow tie and cummerbund and turn on my lights when I left the parking lot. So, two cops pulled me over.

"Have you been drinking?" they asked.

"Drinking? I wish!" I shrieked. "I haven't been drinking. I've been *catering*." I got out of the car and modelled my penguin outfit. They laughed. "Do you think I'd dress like this if I didn't *have* to?" They could see how disheveled I was.

"Our mistake," they said. "You are free to go, miss!"

October 22, 1998

I'm shuffling overdue bills like playing cards. My car is leaking oil and just blew a gasket. Between the cost of my photo shoot, retouching, reproductions, postage, parking tickets, and acting classes, I'm living on the edge of bankruptcy. What if I have to get a job on Sunset at *Girls! Girls! Girls!* Oh, that's just ridiculous. I'm not going to become a stripper. My boobs aren't big enough.

Recently, I've been reading more Dorothy Parker. I went in search of her old residence today in West Hollywood. Then I came home and asked her to speak through me. This is what I wrote:

> *The End*
> *I used to dream I'd make them pay*
> *For wrongs done unto me*
> *With the final say on a war with life*
> *That finally set me free.*
>
> *I'd divvy up my treasures*
> *My shoes, my jewels, my Twiggy tote*
> *Then, I'd take to my bed, with a fistful of pills*
> *And a brilliant, farewell note.*

I'd ask to be remembered
For my humor and my song
That I left the world a gift
Of laughter, loud and long.

A pageantry would follow
Of eulogy and song.
My exit would earn infamy
As that's where I belong.

Those bastards who'd been monstrous
Would finally see the light
And long for one last chance
To tell me I was right.

But that was when I cared
What people thought of me.
In the end, I'll be at Moulin Rouge
Thigh deep in liberté!

They'll all read of my passing
As I set sail for Xanadu
On a golden ship with sails of silk
And a well-hung, handsome crew.

November 3, 1998
Had an audition for a Lexus commercial. A group of four of us had to run in slow motion in our pajamas. Nothing surprises me anymore.

November 4, 1998
Today I had an audition for *America's Most Wanted*, and the other actor had to strangle me on camera. It didn't go that well. I wish I'd been the one doing the strangling.

November 26, 1998

The bulimic girls vomiting is so loud, people can hear her when I'm on the phone. So, when Lawrence called me to say the pipes are clogged, I had to tell him. He was concerned that I was throwing handy wipes down the toilet.

"It could be the bulimic girl downstairs," I said. "She pukes every day, usually when I'm on the phone. Oh listen! There she is now."

November 28, 1998

Well, the truth comes out. My mother is embarrassed of me because I'm not married with children, so I'm a "failure." She calls artist types "you people." She has that "us and them" mentality.

"You don't respect that I've been doing commercials and musicals? I just did a show with the producer of *Rent*, for God's sake!"

"But you do it once and then it's over!" she said.

"THIS is the nature of the beast," I said. I brought up how unsupportive she was during my high school years when I was the editor of the high school paper, wrote and hosted cable television shows, and played the violin in two orchestras. You know what she said?

"Oh, I just didn't want to be bothered picking you up from school."

December 13, 1998

This street cleaning is making me crazy. The parking Gestapo waits in front of my apartment for the stroke of 10 a.m. so they can slap a ticket on me if I don't move my car by then. The tickets are growing in my glove compartment like a fungus.

January 1, 1999, my birthday, 6 a.m., Rose Parade

Today's gig wasn't half bad. We basically served people breakfast in a tent near the street where the Tournament of Roses Parade goes by. I'm so relieved it's an easy gig. Of course, it doesn't feel like my birthday.

Last night I catered a private party for a couple in Beverly Hills whose child's playroom is bigger than my apartment. He's a big shot at one of the studios. They treated us like garbage. Five of us worked

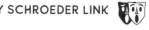

constantly, handing out hors d'oeuvres, opening and pouring bottles of wine, etc., until 2 a.m. They never fed **or** tipped us. They didn't even *thank* us. Tis' the season.

One of the other actor caterers—Max—pulled me into the linen closet at the stroke of midnight. Disgusted by the rudeness of these people, he opened up a bottle of champagne for us.

"Fuck them!" he said, grabbing me and kissing me.

"Yeh, fuck them!" I said, savagely kissing him back. "We should just make out in this closet to spite them!" he said. We drank all the booze and shared a handful of coconut shrimp.

"Why does money turn people into monsters?" I asked him. "We should smear the foie gras all over their dining room." Then we laughed, and he asked for my number. So, I made the best of the night. What a memory!

February 14, 1999

I'm struggling with the reality of life in L.A. and called home for some emotional support. Dad said, "You know what Charlie Obringer does when he's down? He walks around the block. What do **I** suggest? Get a job with the Republican Party!"

February 17, 1999

Today, I auditioned for a pharmaceutical company training film. The role is a lounge singer named Marlene Diabetes.

February 20, 1999

I will NOT end up as yet another desperate actor. I don't feel I have to prove anything to anybody, so I refuse to hand my power over to casting directors and agents—most of whom I don't even know. And just because other actors take the abuse, jack up their credit cards, and end up in rehab doesn't make it the lifestyle of choice for me. I don't have to prove anything to anybody. But I do think I should stay for pilot season.

February 21, 1999

Every day, I feel a churning in my guts, so I went to China Town, to see a doctor. He sent me home with six bags of roots, sticks, and berries. For six days I must boil these herbs in a clay pot of water and drink the tonic. The stench of the herbs is enough to peel the paint off the walls. Scott told me he's moving out if I don't stop making stick water.

March 1, 1999

I found a way to make an extra $100 a week by participating in a study on depression with California Clinical Trials. After I spent an hour filling out paperwork, I learned that I'll have to have my blood drawn every week. Had I known that I wouldn't have signed up. My vein walls roll. Well, I guess I'll have to get used to it.

April 1, 1999

Today I temped at a Beverly Hills law firm. The highlight of my day was typing Betty White's will. She's leaving a lot of dough to animal organizations. I've always known she was a remarkable dame. I hope to do the same someday.

April 20, 1999

My friend George and I went to the Kasbah in West Hollywood for "several" glasses of pinot grigio. I thought I was perfectly fine until I was on the way to the bathroom and smacked into a mirror. Thank goodness Scott dropped by for some conversation because without him, George and I would have ended up in the gutter.

By 9 p.m., George was falling down drunk. Scott was amused, until he realized he was the only one capable of driving George and me home. Still functional, I took George's jangling keys and tripped up and down the street peeking into windows. I spotted a script on the backseat, tried a few keys, and voila!

Scott and I positioned a staggering George between us, and I covered George's head with a napkin to save face. The steps were tricky, but George took it in his stride, mumbling and snorting the whole time. We put George up front so he could do what he's always wanted to do— direct.

George couldn't remember his street address and peered at us as if he were wearing bifocals.

"Is it north or south of Doheny?" Scott asked sweetly.

"N-n-n-n-south!" George said, poking Scott in the shoulder with his index finger. I realized I had to puke and scrambled for the door handle.

"I've got to. . ." I squeaked and threw up on the floor. "There's no car mat," I moaned. Scott put his head into his hands, and George pointed at a mongrel peeing on a parking meter.

When we got George home, he didn't recognize his own place, so we led him to the bathroom. Scott toured the sparsely decorated apartment shaking his head.

"George, you are so straight." George leaned against the wall with his eyes closed, listened intently and nodded in agreement.

When I opened the bathroom door on George, he was leaning against the wall, aiming his penis at the toilet bowl.

George looked at me and slurred, "Do you want to make love?"

Scott lost his patience and jostled George into bed. Suddenly, George reached up, grabbed the front of my dress and pulled me down on top of him.

"Marry me," he said. "Please, Holly, marry me."

Scott reached down to unzip George's tight jeans so we could get him under the covers. No underwear.

"I forgot," I said. "He often doesn't wear underwear."

"I'm not peeling those off of him with that thing jingling around," he said as he threw the comforter over George's head. "Just leave him in his jeans," he added, waving it off and slipping out of the room.

The following morning, I couldn't walk any further than the bathroom and threw up six times. George called and said, "What is it about you that every time we get together, I lose all control. I profess my love to you and simultaneously humiliate myself?"

We went to lunch at a Jewish deli. The waitress, who knows George, said to him, "Now this girl I like. Have some pickles." But I couldn't eat them. Pickles aren't appetizing with a hangover. But George was able to keep a few down. He was so cute, with his tousled jet-black hair and handsome bone structure.

April 27, 1999

Even the illnesses are more intense out here. I've had what I call the "Hitler Flu." It took me two rounds of antibiotics to get over it. I went to Urgent Care, where my hands were shaking so badly, I couldn't write my name. After the nurse took some blood from me, she had me feel the tube. It was HOT. I was one degree away from brain damage.

Scott's boyfriend Simon is a nurse and said to take a cool bath to lower my body temperature, which I did. Scott was tickled with himself when he pulled open the bathroom door and hurled a tray of ice cubes into the tub.

May 1, 1999

I've been dating a producer I call "Hebrew David," and today Mother asked me why he hasn't asked me to marry him.

"Because I'm not Jewish and we've been dating three weeks."

"I think you'd make a great Jew," she said. "God knows you were never a good Lutheran."

May 15, 1999

Before I moved to L.A., I was proud to be an actor. But in L.A., I'm embarrassed to admit it because we're such a dime a dozen. The other day I saw a sign at a casting director's office: "No actor parking allowed. You will be towed!"

May 16, 1999

Been at the Bodhi Tree a lot lately. Made some great notes in my diary like this. . . *How many of us can get out of our egocentric predicament to experience our identity as part of a system? I intellectually know more than I live as if I did. How do I integrate all the realities I know and have touched? The awakening is the realization that the constellation of thoughts of who you think you are is a limiting condition.*

Enlightenment is the ego's ultimate disappointment. Who I think I am is not who I am.

May 26, 1999

Today I auditioned for the role of a park ranger in a film entitled, *What's a Natural Resource?* The director told me I was talking too fast for the second-grade audience.

"They're second-graders," I said, "not imbeciles."

I got the part!

June 4, 1999

Someone keyed my car when it was parked on Melrose Avenue. Why are people so nasty? I have no enemies here! The only reason for it I can come up with is my bumper sticker, which says, *"Men are not pigs. Pigs are kind, gentle, sensitive creatures."*

June 5, 1999

John Howard took me to lunch at the Mexican restaurant on Melrose Avenue. Suddenly, I had this bad feeling in the pit of my stomach. I went outside to plug the meter, and there it was—my worst fear come true. The dreaded yellow boot! They slapped a giant orange sticker on the windshield and shackled my car with that evil contraption. My heart fell to my ankles.

John drove me to the license bureau, the whole time complaining about the Koreans.

I took every last penny I had, $300, and slipped it to the sweaty man behind the scratched plastic window and said,

"This town is **ridiculous**. I'm getting the hell out and going back to the Midwest where there's a SOUL!"

"Can I come with you?" he asked. John had to pay the last $20 because I didn't have it. Two years in Los Angeles cost me every dime I had.

June 6, 1999

I went for broke, and L.A. broke me. I've had it. This is ONE TOUGH TOWN.

Joseph Campbell said, "The journey is meaningless unless the hero brings back the elixir, a lesson from the special world." So, what's my lesson? It's not enough to have talent in Hollywood. You also need connections, energy, and money because it's a ten-year plan and you can't give up after two, like I'm about to do. Will I regret this choice, years from now? Probably.

I had some illuminating adventures in Hollywood, the "Dream Factory," a town where someone's interest in you is directly proportionate to what you can do for them. The City of Angels, a spooky, surreal universe in the desert, where people talk big and deliver little. La La Land, where the rich and famous are out of reach and desperation never far away.

In the words of Irving Berlin, "There's **no** business, like show business." The magic of Hollywood is like stardust. It floats in the atmosphere but is impossible to grasp and hold onto. In an industry based on illusion, things are rarely what they seem. I can see why people get hooked on Hollywood, though. If I were connected and booking a lot, I know I'd like it a lot more. But it **is** like another planet. I never realized just how Midwest I am.

I am willing to risk my significance, but I can't rot away, sacrifice personal relationships, sanity, and years of my life, hanging on for that "big break." All I'll ever be is one big break away from fulfillment. I want to be happy **now**. I became a performer so I could express myself. Creativity is my quest, not necessarily fame. My revised, revised, resolutions:

> Find happiness within
> Enjoy the journey

THE CANE MUTINY

Most actors have "survival jobs" and one of mine was writing advertising and marketing. I spent 20 years coming up with product descriptions no one reads. Name an object in your home and I've written about it—apparel, electronics, home décor, toys, jewelry, collectibles and novelty items. I've written for Spiegel, Warner Bros., Montgomery Ward Direct, Damark, Rivers End, Dept. 56, etoys, and Fingerhunt.

Back in the day, Fingerhunt produced an astounding volume of catalogs. Most Minnesotan writers, art directors, and photographers worked for the catalog at some time or another. It was a forgiving work environment. As one designer said to me,

"Only Fingerhunt would hire a color-blind art director."

June 8, 1999, Minneapolis, MN.
I called the folks at the Fingerhunt catalog to see if they need copywriters.

"Come on back!" they said. Oh, to be needed again. It took two years of unrelenting struggle in Los Angeles to make me appreciate my catalog copywriting jobs. So, it's back to the Midwest for me. Back to "the corral," the freelancer den in the poorly-ventilated basement. Quite frankly, I am THRILLED to do honest work with real people again. I've always felt comfortable there.

June 13, 1999
The fodder for my memoirs is priceless. Where else can you write about grease bowls, toilet bowl brushes, Virgin Mary crying lamps, and spray-on hair? Or my personal favorite, the vacuum cleaner cozy that comes in several incarnations: Pig, Cow, Bear, Maid, and Butler.

Discussing demographics at a meeting, our customers are termed "shut-ins." Our primary market is people on welfare who don't have credit cards. Customers pay for merchandise in monthly payments.

A toilet bowl brush can be paid for in monthly installments of $1.12, for example. In the end, it's more expensive than just paying in full, but our customers, aren't good at math.

June 22, 1999
Very proud of the headline I wrote today for a cookie jar of a bear dressed up like a policeman. The lid is his hat. "Serve and Protect Your Cookies!" I wrote. It's the little triumphs.

June 25, 1999
A tall, wild-haired man with a loping stride waves to me in the hall every day. The phrase "shoot from the hip" comes to mind. He always has a morose expression and holds his arms stiff at his sides. As he lumbers towards me, with his hands held near his hips, he flashes me a little wave. I've never formally been introduced to this character, but I always nod his way politely.

Turns out, this sauntering fella is known by many. His stride and signature wave are known as "The Bob Spidey Stroll."

"Something happened to him," Pat, my coworker said. "He's on medication. He was in Vietnam, you know."

"What happened to him there?" I asked, totally intrigued. Pat paused dramatically.

"He worked on weather balloons."

July 1, 1999
Got some good gossip today. The most famous Fingerhunt legend took place a year before I arrived. A mentally unbalanced copywriter, pushed to his limit, "lost it." He went into the bathroom, stripped, and placed his clothes in a pile, with his wallet on top. Then, wearing only his tennis shoes, he tore through the maze of beige cubicles and fluorescent lights, smacking the burlap walls with his hand and whooping like a lunatic. He ran so fast he wiped out turning a corner. Then, he ran down the hall to the front entrance, where visiting vendors watched in amazement. He ran into the glass window like a dazed bird. Fumbling, he found the door and streaked

down Highway 7. The cops picked him up shortly thereafter. He had to take some time off after that. But here's the thing about this company: They forgive and forget. This guy took some time off and came back to work there a year later.

"Jesus. They'll hire anybody," said my friend Melissa.

"Thank God," I said. "Otherwise, I might not have a job."

July 10, 1999

There are a number of people here who need canes. Dan in Receiving broke his leg in several places over his lunch hour the other day. He was in a nearby pasture. In an attempt to climb over a fence, he clumsily toppled over it instead. Rumor has it he crawled back to work. Poor Dan.

July 20, 1999

Today, Melissa came to my cube and said,

"I think they're even hiring freelancers with canes. It's a cane mutiny!" Several of us from the corral met in the hall to discuss the mutiny.

"Are they only hiring cripples now?"

"I've never seen so many damaged people in my life," said Kitty. Melissa, having given her two-weeks' notice, shook her head.

"Let's face it," she said, "This whole place is a god damn booby hatch."

July 26, 1999

I met Richard Simmons today at work. Richard is selling some of his products in the catalog. My friend Paige used to go to his workout class in Hollywood, where he would rifle through purses and wallets during class and make jokes. My buddy Phil Bolsta filmed me and Richard meeting in the gym, where I cornered him. I gave Richard flowers and a grease bowl, one of the catalog's big sellers.

"This is for storing cooking grease, Richard. You know, after you fry some bacon, you just put the bacon grease in the grease bowl and use it later!" The bowl was wedged in Styrofoam with the price tag still on it. "Oops!" I said, as I pulled off the price, right before I gave it to him. He got the joke and we laughed and embraced.

August 27, 1999
I had an incredible Tarot card reading with my pal Deb Pierce. Very powerful. She pulled the following two cards.

The Ace of Wands—Second biggest energy card says it's very important I maintain my creative outlet. Find the right framework in which to set it. All security and certainties I've been clinging to will be shaken and destroyed by the impact of the energies breaking through. I can only use the incredible energy and power I have if I have a goal, toward which I can direct it.

Death Card—Oh, boy. Signifies radical external transformation. Let go of the old. Hang or cling onto the past and I'll have agony. Let the old die. Let everything go.

October 10, 1999, Minneapolis, Minnesota

I'm doing a sexy bad girl review called *Vixens*, created by actress/singer turned producer Perrin Post. She and I met when I starred in an interactive class reunion she wrote called *Ten Years Later*, a show about a 10-year class reunion. I always wear something of my own in a show, and this time, it was my mother's cat eyeglasses. I played Mary Lou Nelson, who falls in love with Jerry when they reconnect at the reunion. It's a whole different ballgame doing this type of show. *Tony and Tina's Wedding* is another popular interactive show that's done very well in Chicago and Minneapolis. It's all about improv and being on your game because your "stage" is a ballroom full of audience members, who are also attending the reunion. My favorite part is when Robbie Mancina feels the disappointment of not getting the guy, yet again, and stuffs her face full of cake.

Vixens, Perrin Post's next production, is the sexiest show I've ever done. I'll be in fishnets and high heels. As Jim Faust said, "Jacked up, cinched in, shaved high, and thong ready." We'll be doing songs from *Cabaret*, and *Chicago*. Working with other strong women is empowering. One of my numbers is the "Call from the Vatican" number from *Nine*, which I do entirely on a table, in high heels. That should get me a few dates.

To promote the show, we are performing at the Mall of America, for a senior citizen job fair.

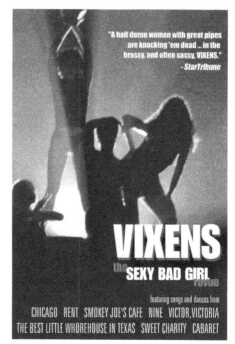

"A half dozen women with great pipes are knocking 'em dead ... in the brassy, and often sassy, VIXENS."
- *StarTribune*

VIXENS
the SEXY BAD GIRL revue

featuring songs and dances from
CHICAGO   RENT   SMOKEY JOE'S CAFE   NINE   VICTOR, VICTORIA
THE BEST LITTLE WHOREHOUSE IN TEXAS   SWEET CHARITY   CABARET

Photo by Rick Spaulding

November 10, 1999

I went to Chicago for the weekend to hang out with a guy I'm dating and see my parents. Chicago always lifts my spirits, with its palpable energy and sophisticated skyline. I'm attracted to this new fella but he's another bad boy.

I took the South Shore to Michigan City and my mom picked me up. I was futzing with my hair and makeup in the bathroom when Dad walked by the door and paused in the doorway.

"You look really good," he said. It wasn't like him to say something like that. "Smile!" Then he walked away. There was an odd feeling that lingered. I don't know how else to explain it. Mom and Dad and I had a nice visit together. It was less stressful than usual.

GOD CLOBBERS US ALL

There's nothing like death to interrupt life. The impermanence of life has knocked me over again. My brilliant, kind, sometimes bumbling Father died a week from his 71st birthday, of a heart attack. He served in the war, buried his only son, and dealt with my mother and her pain for 45 years.

December 10, 1999

Thank God I saw him last month. Dad died in bed of a **heart** attack, next to Mother. No surprise there. Mom told me the story of how she woke up to the sound of air coming out of Dad and that his eyes were glassy looking at the ceiling. She thought he had a leg cramp.

"Holly, his eyes were open, and this air was coming out of him, and I thought, oh, my God, it's happened to me . . . I'm a widow."

I was speechless.

An ambulance came, and the cats stood nearby as they tried to revive my father, but he was gone. My mother called me and said, without emotion,

"Your father is gone. Come home."

December 16, 1999

The funeral is a blur. My mother was happy with it, but I thought it was bland. I suggested bag pipes, as my father loved them, but she put the kabosh on that. Pastor Shoop was dry and dull in his delivery and words. Jodi Scutchfield Thyen came and leaned in at one point to whisper in my ear, "He really goes by the book, doesn't he?" Later at home, I sat at the kitchen table with my mother who asked me if I believed in reincarnation.

"The soul is energy, so it has to continue. I'd like to believe in reincarnation because then I'd have a second chance at getting life right." My mother thought about this.

"Oh, no," she said. "What if Dad has gotten to heaven and Danny isn't even there because he's been born to a family in Ohio?" I pondered this.

During the funeral I thought about how my father was usually the smartest person in the room and didn't have a mean bone in his body. He taught his children, when they would listen, valuable life skills, and the animals loved him. People in the various kennel clubs he and my mother joined really appreciated his humor and willingness to work for the benefit of others.

In 1946, he entered the Army Air Corps and served with the Air Sea Rescue Research Group. Then he was reassigned to Hokkaido Japan and worked as an aircraft mechanic. He was discharged as Crew Chief in 1947. I would have loved to hear more stories about that time in his life, but Mom often shut him down.

A saint in many ways, he never stopped believing in God, even after his only son died at 31. With no more men left in the Schroeder family, there won't be a rational thought in the room during the holidays. Thank goodness I squirreled away some of his letters and his recipe for dandelion wine. I recall a particularly funny incident from June of 1997.

June 20, 1997

I went home to visit Mom for her birthday and the funniest thing happened. Porsche and Alex, the Moluccan cockatoos, were in their cage in the garage because Mom and Dad put them out in the driveway for some sun when the weather is nice.

So, Mom and I leave the house to head to LaPorte. Mom remembers that she left the garage door open and turned around to go back and close it. As we pull into the driveway, she pressed the remote-control garage door button. At that second, Dad was pulling the birdcage with the birds in it back into the garage. He had no idea Mom had come back and pressed the button, so he was caught off guard by the door coming down onto the birdcage.

"Press the remote, MOM!" I said to her as the door came down on the cage. Dad ran for the garage door console on the garage wall. It was like a cartoon. When he realized that she, once again, had shut the door on top of him (the other day it was his car), he threw up his hands. My Mom and I started laughing. It was so funny we couldn't speak. Then he started laughing and we all just wheezed for five minutes. It was the best five minutes ever. The next day, Alex the cockatoo flew away into the woods and has been living there ever since.

December 20, 1999

Why do our family members die during the holidays? The only grandmother I ever had, my father's mother Lydia, died on my birthday. Looking at photos and history from my Dad's old photo albums, I want to hear his stories again. I'm thankful for the family reunions my father's family hosted, in Hammond Indiana. I was just a kid, so I didn't realize then how much those reunions would impact me.

Held outside a modest pre-war home, in late July, about 25 people attended the reunion.

Aunt Phyllis, my father's aunt by marriage, was damaged. When she was in her 20's, Phyllis contracted polio, which scrambled her brain. She had short, spikey gray hair with bangs, and black cat eyeglasses covered in rhinestones that often swung on a chain around her neck. Dad said what happened to her as a girl was a shame because Aunt Phyllis used to be beautiful and smart before she got polio and her husband went off to war.

When she spoke, her head bounced around on her neck. Kooky and full of jokes, she was the female version of Red Skelton. Thankfully, the polio didn't kill her spirit. I had no idea she was mentally disabled. I just thought she was funny.

Every year, Aunt Phyllis brought nine of her angel food cakes to the family reunion. You'd slide up to the spread of casserole dishes and slop some green bean casserole on your plate next to shiny slices of ham, coleslaw, and a devilled egg, and there was Aunt Phyllis, promoting her nine angel food cakes. There was something for everyone: orange, coconut, strawberry, blueberry, chocolate, banana, cherry, bubble gum, and vanilla.

Hovering over the table, like a carney barker, passing the knife hand to hand, she reminded us, "Save room for cake! Eat 'em up, eat 'em up, before they're all gone!" Nine angel food cakes is a **lot** of cake. They were never all gone.

At 3:30, it was officially time for our annual trek to the Five and Dime. Uncle Earl, bursting out of his denim overalls, sat on a wooden stool under a mulberry tree playing the accordion.

"Roll out the barrel. We'll have a barrel of fun!"

All the kids lined up single file behind Aunt Phyllis, who saluted and marched. She lifted her black orthopedic shoes and white athletic socks high in the air. We took orders and followed her three blocks to the Five and Dime.

"Left, left, left, now left!"

That two-block walk to the store with all these kids filled me with anticipation. I could almost taste the Zero candy bar I was about to buy. Once we filed into the Five and Dime, we scattered like marbles across the linoleum, snatching up Boston Baked Beans, Atomic Fireballs, Honeycombed Peanuts, and Hot Tamales. Aunt Phyllis continued clowning, marching in place at the register, grinning from ear to ear, like Alfred E. Newman.

Holding tight to our paper bags stuffed with sweets, we marched back to the reunion with our stash of *Mad* magazines, candy cigarettes, Boston Baked Beans, Lemon Heads, Mike & Ikes, Good and Fruity, Razzles, and Astro Pops. Aunt Phyllis returned with a pink bubble gum cigar, a Scooter Pie, and a box of corn pads. Back at the reunion, she smoked her bubble gum cigar.

For a kid who had no cousins to play with, the pilgrimage to the Five and Dime with the other kids and kind-hearted Aunt Phyllis meant the world.

LETTER FROM DAD

July 26, 1986, 7:30 a.m.

Dear Holly,

I'm using company paper because it's cheaper. We got a letter?? from your $orority. Apparently the "S" key on their typewriter is broken, so they used the $ key instead. They must have learned about rate increases from NIPSCO. However, Pi Phi attorneys have better contracts. The Pi Phi$ have an excellent credit department (Mafia type). The dog show is over, thank God. We had some of the sheriff's cadets to handle traffic. I asked for four and got six, plus one very bossy lady who thought she was in charge of them and <u>ME</u>. When it came to me, she was not correct. I think I made her unhappy. I told her that the exhibitors are not convicts and the cadets are not Hitler's storm troopers.

I have flowers to plant and beans to pick so I'll get with it. Oh, Mom's basset Jeremy has a $150 stud service this morning. I hope he performs. I like that type of work but could never get paid for it. Nothing else new in LaPorte, just a few robberies and an occasional murder.

Love, Dad

TURTLE GIRL

Minneapolis, Minnesota, January 15, 2000

I've started a job working with photographers and stylists at Dayton's photo studio. Our male creative director Mark happens to be very kind and transgender, so he wears long fake fingernails and barrettes. It's comforting to work for a company that allows people to be who they really are.

My job is to prep and label merchandise for the Sunday circular ads. Today I learned how to stack a pile of shirts, so they look great on camera. Felt, foam core, and Polyfill make each shirt look flawless. Then, I prepped chocolate Easter bunnies using an Xacto knife on the seams and small brushes to clear away stray flecks of chocolate. I wanted to take a bite out of those bunnies all day.

As for my personal life, I'm dating a wry detective named Chris who works for the state of Minnesota. We met on Match.com. His contact with the underbelly of life (bottom feeders he calls them), fascinates me. Our perspectives are completely different and he shocks me with what he's experienced. On our second date we had dinner.

"Today I had to write about Big Billy Bass, a motion-activated trout on a plaque that sings 'Don't worry, be happy.' How was your day?"

"I've got to wash my hands. I just got out of a house full of maggots. The neighbors were complaining about the smell. Well, no wonder! The guy had been dead for two weeks. He'd used a shotgun and blown his head clean off. I thought he had a head when I walked in the door, but it was really just a swarm of maggots. No head."

January 18, 2000

Steaming fabric is fun when it's glorious satin, silk, cotton. This may be the ideal job to fit with my writing and performing. Today, I cleaned crystal, silver, made swatches, prepped garden merchandise, kitchen gadgets, and ran an errand to buy cream and find tomatoes for a shoot. January is not the time to shop for tomatoes. First, I went to Lund's and then to Whole Foods to pour over vine-on tomatoes, to find the right hue and plumpness. People have no idea what goes into those Sunday circular ads.

As for the detective, he's unlike anyone I've ever dated. He makes me happy to do what I do for a living. On our second date, he told me about an accidental suicide on one of the reservations. Two Native Americans, pie-eyed from pouring on the sauce for hours, played Russian roulette with their own pistols. One poor guy accidentally shot off his own head. There were scattered bits of skull and teeth stuck in the ceiling tile. I would never be able to get over seeing such a thing.

February 20, 2000

At the photo studio, I love perusing all the antiques and home décor in the prop loft. The stylists are wildly creative, and Jim Faust never disappoints with his unbridled wit.

March 10, 2000

I'm learning that traumatic experiences in the field have hardened Chris the detective. How could they not? He once held a woman in his arms as she died. She literally died in his arms. In her last breath, her daughter arrived on the scene, just in time to see her mother pass. That's a job you can't leave at the office.

When he was a police officer, one of his first jobs was to check out a complaint at an apartment building. He and three officers found the source of the smell. A diabetic man had died in his bed two weeks before—and it was summer.

"There was a hair in his ear that kept moving," he said. "The gases escaping from his head kept this hair dancing in his ear."

Then, he explained what happens when a person has been dead for two weeks.

"You can't touch their skin," he said. "So, the other officers and I had to remove him by each taking a corner of the bed sheet. And then he leaked all over the floor of the elevator."

I am attracted to him, but we have different priorities. After living in California, I'm so conscious of where my boobs are going. Real ones don't stand at attention. Real boobs flop into your armpits. But if you prop yourself up on your elbow, using it like a kickstand, they fall forward. Far more flattering. When in bed, he'll try to push me down, and I'll pop back up. He'll push me down, and I'll bounce back up. Down, up, down up.

"What are you, a turtle?" he said. "I'm going to call you 'Turtle Girl.'"

"Okay!" I said. "I like turtles."

April 13, 2000

Heard a hilarious story today from the detective involving a Podunk precinct, in Kentucky.

"This precinct was as hillbilly as you could get. Think *Deliverance*," he said. "There was a spittoon in the middle of the dingy, one-room station." When he walked in, there were four police officers, legs up, spitting approximately eight feet into the spittoon. A portly dachshund wandered around the room.

One cop said, "So, what's yer state bird?"

"The mosquito," Chris said, attempting a joke.

Cop says, "Skeeters? We got skeeters. Some of them get so big they been known to sneak up behind a man, stand flat footed, and fuck 'em." *Spit!*

May 22, 2000

It was fun while it lasted. The detective is chasing a pension and I'm chasing dreams. He told me I have no anchor and that I'm "high maintenance." I called Mom and she cheered me up.

"Holly, forget the cop. All he wants to do is fight crime. As for being high maintenance, I don't think that's an insult. I think it means you're fancy!"

June 5, 2000

Today I went to Jim Faust's house, where we talked about our families. He told me the following and I typed it as fast as I could. It is extraordinary. And the fortune Jim got in his cookie? Wow!

MIDDLE FLAT

When I was a kid, we used to go on tours with my grandfather. We'd go to the Obrien Road, which was an old Indian trail that had been obliterated by the 1960's. If he saw a puddle, he'd stop the car and get out to measure it with a stick to make sure it wasn't too deep. It could be the size of a dinner plate and we were convinced the car would fall through to China. My cousins and I would scream, "No! We can't drive through that puddle, Grandpa!" He'd be smoking his big cigar, wearing his stained undershirt. He always smelled boozy and smoky, which was comforting to me. I liked it. It made me feel secure that he was all liquored up.

Then, we'd go to the dump. For me, going to the dump then was like what going to New York is now. There would be other kids there shooting rats with BB guns. We'd walk around, poking in the garbage with sticks. There were always at least three smoldering fires burning in the dump—like pagan fire pits. There was also a hut, an old ice-fishing house, where people put the good junk. We'd look around in the hut like we were at the Met and be at one with the dump. Then, we'd go to The Bug House, which was the mental hospital farm. This was not just an expression: It was called The Bug House, and that's where Grandpa worked.

We'd check the crops in the fields behind The Bug House, and then we'd go to the criminal ward yard. This was like going to the movies. It had thirty-foot fences with razor wire coiled at the top. Behind the fences were picnic tables. We'd sit and eat candy and popcorn, watching the patients. The patients would get pissed off and start rattling the fence, yelling at us. We didn't care because my grandpa was there to protect us.

Once, a patient threw a shovel at my grandpa and almost cut off his left ear. My grandpa also caught hepatitis from bad chicken salad.

My mom was an X-ray technician, and my dad was an orderly at the State Mental Hospital, which was first known as the

Minnesota State Hospital for the Criminally Insane and Feeble-minded. My mom eventually referred to patients not by their names but by the body part they had to x-ray. She'd say, "Send up that right hip." She was once trapped in an office with a patient who was 6'5, weighed 280 lbs., and tore radiators off the walls. She saved herself by talking to him about the accommodations at local luxury hotels.

To this day, she refers to people in her everyday life who appear to be manic or clinically depressed or neurotic as "Middle Flat." Outpatients are referred to as "Lower Flat." And "Upper flat" is for those with severe levels of psychosis. These are the schizophrenics, hebephrenic, and catatonics—who are often naked and shit on the floor. Hence the term, "hose down the ward."

My father was an orderly on Upper Flat, where Phenobarbital was dispensed in a water cooler in the hallway. The orderlies occasionally tipped back a few Dixie cups. Then, they would reposition the catatonics in the hallway in provocative positions leaning on the wall. They'd stay that way for hours.

There was a patient in Upper Flat who got a hold of a box of kitchen matches and burned every hair off his body without burning his skin. Every hair. Eye lashes, pubic hair, armpit hair. They guessed he'd had the matches all day.

Then there was the guy in Middle Flat who'd been molesting his daughters for years and called it, "playing leapfrog."

Since my childhood, I've learned that my father, a former Lutheran minister, is a mentally ill, latent homosexual. I was told he has a narcissistic personality, which is complicated by avoidant and dependent characteristics. When he was 55, he had a quintuple bypass. I suspect they cut him open and his personality fell out.

After he'd been institutionalized for two years, I was in a Chinese restaurant and when I cracked my cookie in half, I read my fortune which said:

He loves you as much as he can, he just can't love you very much.

July 20, 2000

Thank goodness I bought that tape recorder from Radio Shack years ago. I lucked out and recorded a phone conversation with my mother that is gold.

Telephone rings...

HOLLY

Hello?

MOTHER

I have to have an operation.

HOLLY

Hello, Mother.

MOTHER

My bladder has fallen. Or my uterus. I don't know which, but I'm hoping it's the uterus because I don't need *that* anymore.

HOLLY

What do you mean its *fallen*?

MOTHER

Well, I was on the toilet and it just sort of fell out.

HOLLY

FELL out? Did you fish it out?

MOTHER

No, it didn't fall in the water. It just sort of . . . hung there.

HOLLY

What did doctor Battle say?

MOTHER

Oh, he doesn't know.

HOLLY

You didn't call him?

MOTHER

I'm a little busy right now.

HOLLY

Doing what? You don't have a job. Your organs are dangling in the toilet! Call the doctor.

MOTHER

He might want me to have surgery and I have a dog show next weekend, Fond Du Lac.

HOLLY

And you wonder why I always had to be the adult.

MOTHER

Sigh. Just so you know, I talked to Lorraine and found out it's common. If you would've had children like you were supposed to, you would know that it happens. I'm going to have a surgery where they tack it up. So, I need you to come home. The surgery is a week from Thursday.

HOLLY

What if I have something going on? What if I have an audition?

MOTHER

Well, cancel it. This is more important.

HOLLY

How do you know that? You don't even know what it's for, Mom.

MOTHER

I don't give a shit if its Martin Scorceezey. Your mother is more important than any audition you will ever have. And let's be honest. You never seem to get any of those so why even GO?

LARGER THAN LIFE

Children's Theater Company, Minneapolis, Minnesota
July 8, 2001
I'm working for a theater that has money. I've started rehearsals at the Children's Theater Company for *Charlie and the Chocolate Factory*. The grants, the donations, the subscription audience . . . it's a big step up from doing cabarets at the Bryant Lake Bowl. The resources at CTC are astounding. I know for a fact that CTC child actors are not typical children. Connor, 12, who plays Augustus Gloop, knows far more about opera than I do.

I am playing Mrs. Salt, mother of Veruca. In the stage version, she is more prominent. Me, Mr. Salt played by Eric Eagleson, and Veruca, played by sassy Sabrina Crews, are a visual assault. We are Euro-trash in pink and electric blue couture trimmed in Muppet fur, which is very expensive.

The CTC wardrobe department is the closest I've gotten to working with Muppets. Many of the costumes are custom made. The wig mistress told me my head is smaller than most of the kids, so they are making my wig from scratch.

July 15, 2001
Our director David Schweitzer resembles a mad scientist and is an advocate of improvisation. Hooray! I was concerned about upstaging or stealing focus, but he said in this show, there's no such thing. My dream job. Can't wait to see his interpretation of the Oompa Loompas.

July 16, 2001
Well, the Oompa Loompas weren't in the budget. So, they're usually offstage. When onstage, WE are actually the Oompa Loompas, but playing them behind a scrim, to create shadows. Totally different

interpretation. But that's the challenge of theater versus film. Plus, little people these days are not "p.c."

July 20, 2001
As golden ticket winners, all the families have to walk in with the public and find their seats in the theater at the start of the show. As we stumbled down aisle J to our seats today, a couple of kids reached out to touch us, like we were royalty. One little boy said to me, "You're awfully small to be a mother."

Left to right: David Cabot, Eric Eagleson, Sabrina Crews, me.

Sabrina Crews, my daughter, was so well cast, I feel like she is my daughter. This kid doesn't miss a beat. There's a swarthy crew member who flirts with me backstage and Sabrina catches every innuendo and eyebrow. I think she knows Mr. Salt and I are "involved." We maintain a professional distance at the theater, Mr.

Salt and I, but I think she knows. If I could have a daughter like her, I'd welcome motherhood with open arms.

September 11, 2001

When I got to the theater today, there was no one in the dressing room. For a moment, I thought I'd read the schedule wrong.

"Hello, Possums!" I shouted down the hall. Nothing. Then, I dashed to the Green Room, where everyone- kids, parents and cast were staring at the small television.

Connor was bawling. Parents were stricken. Just as I joined them, a plane hit one of the Twin Towers. It was inconceivable, like watching a disaster movie.

Artistic Director Peter Brosius came downstairs and led us in a prayer and moment of silence. He was so gracious. At first, Peter said we would cancel the show, but then we found out the buses of kids were on their way. So, Peter said to go ahead and get in makeup and costume. I felt ridiculous donning my Muppet fur in the face of a national tragedy of epic proportion.

Turns out, the buses were directed back to the schools and the show cancelled. In this particular case, the show did not go on.

September 19, 2001

Mickey the stage manager told me I'm stealing focus in the nut room scene, during which my daughter Veruca falls down the garbage chute, and I thrash around with an orange squirrel on my head as ten rodents pelt me from all directions, concluding with me falling down the chute. How could I NOT steal focus? I mean really.

"Stealing focus?" said Lynn Rotto Nelson, playing Mrs. Gloop. "I should hope so!"

October 12, 2001

Had my first fitting for our next show, *How the Grinch Stole Christmas*. As Grandma, I have the biggest boobs of all. And my wig looks like the Chrysler Building.

Left to right: Dean Holt, Holly Schroeder, David Cabot, and Kimber Lee

October 16, 2001

Our color-blind cast includes one little black boy named Donovan Tyson, who plays Brother Boo. Can't wait to hear what my mother says about that. He's really comical and will say something only a child would say or ask a ridiculous question every day before rehearsal when our illustrious director Mathew asks, "Any questions?"

We all wait with anticipation for Donovan's next observation.

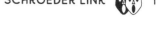

Today he said, "I've noticed that I don't get mail at home or at the theater."

October 17, 2001
The shopping number where we dance with wrapped gifts is very 42nd Street. There's also a smokey, jazzy, Fosse-esque song that makes me want to rub against Grandpa.

October 19, 2001
Worked on the scene in which Cindy Lou witnesses the Grinch stealing the tree. When she sings to him, everyone melts. For a moment, you believe she's gotten through to his core. It is so sweet, it brings all of us, director and Grinch included, to tears.

Sweet little Cindy Lou, who has a mean streak and tortures Donovan. Yesterday, she trapped him in an upside-down laundry basket and told him he had to stay there until intermission.

November 3, 2001
Thank God the run of *Charlie* is over. I'm falling apart like a meatloaf sandwich. Several layers of overzealous costuming with dancing, running, hopping, posing, and miming and we're all drenched by the end of the show. My knee injury from over a year ago is worsening. I found out my ACL is ripped in half. Must have happened when I was doing ballet leaps on that raked stage at Timberlake Playhouse. Or perhaps it was all the dancing in high heels and fishnets during the three runs of *Vixens?* Who can tell? The doctor said it probably happened gradually over time. If I hadn't built up the muscles around the injury, I would not have been able to perform nine shows a week in high heels.

November 30, 2001
It is tech week and even the Who's are grumpy. A glitch in the computer erased all the light and sound cues, so we had to spend the day backtracking and reenter all the light and sound cues. Sitting in a Who pod is different than sitting on your ass. There we were, lolling about on the floor, steps, and stage like walruses.

December 1, 2001, Opening Night

The opening number makes my heart swell with joy. I'm so thankful to be able to share this with my dear friend Doug Trapp, who is playing Father Who. He stands right next to me. When the drop rose to reveal the entire cast hand in hand swaying and singing, the audience gasps. The magnitude of so many Who's in their large pods, Seuss hair and makeup, is visually spectacular. I could feel the waves of energy flowing from the audience.

They clapped for the wild ride and the Grinch's transformation. And as the snow came down and the Who's of Whoville sang to a tear-stained Grinch, the audience was spellbound. At the end, they jumped to their feet for a standing ovation. Pure Magic! Big success! Hugs all around!

December 2, 2001

The day after a successful opening, there's usually a bit of a let-down and perhaps a flub onstage. No one lost a line today, but Grant Sorenson (mini-Grinch) lost his whip. During the wild ride, Grant whips CJ (mini-Max) as they barrel down the mountain towards Whoville. They're up in the air so it is quite exciting. Well, Grant lost his grip on the whip and it flew across the stage.

Then, during the closing number, Cindy Lou hiccupped on her lyrics. "'Specially when the snow is falling *(hiccup)*, I'll be calling."

December 4, 2001

During the quartet today, when Doug and the incomparable Dianne Benjamin Hill as his wife embrace and sing to each other, a kid in the audience said out loud, "If they kiss, I'm outta here."

The Q&A session after the show this morning was great. One kid asked, "If the Grinch has a heart two sizes too small and it grew three sizes that day, wouldn't it be one size too big?" He has a point.

December 7, 2001

Before the show tonight, the Grinch entered the women's dressing room wearing only his padding, wig and makeup. He leered at us, growling through his phlegm, tormenting us with his furry, floppy fingers.

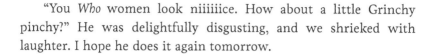

"You *Who* women look niiiiiice. How about a little Grinchy pinchy?" He was delightfully disgusting, and we shrieked with laughter. I hope he does it again tomorrow.

December 9, 2001
Dianne's car broke down on her way to the theater. David wanted to go as the Grinch to pick her up but two of the mom's went instead. When Diane finally rushed into the dressing room, panicked, Dean (Max) in his dog makeup was standing there in her dress. He said he'd been going over her part and was ready to go on.

December 11, 2001
Today, the show was signed for a hearing-impaired audience. Grandpa (Tony Thomann), whose character is hard of hearing and always says, "What?" and "I wish he'd speak up," said, 'I've been dreading this day." There's nothing like making jokes about deafness to the hard of hearing.

December 13, 2001
I walked onstage tonight with the pie—and a bright green label attached to my left breast. Grandpa followed me to the fireplace and ripped if off before the audience saw it. I had no idea it was there. Must have stuck to my boob when I leaned on the prop table.

December 14, 2001
A couple of funny mishaps today. During the opening number, Allison's antennas fell and hung down by her ears. Then, while talking to the Grinch, Cindy Lou belched on the word "frog."

JP Fitzgibbons had a major brain fart today. Usually, he says to the Grinch in the town square, "It's a custom this time of year to wish all your neighbors health and good cheer." Instead, he said some long, jumbled mess, which he then tried to rhyme but it only got worse. We all stood there, witnessing a train wreck, as the color drained out of his cheeks.

December 20, 2001

My mom came to Minneapolis so she could see the show, which I appreciated. She had no interest in meeting cast members and acted cold. When we got home, she said, "Why did they cast that little black boy? Everyone KNOWS he's not a Who!"

I tried to explain color-blind casting to her. She rolled her eyes and said, "Whatever."

I talked to my therapist, who said, "The theater is your world, not your mother's. She is only interested in things that involve her." I looked up more on narcissism.

> *Grandiose and arrogant.*
> *Voracious—you belong to them.*
> *Exploitive and threatening, prone to rages, like a child.*
> *Irrational and immature, a perpetual toddler.*
>
> *They live in their own distorted version of reality. The more power they have, the more they impose their reality on those around them. They'll exploit others without compunction and rationalize everything they do.*
>
> *Rarely do they admit mistakes or take responsibility for what they've done.*
> *They lack empathy for most people yet can feel so sorry for themselves. They don't express much gratitude.*
> *They need to feel special. If you fail to acknowledge them, they will feel a narcissistic injury.*
> *They don't recognize personal boundaries. Reminding them you have feelings and needs is just tiresome to them.*
> *If another person is more talented, smarter, or successful, the narcissist experiences envy.*

December 23, 2001

I tripped on my dress trying to get away from the Grinch and fell flat on my boobs. The crew said I bounced. I could see them offstage pointing and laughing at me. There's no way to crawl into the pod because I can't get my knees up. All I could do was flounder, flop, and finally, just roll off stage as the Grinch pointed and laughed.

January 5, 2002, Closing Night

I watched Mama Who during the scene when she kisses all the Who children and sings a gorgeous lullaby. She was really emotional because this is the last time she'll be Mama Who. I teared up backstage. Between Dianne's gorgeous voice, the lighting, and the costumes, it IS sheer magic. SO thankful to be here. This has been a Christmas to remember.

We earned a standing ovation. Diane and I squeezed each other's hands through it all as we swayed and cried in front of 600 people. To be part of a large cast in a beloved show is the only Christmas gift I need. The mirth we created in that theatre buoys my heart above all the pain I usually feel at this time of year.

Matthew Howe our director came to the dressing room and cried with us. We did 78 shows in two months. Oh, the satisfaction! The camaraderie and family that evolved changed my negative core beliefs.

The kids are devastated that we are closing, and so am I. Weepy, we all wandered around cherishing our last night together. For six months, I was part of the CTC family—a wonderfully fulfilling, joyful experience I couldn't forget if I tried. I am better for having been there.

IN SEARCH OF HOME

"Sometimes the only realists are the dreamers."
—Paul Wellstone

All I wanted was to find a home for myself where I could be me. When I returned from Los Angeles, I told a musician turned realtor that I wanted to buy a condo and pay nothing. A week later he called me, incredulous that he'd found a "condo" for a song. It was near the Children's Theater Company where I worked, and the price was right, so I bought it and transformed it with paint, pillows, and antiques à la shabby chic. I did all the work myself and three years later, sold it for double what I paid for it. By then, I'd found a bungalow with the help of a coworker from the Dayton's Photo Studio. It was on the edge of a dicey neighborhood but had great potential. I was beside myself with the anticipation of owning my own home on an artist's salary.

October 25, 2002
Today was the closing on my bungalow. I had an anxiety attack in the car before walking in. An hour into the process, the receptionist came in with some horrible news. Senator Paul Wellstone, his wife Sheila, and daughter Marcia went down in a plane crash in northern Minnesota this morning. They're all dead. None of us could even speak. This is a horrible loss. It was impossible for me to concentrate on signing all the paperwork.

The Wellstones were on their way to a funeral. If only they'd stayed in town for the rally and fundraiser. He was an extraordinary man and not a typical politician. Paul accepted everyone. I'll never forget singing at his birthday party with a group of liberals. All walks of life attended. Two transvestites stood next to me, big men who had squeezed their large masculine feet into women's sandals. Paul Wellstone brought people to tears with his enthusiasm and compassion.

August 2003, Loring Theater, Minneapolis, Minnesota

I've been in rehearsals for *Falsettos*, a musical directed by Jef Hall-Flavin for Outward Spiral. Getting the role of Trina is huge. The first time we read through the script and worked on music, Joe Leary, who plays Whizzer Brown, said, "I'm going to earn all three letters of my BFA doing this show."

This is the fourth show I've done in this theater and there is an energy here. So, I looked into the history of it. The Loring Theatre opened December 4, 1920, as a silent film theater and vaudeville house. Because of the expansion of the streetcar line, the Loring Theater had great success throughout the 1920s playing silent movies and seated 1,116.

The auditorium ceiling was topped with a huge dome, and it had the most up-to-date projection equipment, "refrigerated air," a pipe organ, and a house orchestra.

Television caused its downfall. It rapidly fell into decline in the 1950s and closed in 1958. Then it reopened as a church—the Minneapolis Evangelistic Auditorium, for over two decades. In the 1980s, the Loring Theatre became a legitimate playhouse and transformed into the Music Box Theatre. It was made to resemble a Victorian era music hall inside. In January 2010, it was again re-named the Loring Theatre.

No surprise then that it is haunted! The ghost, believed to be a man, walks up the ramp and into the sound booth. Tom Bothoff, a sound man who has worked in this space a lot, has seen the ghost. Stage lights that aren't hooked up often flash on and off. And when we have gatherings after a show near our bar, there's an energy present.

Our stage manager has seen the Guthrie Theater ghost numerous times. The ghost used to be an usher at the Guthrie and likes to sit at the top right of the giant frame during *A Christmas Carol*. She said he sits in his uniform, watching the show from above, perched on the tippy-top of the frame.

It reminded me of the story I heard in Chicago about a summer stock theater doing a production of *Quilters*. One particular audience member loved the show so much she came every night and always

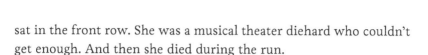

sat in the front row. She was a musical theater diehard who couldn't get enough. And then she died during the run.

There's a part in the show where all the women make a circle and join hands. Then, they run, turning together as a circle around and around. At the last show, the ghost of this woman joined the cast onstage and every cast member saw her spinning with them.

August 2003

Mother said she has a dog show and a doctor's appointment the week my show opens. She wants to come during tech week—the worst time for her to visit. I explained that visiting during tech week is bad timing. It's a stressful, nerve-wracking week that leads up to opening night. No compromise. She is impossible.

I am quite sure she won't enjoy *Falsettos*, as it is quirky and long. William Finn and James Lapine wrote the book and Finn wrote music and lyrics. It's a combination of *March of the Falsettos* (1981) and *Falsettoland* (1990). The story is about a modern family. My character Trina loses her husband Marvin, who is gay, to another man. We have a son who's about to have his bar mitzvah. Our psychiatrist is a big part of our lives, as are the lesbians next door. This show is **not** for my mother.

She said she wanted to go to rehearsal with me, but I should've known the wiser. I hated to hurry her, but I had to because the stage manager asked us to **please** be on time and I'm often late.

"Mom, can you hurry a little? I can't be late, AGAIN," I said. "I make other people wait when I show up late. Its rude and unprofessional, and I can't afford a bad reputation for being late."

"All right, all right," she snapped at me.

We arrived at the theater five minutes late, and I apologized to the stage manager who said, "It's okay. You weren't the only one."

My mom says, "Seeee?" I wanted to strangle her.

Our director Jef Hall-Flavin said, "They need this room tonight, so we will have to rehearse downstairs in the basement and the acoustics aren't as good." Joe Leary kills me with his hilarious comments.

"Oh, great. It's closer to hell."

And it was. We had a really rough rehearsal, and my mother was there for it. WHY couldn't she come to the real show and not a rehearsal during tech week? This will be her version of "seeing the show." So, she sat on a folding chair, clutching her leather purse to her chest, watching our disjointed, stressful rehearsal. Joe, with his flushed cherubic cheeks and blonde curls, looks like a Hummel.

He leaned over to me and whispered, "Is it THAT bad? Look at your mother's face!" Then, he picked me up like a child and swung me around. And then, Phil Callen (Marvin) picked me up and swung me around. God, I love those two.

Anyway, after we had worked for two hours, my mother interrupted the rehearsal when Jef made suggestions to myself and Phil. My mother motioned me over with her trigger finger. Jef was good natured about it and called, "Ten minutes."

My mother was testy. "How much longer is this going to take? I have to eat! This show, how long IS it??"

"This is just the first act," I said.

Her head rolled. "Oh Holly, that is too long. Waaay toooo long. Listen, I have to EAT, on a regular schedule. And I can't walk very far, remember, so we have to park close. When can we eat and how close is it?"

"Mom, I told you this would be a couple of hours. As soon as it's done, we'll go. I told you the time of the rehearsal and you agreed to it. As soon as this is over, I will personally drive you to Palomino, where I'll bust through the plate glass window on Hennepin Ave., drive you up the escalator, and park you on top of the hostess desk. "

"And it's close?" she said, missing the joke.

The second rehearsal was over, we made a beeline for Palomino. Bread and their crack cocaine butter blend soothed my mother.

She said, "Well, those boys seem to like you." This is a surprise?

During her visit, I had a small gathering of people at my house, including handsome actor/singer David Anderson.

On my back porch, David said, "Well, Mae, what do you think about Holly's show *Falsettos*?"

Mother rolled her eyes and said, "Don't ask."

September 2003

I think our ghost joined our opening night of *Falsettos* during that chaotic, over-choreographed overture. Right before I was to enter pushing a vacuum cleaner, I hear Barbra Streisand singing "Putting It Together" from the Broadway album. My eyes darted around, looking for Joe and Phil. Did they hear Barbra too? No one can figure out how it happened because the DVD player was not plugged in.

Falsettos is the hardest show I've ever done. I'll never forget the night Joe came up to me, trying hard not to laugh.

"Where are we in the show?" he asked.

"We're not even halfway through the first act," I said. But the hard work paid off with great reviews:

> *"But the most striking performance, both from a musical and theatrical perspective, comes from Holly Schroeder, an actress I've not seen before. Playing Trina, she has a versatile singing voice that's at home in a range from brassy to ballad and lots of different and interesting places in between. She sparkles in many moments as a comic actress as well, delivering a sweet-and-sour performance that's a terrific calling card."*
> —Dominic P. Papatola, Theater Critic of St. Paul *Pioneer Press*

> *The cast is uniformly strong, although Holly Schroeder stands out as the jilted wife. Schroeder's comic brio, her facial expressions and gestures stop the show in several of her solo numbers, particularly the manic "I'm Breaking Down."*
> —Graydon Royce, *Star Tribune* Staff Writer

> *The comically-gifted and big-voiced Schroeder particularly excels in the nearly-show-stopping "I'm Breaking Down."*
> –Dylan Hicks of *City Pages*

Great theater requires a tremendous amount of commitment, talent, and direction. Our cast learned so much with Jef Hall-Flavin's brilliant direction. In Jef's words:

"Ten years after its Broadway run, and more than a generation after the events in the play take place at the dawn of the AIDS epidemic, Falsettos was still breaking ground, redefining what makes a family. I've always loved the twists and turns of Bill Finn's quirky lyrics and unexpected five-part harmonies. His words and music need each other, and they burrow their way into your heart.

I was particularly proud that our "teeny tiny band" of actors, musicians, and production staff created a completely microphone-free musical... something that's increasingly difficult to pull off. To me the humanity of this piece—the joy, the love, the loss—was felt more acutely as an acoustic event. Critics agreed."

Left to right: Carl Schoenborn, Jared I. Smith, Holly Schroeder, Philip Callen, Joe Leary, Gillian Martin, Tina Miller

Photos by Michal Daniel

June 25, 2004, Plainview, Minnesota

I'm back staying at the farmhouse in Plainview, Minnesota, where I lived two years ago while doing *Honk* at the Jon Hassler Theater. This time, we'll be staging *And the World Goes Round*. Nicole Stefanek and I get to be in cahoots again. Marshall our pianist says, "It's the second coming."

Director Peter Rothstein is on the porch reading *The Bohemians*, Nicole is in the living room knitting Marshall, our music director, a scarf for Gay Pride, and I'm on the front porch reading this quote from *Backstage Broadway* "Behind the Curtain."

> *Whenever I do live theater, I am ever so grateful to hear that laughter and that "thunderclap." There can be no aphrodisiac in the world as wonderful. "The smell" and "the roar" are everything they're cracked up to be.*
> *–Carol Burnett*

Tomorrow, Nicole and I are going on a vision quest in Rochester. Heaven is here. I was looking at the rich, umber-colored yolk of the farm fresh eggs we cooked for breakfast and said to Peter,

"Aren't these eggs beautiful?"

To which Peter said, "Isn't God something?"

July 2004

Kander and Ebb material is my cup of tea. It has the edge and message that says life has kicked the shit out of me but I'm going to keep going.

Peter Rothstein has amazing attention to detail. We rehearsed at night in Minneapolis, and by day, I wrote theme proposals for Design Group, the event planning company. It's like when I wrote catalogs for Montgomery Ward Direct during the day (taking a nap during lunch hour in a church parking lot), rehearsing *Vixens* at night.

Clark Cruikshank is the artistic director at the Hassler Theater. I've known him for years.

"I suspect sometime in the future they will isolate the actor gene," he said. "It'll be some gnarled, nasty-looking thing."

Left to right Nicolle Stefonek, Bill Scharpen, Jody Briskey, Joe LaForte, Holly Schroeder

March 3, 2006

Paige Claire, my wildly creative, talented, beautiful friend is dead. At this point, she's a pile of ashes. I cannot believe it. Her sister Penny tracked me down through my agent. After a long battle with alcohol and depression, Paige fell down the basement stairs and the doctors couldn't stop the bleeding. After three blood transfusions, she bled to death. I am sick over it. What a surreal feeling. What's odd is that I've been thinking about her for months. Out of the blue, she popped into my head, so I tried to find her online. A week later, I came home to a message on my answering machine from her. I couldn't believe it. We're still linked psychically after seven years of not speaking. The last time we spoke, I finally told her that her anti-depressants won't work if she keeps drinking. She didn't want to hear it and was furious with me.

Paige said in her message that she thought about me a lot and saw some of my TV commercials. She said she was proud of me, but the tone of her voice was low energy. She didn't leave her phone number and mumbled a web address which I tried repeatedly with no luck. My cordless phone battery was dead, which rarely happens, so it didn't register her phone number, so I couldn't call her back! I let out a scream of frustration. It was as if she was saying goodbye, not leaving me any options for contacting her.

Paige and I were so close at one time, but distance, jobs, and addictions got in our way. Her sister Penny says Paige was bi-polar. The family had an intervention to get her to stop drinking. She was getting different prescriptions filled by different doctors. She tried covering up her skin with self-tanner when she was jaundiced. I saw the last photos taken of her and it wasn't the Paige I knew. Her sister Penny put together a wonderful memorial video with photos and songs.

I reminisced about the time she flew me out to Whidby Island to see her after I moved to Los Angeles. We had a ball with Vivienne Pea Face the Weiner Dog. We ambled around Seattle in her RV, which had belonged to her Dad, cooked some great meals, went out for drinks, and laughed a lot. Now I'll be returning to Whidby Island for her memorial to sing, "Somewhere Over the Rainbow," as we throw Paige's ashes into the sound. This is tragic.

I wish I could've saved Paige. I knew she was a tortured soul. Just think, she's with Danny now and free of emotional and physical torment.

For Paige. . .

The day we met, you recognized me, as kindred spirits do.
You were a woman. I was a girl. And I wanted to be you.

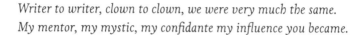

Writer to writer, clown to clown, we were very much the same.
My mentor, my mystic, my confidante my influence you became.

You always gave more than you took. This truly was "your way."
What I'd give to thank you now. What I'd give for one more day.

I'd tell you how much you live in me. And how the caged bird sings.
And for all the gifts you gave the world, God's granted you your wings.

December 14, 2007

Its winter, and I'm having a hard time. I feel hopeless, fearful, unmotivated, uninspired, regretful, empty, sad, and afraid of the future. I know I have a lot to be thankful for and I've been this low before, but if don't find a way to pull myself out of these slumps and thoughts that torment me, I'm going to do myself in. I would do anything to be free of my negativity and depression. Anything.

TO BE OR NOT TO BE

Most people have no idea of the reality of being an actor. Truth is, only 2% of working actors make enough to earn a living. 90% of actors are unemployed at any one time, and 70% of actors have a career that lasts for just one year. How many industries have those statistics? You must have moxy and be a little crazy to endure.

A big part of working in show business is *not* working and some actors make a career out of collecting unemployment. No matter how wonderful a production is, at some point it will close and then it's back to square one—finding another job. When a show or film closes, it's like a death. Many performers are plagued with self-doubt when they don't get a role they're right for. I fall into that category. My life was a roller coaster ride for a long time.

It was never easy, or boring. What I learned eventually is that no matter how dire things became, just in the nick of time, a project with a madcap troupe of show folk with pluck, would come through. I learned to trust the universe, but it took a long time.

February 5, 2007

I've been cast in a very popular show called *Menopause the Musical*. I will play the fading Soap Star. Now that I'm older, it is time to play women in decline.

The characters don't have names. We're stereotypes. Perky Laurie Flanigan-Hegge is the Iowa Housewife, and Brooke Davis is the Earth Mother. The Power Woman is played by Cynthia Jones-Taylor from Seattle. It's an Equity contract, so I'm going union. There's far more non-union work in Minneapolis so I hope I don't regret this.

Our choreographer is a Latina spitfire named Daria. She. Is. Fierce. The specifics of our hands, feet, and hips are maddening at times. It's all about the details, and we are in constant movement.

April 15, 2007

While this show is a sell out in other cities, advance tickets sales for the summer aren't looking good. We are all gainfully employed for five months, but now, because of low ticket sales, the producers are postponing the show until fall. What they didn't realize is that Minnesotans endure such hard winters that when summer comes, they want to be at their cabins and on a lake.

Autumn 2007

Someday, I'm going to write a show that happens entirely in the dressing room. I've always loved the banter that organically occurs as women doll-up. "Although they don't speak of it at school, we must labor to be beautiful."

As we put on our faces and do our hair, we discuss men, careers, family, health, and other shows. Now that I'm doing a show about menopause, with some of us actually **in** menopause, the conversation is illuminating. Monica Heuser is now our Earth Mother, and Cynthia Jones-Taylor from Seattle is playing the Power Woman. She has educated us fully about the horrors of menopause.

At the beginning of the show, we line up before our entrance stage left. Cynthia says the show is a train ride and once you board, it's a 90-minute ride with no stops, in high heels. And it is.

Left to right Cynthia Jones-Taylor, me, Laurie Flanigan-Hegge, Monica Heuser

January 2008

People I know whose spirits are low, are all in the same sinking boat.
We've jumped through hoops, joined networking groups,
Our economy has come to blows.

Wrote this little ditty to distract myself from impending reality, which has me wigged out. If what I did in the past as an artist was struggle, what I'm doing now is *flailing*. Would someone throw me a lifejacket? A line? How about a floating door?

With the unemployed masses scrambling, it's hard to be "positive" but that's exactly what you have to be in order to interview and land a job. Before pursuing the most menial job (many of which used to be done only by teenagers) I have to talk myself "up." Days become weeks become months, and all the while, the bills are lining up like ants at a picnic.

Being unemployed for months is debilitating to ALL of my reserves. Recently, I collapsed in a heap on my bed and sobbed for five hours. I really thought it was a psychotic break and that I'd end up in an asylum like Zelda Fitzgerald.

I'm sick of myself. I spend hours every day evaluating my skills, revising my resume and website, and networking. Who do I know who knows someone to get me through the door to the inside track? I hate to sound like a downer, but it is *who* you know that matters most. It's a good thing I'm an extrovert.

May 3, 2008
It's Mia's 18th birthday. He is now almost deaf. If I stomp on the floor or wave my hands, he senses that. If I startle him, he yells at me. It breaks my heart. My little man can no longer hear me sing. I remember how he used to run into the living room when we lived by Wrigley Field and jump onto the couch, eager to be my audience. Now, he wanders around in a world of silence and vibrations, watching my mouth closer than ever before.

> I called my mother and said,
> "Well, Mia's ready for college now. He's thinking Harvard. What do YOU think?"
> "Oh, Holly, don't be silly," Mom said. "Mia can't go to Harvard. He should go to Purdue, like you did."

June 10, 2008
I've decided to stop doing other people's monologues for auditions, so I'm writing my own about two things I know a lot about—boobs and shoes.

Boobs

If you have a "C" cup or higher, a bra is a vital foundation garment because a nice pair of knockers comes with responsibility. All that jiggling, bouncing, and swaying can cause traffic accidents. Bigger boobs are not necessarily more desirable. I would never want to be a DD—that's a full house. Breasts that big make most men nervous. I would never pay money for a big set of knockers because I don't want to attract the wrong kind of man. I'm fine with what I've got. Mine can fill a champagne glass, and I can jog without chafing.

One of the downfalls of real boobs is that they don't stand at attention when you lie down. For example, when I lie on my back, they fall into my armpits. So, I have to wear one that cinches me in, jacks me up, and gives me leverage.

There is an arsenal of bras on the market—the Wonderbra, bandeau, built-in, bullet, bustier, contour, convertible, demi cup, front-closure, full-support, hard cup, soft cup, jogging, leisure, long-line, nursing, strapless, racerback, underwire, water, shelf, push up, padded. and plunge.

My favorite bra of all time was the Maidenform Chantilly. I wore the Maidenform Chantilly for 20 years and it was the most exciting 20 years of my life.

Shoes

A man does not complete me. Shoes complete me. They're the most important part of my ensembles. An exquisite pair of shoes can transform anyone. If I slip into a pair of shoes that don't fit the style or mood of dress I'm wearing, I feel common and incomplete. It's like wearing gym shoes with an evening gown. You just don't DO it. Everyone will question your credibility as a well-dressed woman.

If you're a clothes horse, you need a lot of shoes. I can tell you that there's nothing like a sexy sandal to make me feel more feminine or a pair of platforms to give me confidence. There are a few practical pairs of shoes in my closet, but I'm partial to shoes with an attitude. How can I strut my stuff in a pair of Birkenstocks? I can't.

In the same way a pair of shoes can make you, they can also break you. A pair of stilettos that impair your walk (with or without alcohol), can put a damper on your mood and the evening. It's hard to be glamorous when your feet are on fire. And if my feet are in agony, I'm miserable. That's why I prefer Italian made shoes—architecturally superior apparel for feet that go the distance.

You can tell a lot about a man by the shoes he wears. Forget what's in his pants. It's his shoes that matter. Shoes speak volumes. And what they're saying is that life is too short to wear cheap shoes.

September 6, 2008

New project on the horizon! I'm rehearsing *Legendary Ladies*. Perrin Post has created this show for specific performers that want to honor the grand dames of Broadway—Mary Martin, Ethel Merman, Julie Andrews, Angela Lansbury, Carol Channing, Bernadette Peters, Patti LaPone, Barbra Streisand, Elaine Stritch, Liza Minnelli, Chita Rivera, Audra McDonald, Heather Headley, and Barbara Cook.

We will honor the icons who inspire us. What I love is that we're not just performing the material. We're integral to the whole process, writing the intros and involved with costumes and choreography. It is fate that I do this show, since Barbra Streisand is the reason I became a performer in the first place. Every time my mother asks, "WHY did you pursue something so unstable?" I answer, "It's Barbra's fault. Take it up with her."

Left to right: Kerston Rodau, Jody Briskey, Kathleen Bloom, Michelle Carter, Holly Schroeder, Ann Michels.

Diamonds are a girl's best friend. Left to right Zoe Pappas-Cipriano, Kathleen Bloom, Stacey Lindell-Bannick, Jen Burleigh-Bentz, Holly Schroeder

October 5, 2008

Because we're a cast of dynamic, beautiful women, people love to think all of us women are fighting like cats. That happens all the time in the corporate world, which is why I hate working in an office. Women are supposed to support each other, not tear each other down. On occasions like this, when I have the honor of working with strong, gifted, gorgeous women who don't punish me for having talent and beauty, I am the best I can be. This show meant the world to me. Every night I got goose bumps bringing to life the gems of musical theater with other strong, gifted women. My favorite part is the Elaine Stritch segment. She and I are kindred spirits, so I'm leading that part of the show.

My lead in to "Travel" by Noel Coward:

Elaine Stritch is known for her unique delivery and biting wit. She's also been known to throw back a few. In her recent one-woman show, At Liberty, Elaine admitted that for 58 years she never set foot on a stage without a drink. "It's scary up here, okay," she said. "I need a friend out here with me." Through the years, she's had a variety of friends; for Angel in the Wings, it was Canadian Club, On Your Toes—Dewars, Sail Away by Noel Coward . . . well . . . Dom Pérignon! Bus Stop? Schlitz! Goldilocks . . . anything she could get her hands on.

Left to right: Michelle Carter, Jody Briskey, Jen Burleigh-Bentz, Holly Schroeder, Ann Michels, Kathleen Bloom

"Don't Rain on My Parade" Left to right: Kathleen Bloom, Jody Briskey, Holly Schroeder, Jen Burleigh-Bentz, Stacey Lindell-Bannick, Zoe Pappas-Cipriano.

Legendary Ladies photos taken by Craig Martin Stellmacher

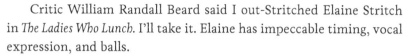

Critic William Randall Beard said I out-Stritched Elaine Stritch in *The Ladies Who Lunch*. I'll take it. Elaine has impeccable timing, vocal expression, and balls.

"Many songs were overly truncated to keep the show to a reasonable performing length. I would rather have had fewer songs, sung completely. What I wouldn't give to hear Holly Schroeder sing all the bitchy verses of Noel Coward's "Why Do the Wrong People Travel?" from Sail Away. *Schroeder, an expert belter, demonstrated that she also knows her way around a ballad with a touching "Quiet Thing" from Liza Minnelli's breakthrough,* Flora, the Red Menace.

October 18, 2008
My mother came to Minnesota with Phyllis to see *Legendary Ladies*. I knew she would love the show. Afterwards, she and Phyllis came backstage.

"That was a wonderful show!" Mother said. "Every one of you was great. I don't know who I liked best?! Oh . . . you, I guess!"

I burst out laughing. It's okay. I know who I am.

October 26, 2008
The show closed today. We got a standing ovation after the first act and at curtain call. Everything was ON. I really love group numbers. It's so empowering. Singing the harmonies in "Sunday" was like a religious experience every night. "Don't Rain on My Parade" was especially meaningful for me. I've decided the next time someone attempts to squash me and my enthusiasm, I'm going to burst into that song complete with choreography.

We had a wonderful party at Perrin's house. Patrick, our accordion player, is wise beyond his 23 years. I will miss every single person involved in this show, the music, and that connection with the audience.

February 16, 2009
I've been doing voiceovers at Marketing Architects. Most of them are "testimonials." If I could just do voiceovers all the time. I love being in the booth with headphones on. It demands so much less. Nothing is harder than being "a triple threat"—a singer, dancer, **and** actress.

Spring 2009

When I look back at the giant collage of people, places, and projects that were my life, Mia my cat is in the center of it all, sitting perfectly still, my rock of Gibraltar. I was 24 when my mother gave him to me. Mia saw me through the tragic drowning of my brother, my father, who died of a heart attack, the breakup of an engagement, nine moves (two cross country), near bankruptcy, two robberies, theater openings and closings, countless freelance projects, and God knows how many hangovers. He's been my constant.

November 2009

My dear friend John Halstrom came over to photograph Mia as it was our last day. It is hard for me to even write the words . . . my little man Mia has passed. He would've been 20 in May had he not died in November, on a Friday. I am grateful the moment was exactly how I'd always envisioned. He was safe in my arms, looking calmly into my eyes, and we both knew. I was wearing a brave face but shaking.

"I love you like crazy, Mia," I whispered as the tears fell. And poof! The light in his eyes went out. Inconceivable. I have never loved a cat like this. In fact, I don't think I've ever loved a human being the way I love Mia.

I SLEEP WITH ALL MY CLIENTS

Theater saved my life and was my drug of choice. My kooky, expressive self was rewarded in that world. No wonder I refused to accept that even with wonderful reviews, it couldn't sustain me financially.

To tell stories on stage and on the page, I became a survivor and suffered and shone for my art, negotiating with gatekeepers, nepotism, rivalry, jealousy, and inevitable periods of unemployment. It was a constant hustle. There are so many elements that factor into whether an actor gets cast, so it isn't wise to take it personally, but it does seep into the subconscious. I missed out on roles because I wasn't married to the artistic director, related to the producer, young enough, old enough, too pretty, not pretty enough, too short, too skinny, and had the wrong hair color. Year after year, a true improviser, I flew by the seat of my pants. And like my mother, those pants were in style.

To pay my bills, I did commercials, training films, print work, and voiceovers in a predominantly non-union market. I worked as an actress, writer, and coordinator in the events industry for corporate parties. I wrote feature stories and profiles for magazines when I could and worked for Aquent and the Creative Group as a writer and proofreader. I helped my neighbor with her cleaning business. I hustled.

And then I reached my 40's and everything changed. I felt frustrated with another failed relationship, the harsh winters, and the lack of work in the Twin Cities. I had moved to Minneapolis for a man, and when that went south, I stayed because of the arts scene. I'm so glad I did. Because the acting industry was changing and many performers were struggling, *The Minneapolis Star Tribune* did a story on me for the arts section titled "Exit, Stage Left."

It was a hard decision, but my mother's health was failing, and I'd be closer to her. I rented out my Minneapolis bungalow and moved back to Chicago. My song and dance pal Gypsy Vegan Cindy Benson was in Chicago performing in *Billy Elliott*, and we decided to room together.

I'm pretty sure Cindy was Chinese in another life. After she does laundry, she hangs it all up in her bedroom doorway and then ducks back and forth in and out of her bedroom, like a little Chinese woman in a laundromat. In the morning, I wake to the sound of her quickly chopping and dicing vegetables. Thanks to Cindy, I have a whole new appreciation for bok choy, Japanese eggplant, parsley, papaya, and watermelon. Sometimes she makes date shakes, which are such a treat. This is the second time we've lived together. She lived in my attic in my Minneapolis a few years ago when she was in town playing Madame Thenardier *Les Misérables*.

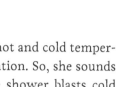

When Cindy takes a shower, she alternates hot and cold temperatures three times each, to increase blood circulation. So, she sounds like she's having sex in the shower. When the shower blasts cold she says, "Oh, oh, oh, oh my God, that's cold." When she's blasting the hot water it's, "Ahh, ahh, ahh, hmmm, oh, that's good." I like to just stand at the door and listen because Cindy Benson is even entertaining in the shower. I call Perrin Post and let her listen in too. Maybe I should request songs from *Cats*, since she was Grizabella on Broadway for years.

Lincoln Square, Chicago Illinois, The Holly Hotel Bed & Barkfest July 15, 2010

I'm ready to reinvent myself and explore something different. I'm still auditioning for commercials, but they don't fulfill me like they once did. Animal care is booming in Chicago, and since dogs have always been my salvation, I've opened a hotel for dogs. In my apartment.

I'm now an official "Pack Leader" for dogvacay.com. My pal, KTLA camera man and editor Michael Joseph James did a piece on the owners of dogvacay.com in Los Angeles and connected us, so I'm getting into the game early.

I came up with the tagline: "I sleep with all my clients" and discovered that starting The Holly Hotel Bed & Barkfest has many rewards. Instead of applause I get unconditional love and wagging tails. It thrills me to no end to make them happy and comfortable. I thought for sure my mother a.k.a. Dog Lover Extraordinaire, would approve of this new venture, but no.

"You're going to board dogs? You're wasting your college education."

"I'm not doing this forever, Mom. Just temporarily."

These dogs have taught me how to just "be." They live in the moment, roll around on the floor, have treats, take naps, take walks, and meet other dogs. I now have several regulars, and Bailey is my favorite. His mother Athena travels a lot for work. No matter the weather, Bailey and I trod the toddling town. We tool around Lincoln Square, Andersonville, and Wrigleyville to run errands together, which includes going to Pet Smart for treats, toys, and conversation with the parakeets. And Bailey likes to wear hats too.

Rosehill Cemetery, our favorite haunt, allows us to walk with no traffic, sit by a lake where turtles sun themselves, and read gravestones. Bailey and I go everywhere together. He even went to the dentist with me and rested calmly on my lap for two hours through another root canal.

When I go to the Jewel supermarket, Bailey goes with, inside a bag I wear over my shoulder. At the deli counter I ask to sample cold cuts. I take a bite and slip him the rest. He knows not to pop his head out until we are at the checkout, when I pull out my credit card. Then he pokes his head out to say hello and delight the cashier. His adorable face brightens everyone's day.

Yesterday, about 3 p.m., he had to do his business and chase a biker. We descended the stairs and got a blast to the face as we went outside into the oven, the air was buzzing with the whir of busy, sweaty air conditioners. It was a scorching 100 degrees in the shade. A block later, I ran into Daisy, my mail lady, who was pulling her cart and delivering mail.

"Holly dog lady?" she says. Like me, she is damp.

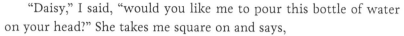

"Daisy," I said, "would you like me to pour this bottle of water on your head?" She takes me square on and says,

"Girl, I LOVE the heat. Hell, the summer's half over. Pretty soon we'll be shakin' in our shoes, it's so cold."

"You're right," I said. "I don't know what I was thinking."

Then I said, "Oh, Daisy, do you know the Asian woman at the post office? 'Cause she's snippy. I waited in line for 15 minutes to pick up a package. But people were admiring Bailey, astonished at how well behaved he is, perched in my arm like a parrot. That pinched faced Chinese woman was nasty to us."

"Do you have a license for that dog?" I looked at her and said, "Yes, he's a special needs dog. And I have special needs."

"Where is your license?" she asked, giving me the fisheye.

"I'm not leaving him in a 110-degree car," I said. "That's animal abuse." She tried to give me more guff. I wanted to say, "Of course you're not adverse to cooking him in a car. You people make dinner out of dogs." But I didn't say that. Instead, I slid her the claim ticket and said,

"I'm just here for a package. Mr. Bailey and I will leave as soon as you put it in my paw."

Daisy says, "Oh, that Chinese lady. She likes me. She's nice to me. You know why? Because I'm a mi-nor-i-ty!"

December 10, 2010

Today is Dad's birthday. He'd appreciate my dog whispering but he'd probably say I need to join the Republican party and go to church. But this is therapy for me. With dogs, there is no ego involved. If you make them feel safe and loved, they express their gratitude with boundless affection. Yes, they poop on the floor and sometimes you step in it, but dogs are driven by a desire to please and love. We are comrades.

Debbie Bickford, my pal from my improv days, is now a successful dog trainer with her own business. She's referred a couple from Poland to me, Christopher and Hannah, who have two Yorkies. The Twins, Coco and Charlie, were born in Poland too. The dogs wear matching snow jackets, harnesses, and sweaters. This is the first time I've worked with bilingual dogs, so I'm learning some Polish.

When I pick up Coco and Charlie from Lake Point Towers, Hannah enthusiastically tells them,

"It's your Aunty Holly!" Dad hands me their supplies and a $100 dollar bill as a down payment. He is all business—until he talks to Coco and Charlie. Then, he becomes a different man entirely, which tickles me.

Spring 2011

I've been getting a lot of new clients. Met a wonderful couple at an art fair in Oak Park, where I sold my reinvented cigar boxes. They make and sell a line of delicious chocolate and caramel sauces and have two labradoodles named Fionn and Maybelline. Littermates, these dogs make the shape of a heart with their bodies when they sleep. Fionn is so big, it's like having a sheep in your apartment.

March 22, 2011

I'm heading to Palm Springs to do *Menopause the Musical* for ten weeks! Several of my clients aren't happy about me being gone ten weeks. One of my wealthy Eastern European clients said, "But, who is going to take care of Cookie?"

I am looking forward to working with Monica Heuser again. We've got four days to pull the show together.

I got to the airport with all my luggage for this ten-week contract. My phone rings. They're changing the length of the contract from ten weeks to six. Not good. Now, I won't get Actor's Equity health insurance off this gig, and I must find a place to live for a few weeks when the contract ends because I sublet my apartment. Five minutes later, I get a phone call from *Finance and Commerce*, the publication in Minneapolis for whom I write a real estate column. They require a local person to write it and I've left. Three steps forward, two steps back. Story of my life.

Summer 2011

It's raining outside and I just washed my windows. Rain patters outside my window as a puggle named Murphy with a prominent underbite shares my chair. When I walked in the room, he was drinking my coffee.

I have a new client, a Boston Terrier named Domino and mischief is his middle name. He's jet propelled and quite a personality. Domino loves to steal shoes, gloves, and hats and run with them. When we take walks, he finds a huge stick, sometimes ten feet long and carries it home. He figures out where to pick it up so he can balance it in his teeth. No wonder his bottom teeth are crooked. One day, he carried a ten-foot branch five blocks, strutting through the crosswalk. A few cars honked because he is such a bad ass with his giant stick.

Dogs respond to visual cues, so my expressive face comes in handy. Moments and looks and songs and codes. Domino is also wildly expressive and so full of piss and vinegar it takes two families to care for him. When friends of Roc, his owner, are at their wits end, I pick Domino up and bring him to my apartment, where he steals my slippers and dish towels and shoots down the hallway like he's been shot out of a cannon. His shenanigans fill me with joy. He's a comedien. One morning, I woke up to him grumbling "Rar, rar, rar, rar," as he pushed what appeared to be a slobbery green plastic penis in my face.

"Just what I want to see the first thing in the morning," I said, pushing it away with a finger. He did it again, and I flung it across the room. He retrieved it, chewed on it, and smiled at me with his crooked teeth.

"I'm taking you to the orthodontist," I said. He grabbed my slipper and shot down the hallway.

October 30, 2012

Mother has had quite a few challenging surgeries. During a routine checkup it was discovered she needed a quadruple bypass. The first thing she did was go to McDonalds for a Big Mac.

Watching my mother get old is torture. She was scared before the procedure, of course, and I don't blame her, but she gets a little rude in the hospital. After she survived a brutal surgery, she fell down on the cement while feeding the possums on the front porch and broke her wrist. That was horrible too. Very hard. And because of the diabetes, she has to have an artificial vein put into her leg, from her groin to her ankle.

Dr. Newman did the surgery, which started two hours late. It was touch and go for a while.

Afterwards, Donna Burris said, "Mae, Dr. Newman saved your leg. The surgery was successful!" My mom's response was typical.

"Well, she could've started it on time!" Classic.

Alzheimer's Memory Care Facility, November 1, 2013

I need to make more money to pay for my high rent, so I'm singing parttime for Alzheimer's and dementia patients all over Illinois. I'll be singing oldies and standards slower than normal so patients can sing along. I use my big noise to trigger their memories. What music can do for human beings is powerful.

My Aunt Penny, a kooky redhead who had fabulous taste and a great sense of humor, died of Alzheimer's, and her husband, Uncle Al, died taking care of her. She didn't even know he had passed. Then Penny was put in a nursing home and lived another 10 years. She never recognized my mother or any relatives again.

Today was my first "performance," with three other administrator types. We sang 40 minutes of songs like "Five Foot Two," "Bill Bailey Won't You Come Home," and "California Here I Come" to 30 patients. One woman did the sign of the cross, continually mumbling, "I want to go home." When I gave her a small maraca to shake during the music, she smiled and said, "Go to hell."

One agitated woman took her top off and she wasn't wearing anything under it. The aides struggled to get her sweatshirt back on her. A minute later, she took it off again. Inappropriate behavior runs rampant in these dementia and Alzheimer units. Everyone looks at everyone else and shrugs. During the patriotic numbers, I handed a small American flag to one man, who said, "Get the hell out of here!" and violently threw it on the floor. Then, he grabbed the flag from the woman sitting next to him and threw hers on the floor too.

Mary was the friendliest face in the crowd.

"Honey, what school are you from?" she asked.

"Oh, Mary, I've graduated already. I'm 47," I said.

"Reaallly? You look like a young giiirrrrl!" Then she asked me what school I went to, and I told her Purdue University.

"Well, thank them at Purdue University for sending you here! You are so kind to have come." And then she cried.

Another old woman kept slapping her knee, saying I was so funny and a real "dolly." Quite a few of the people never opened their eyes, which saddened me. I wish they'd let me tickle them.

November 15, 2013

Went to two homes yesterday to sing oldies. On my way to the bathroom, a short, pleasant looking woman walked up to me and said, "Fucker!" The guy behind the desk responded mechanically, "Eleanor, that's not nice. Please apologize." She sneered at me and lurched away.

While waiting for more people to arrive for the sing-along, I made my way around the room with my cheap American flags and basket of "instruments." The heavy-set, antagonistic, blonde woman in the 2nd row threw up her hands and said,

"Just get on with it, will you?"

I said, "I'm with you. Let's get this party started!"

The songs are purposely repetitive for a reason. She got so annoyed hearing the same verse from "Five Foot Two" six times that she thought out loud again.

"Okay, that's enough! Next song!"

"You're right!" I said. "I'm sick of it too. Next song!"

With Alzheimer's patients you don't argue, you just agree, which is like improvisation. Don't argue, just say "yes, and. . ." At the second facility, one gal slumped in her wheelchair and gave me the old stink eye.

"I'm going to make you smile before I leave here today," I told her. She didn't budge.

"Don't count on it," she said. Four songs later, I made her smile and give me a hug. And that's what makes doing this worthwhile. These people are aching for levity and music. I almost feel guilty doing this for money. But I need the money, so I'll take it.

Dec. 4, 2013

Sang to two groups yesterday, about 60 people. "Have Yourself a Very Merry Christmas" made me cry. One woman, too young to be in this home, watched me intently. And then her face contorted, and the tears flowed. Then I started crying.

There was a 99-year-old woman who had survived the Holocaust, and she beamed through the entire 40 minutes. She has a lot to be bitter about, yet she isn't. I hugged her three times. She kind of reminded me of my Aunty Ann.

One woman thought I was her daughter.

"Let's get the hell out of here," she said. "I'm tired." Then she said, "You know, I can't remember everything. There's just too much to remember. You'll have to get us out of here because I don't know the way back."

I can't get her sweet face out of my head. Her great sense of humor is still there. But what really killed me was what she said after we sang, "We Wish You a Merry Christmas."

She looked at me, bewildered and said, "Did I ever have a merry Christmas?" That will haunt me. Alzheimer's is a wicked disease. Is it worse than cancer? Losing your memory, history, and place in the world? I think it may be worse than cancer. I could lose my hair, but I couldn't lose my my history.

December 9, 2013

Today I sang to a man whose eyes reminded me of the veiled chameleon—those lizards with the fascinating eyes that look like telescopes. A handsome man, really, just with telescope eyes. I rubbed his back, squeezed his arm, and sang in his ear, but that did not rouse him. I wanted to reach him but couldn't. He was somewhere else entirely. When I squeezed his hand and put my head next to his, the bulgier eye of the two opened and looked at me. Then it clamped shut again. I don't blame him. Christmas carols and tambourines can only do so much.

The human condition sucks. This might not be a good job for an empath. I HATE that some of these people are so sad and lonely. Isn't there something more I can do? I will never put my mother in one of these places. Thank GOD I didn't have to do that to my father after all the relatives we cared for.

December 10, 2013

Bodily functions get in the way of music in a place like this. While singing "Aint We Got Fun," a scent wafted by that was a cross between an electrical fire and a perm. Ufta, it was bad.

Then, we were singing, *"Then one foggy Christmas Eve, Santa came to say..."* and someone shouted,

"I have to go to the bathroom!"

Hot Flash Reprise

When you've been away from show biz for a while, you realize just how devoted to maintaining the illusion you have to be to work consistently. Sustainability is a challenge. The older I get, the more work it is to be vibrant. When I wake up, I look like I'm dying of consumption. Yet onstage, I play characters that *appear* to have their shit together.

Left to right: Margot Moreland, Liz Hyde, Holly Schroeder and Emily David

So, I was happy for a break from jazz hands and high notes to hang out with dogs and be real. But when the phone rings with an acting job and health insurance, well, you know what they say—the show must go on.

Reno, Nevada 2013
April 16, 2013

I'm in rehearsals for *Menopause the Musical* again, at the Eldorado Showroom, part of the Eldorado Casino in Reno Nevada. Outside in the real world, terrorists have bombed the Boston Marathon, plants have exploded in Texas, and sinkholes have swallowed cars in Chicago.

In here, we're spending 20 minutes over: "The pinwheel needs to be two inches stage left!" and "You must have all your rhinestones on before the reveal!" and "during the blue out, face downstage before the elephant train!"

I'm struggling vocally due to bronchitis, and the prednisone I'm on jumbles my thoughts, bloats me, and makes me moody. In fact, I had a breakdown on stage at one point. These steroids make me crazy! Everyone is stressed about how little time we have to rehearse. Because Wydetta, the woman playing the Power Woman, hasn't

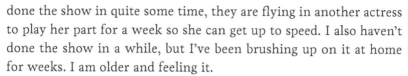

done the show in quite some time, they are flying in another actress to play her part for a week so she can get up to speed. I also haven't done the show in a while, but I've been brushing up on it at home for weeks. I am older and feeling it.

It never fails. The less rehearsal time scheduled, the greater the technical hurdles.

Opening Night—A.K.A. Flying by a Wing and a Prayer.

I've got to give myself credit. I tottered around on three-inch heels I've never worn before. During the closing number, my earpiece fell apart and landed in my cleavage. Arms occupied; I sang louder.

Sue, our wardrobe gal and company manager, is scrambling to get costume needs addressed. When you're doing a show about menopause and you're *in* menopause, a dress that disguises bulges and bumps is in order. There's only so much a girdle can *do*.

April 19, 2013

Went to Wig World. Left with new hair. The climate is so dry in Nevada that eight times a week with a curling iron, will fry my hair. Trying a second pair of shoes (lower heel) for tonight's show.

April 21, 2013

Again with the shoes . . . I'll spring my repaired ACL in these heels at the eight shows per week rate. Sue bought me some ballroom shoes. My saving grace! High heels may look sexy, but my feet don't feel sexy after a two-show day when they're on fire and I'm limping out of the theatre.

April 23, 2013

How can companies charge $100 for a pair of "ballroom shoes" if the straps are going to rip after only two shows? Yes, I spin 220 times during the show, but should that matter?

April 24, 2013

At one time, I was a Diva. But I can't touch some of the women who have been in this show. "Queen Emily," who I did the show with in

Palm Springs, got pissed that the producers wouldn't let her leave for an audition for a Tyler Perry project, so she packed her bags and left in the middle of the night. Not a word to anyone! What balls! I could never do that. I'm too much of an ass kisser.

May 1, 2013

Would you believe there's an actress who used to do this show who ate four dinners at once, threw it all up backstage, and expected the crew to clean it up? She called in sick a lot. She'd say things like, "I don't know why my costumes aren't fitting. All I eat is salad."

One time she said she couldn't go on because she scratched her eyelid with a Slim Jim wrapper. Head of wardrobe was a been there, done that, no bullshit-tolerating queen. When this woman couldn't fit into her costumes and said, "I must be retaining water," he deadpanned, "You're retaining chicken and gravy."

May 2, 2013

What a difference a crowd makes. The yesterday matinee audience was sparse. The evening show, fantastic! One woman had the best laugh I've heard in years. Wish I could put it in a can and save it forever.

May 3, 2013

The other day, a toothless Yosemite Sam right out of the old West came up to me on the street. I was wearing my fluttery false eyelashes and he said, "Did you just wink at me? 'Cause I'm winkable!" I expected him to say, "Howdy do to you and you. It's Ernest T!" He was unkept and a little belligerent, like Ernest T. Tubbs from *The Andy Griffith Show*. After a few challenging performances, the show is gelling. Tonight was "media night" and pretty much a full house. Women were cackling so loud it sounded like a corner in hell. It was a BLAST!

May 8, 2013

Increased stamina. DECREASED jiggly bits around my waist. Left-knee tweaking. Tonight, during the show, after Annette, the Iowa

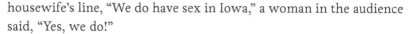

housewife's line, "We do have sex in Iowa," a woman in the audience said, "Yes, we do!"

Last night, before the show, Wydetta looked at my sunburn and said, "What you white people do for color. . ." And shook her head. It is foolish of me. I laid out for two hours and now it stings like hell to pull on my tights.

Then, she and I were looking at the stash of tights that just came Fedex for us. I picked up the box of XL black pantyhose, and what went through my head was, since Wydetta wears a black suit and the Tina Turner bustier/black leather skirt these must be hers.

So, I said to her, "Are these black tights yours?" You should've seen the look on her face.

"Are you fucking kidding me?" she said. "OF COURSE, they're mine, girl. I'm black!"

"Wydetta, I wear black panty hose for certain dresses, so I automatically assumed you might also wear nude hose for certain dresses." She stared at me like my hair was on fire. Then I realized how silly my thoughts were and giggled. I'm just a stupid white girl.

May 22, 2013

At the end of our show, for further female empowerment, women come onstage and join us in a kick line. Last night was a first, when the man whose lap I sat on in the audience as I sing my "Hot Flash Reprise" joined the women onstage!

He squeezed in between two middle-aged bowlers shouting, "I'm on hormone treatments for my prostate cancer, so I'm having hot flashes too!" I wish more of the men dragged to this show had that attitude.

May 23, 2013

The no frills complex we're living in called the Colonial Garden Court is like something out of a Quentin Tarantino movie. The owners said the pool isn't up to code. The only living beings that use it are two mallard ducks who live in the nearby weeds. The female has a nest of eggs behind a bush, and I feed her every day. Yesterday I brought her a plate . . . carrots, saltines (her favorite), some organic peas, and lettuce. Annette does it too. I enjoy fussing over the duck with

Annette and eating free food at the casino cafeteria. They have left over desserts at the end of the day and we often partake.

I promised the owners of the Colonial Garden Court that I'd relocate the mallard to the Truckee River after the ducklings are born but I think everyone is so anticipating it, they might allow her and the brood to become mascots.

May 25, 2013

This morning the female mallard woke me up. She was quacking in the pool because a tenant's cat was lurking. These misfits of society that look like something out of a Herman cartoon don't know ducks like I do. One woman with two teeth in her head yelled out the window to sweet-but-slow caretaker Jim, "Can you shut that damn duck up?"

May 27, 2013

What I've realized lately is that you've got to be drawn to chaos and emotional instability to thrive as an actor. Unless you hit it big, I don't think it's worth it.

June 1, 2013

I'm discovering Reno, "The biggest little city in the world" and getting away on days off to Lake Tahoe and places like Virginia City with the cast. We take trips to the grocery store together as well. Becca, who plays the Earth Mother, has her little girl Nancy with her for the contract, and I wish she was mine. Bright and talkative, she is a delight! Becca and I did a promo for the show at one of the local radio stations, and Nancy came along. After our on-air interview and snippets of songs, we walked down the hallway of the station, and five-year-old Nancy noticed a Beatles poster on the wall. In her little girl voice, she sang out loud, "I am the egg man, they are the egg man, I am the walrus, goo goo goo joob."

June 10, 2013

People love the Zoloft, Prozac, and St. Johns Wart references in the show. How ironic that my character takes Zoloft because I took it in 1996 and it saved my life.

I thought about that really challenging time in my life today. David and I had just split up and I was homeless. At the same time, I was understudying three women at the Ordway for *I Love A Piano* (65 Irving Berlin songs in three different harmonies); writing and performing a one-woman Fringe show at the Bryant Lake Bowl; and Mia broke his leg falling off the winding staircase in the home of my landlady. Couldn't have survived all that without Zoloft.

June 11, 2013
The handsome Czech bartender at the Eldorado bar makes a marvelous drink called A Scooby Snack. I can have one free drink every night after the show if I so desire. But one drink here at this altitude is like three drinks at home and two is my limit.

June 15, 2013
If I could send my girdle and wig onstage to do the show I would. Tonight, a fight broke out in the audience. A very intoxicated "theater patron" created quite a ruckus during the show. He was so belligerent, another audience member (not the ushers) escorted him out.

June 16, 2013
My fun-loving friend Vince came to visit me from Wisconsin. After the show, we were at the bar and a middle-aged fella claiming to own a casino, slurred his words at us.

"What show are you in? The Vagina Monocles?" I nearly fell off my stool.

June 17, 2013
Do not drink "Smooth Move" laxative tea and trust that the move will happen "smoothly" in six to ten hours like it says on the box. Took 20 hours for my gut to process it, and when it did, it was right in the middle of "Hot flash Reprise."

Speaking of Hot Flash Reprise, I'm up to three men per night when I venture into the audience to work the crowd. I usually run my fingers through their hair but the man I sat on tonight was wearing a toupée. So, I just patted his head.

June 20, 2013

Today is Mom's 79th birthday. I asked her what she plans to do today, and she said, "Write my obituary."

June 21, 2013

Tonight, after the show, Annette said, "After this contract ends, I need a break from fluff. Time to do something like *A Winter's Tale.*

June 22, 2013

During the show tonight, when I went into the audience to do my schtick of sitting on a guys lap and stroke his hair, a riled up Latino in the next row yelled,

"That's an old guy you just sat on. Pick me! I know how to treat a woman!"

"I've had younger, believe me," I said between my lines.

Then he says, "Come on, baby!"

"You just calm down!" I scolded. "I don't have time for this. I'm singing with a click track!"

July 1, 2013

Will I EVER stop going off course for a man? It's just like one to show up right now and break my focus. He's quite honestly the most aware, calm, enlightened, kind, considerate, spiritually healthy person I've met in years. He's also a veteran of Burning Man, a recovered alcoholic, and married and divorced three times. He had a challenging childhood and was raised with a silver-plated spoon in his mouth. He practices gratitude and joy. There's no question I was supposed to meet him. The minute I saw him I knew he was an extraordinary human.

He has two redheads in his life now. Toma Tetta Von Herrin Hausen, his female Wirehaired Pointing Griffin and me. I call her Toma Tetta Tutankomon, Von Herrin Hausen. She is threatened by me and wraps her leg around mine, trying to trip me. If Tomma Tetta were a female human, I'd be dealing with superficial posturing, and passive aggressiveness. I'd much prefer a bruised and scratched thigh. I will have to earn her trust.

The old me would say he's been married three times so there must be something wrong with him. The new me says he's been married three times, so he understands women. That's a huge plus because I don't have time to teach him. Plus, I have no right to judge him.

Andy makes the best coffee and prepares "mice" for me. He told me a story about two barn owls. One winter, he was walking past a dead poplar tree that has a hole in it. Inside the hole was a female barn owl. The male owl was on the ground hooting to her. He had placed 15 headless mice in three rows for her to choose from. We both prefer small amounts of food on a plate, like tapas, or appetizers.

Each of our escapes from Reno have been packed to the brim. For example, we have gone to Emerald Bay in the rain and toured the Vikingsholm. We have floated down the Truckee River on inner tubes, bathed nude in the Sierra Hot Springs, camped under the stars, and stood in a circle of crystals. The hippie cowboy has opened up my fifth chakra.

July 3, 2013
H.C. drove me up Windy Hill, where the high schoolers make out. We pulled over, and the Nevada Philharmonic Orchestra played the 1812 Overture to an audience in a pavilion below. Then some fireworks went off in the distance . . . it wasn't even the 4th, and we got fireworks! I figured he'd planned it that way because he's a planner.

July 4, 2013
Andy and I saw fireworks over the Nugget Casino after a burger and fries at In-N-Out burger.

Meeting Andy has been a gift. I'm so high-strung he has been good for me. We study Enneagrams, and when I'm with him, I can just breathe.

He wore his fencing shoes when we rode the Truckee River in inner tubes. It used to be wrestling shoes that turned my crank. Now its fencing shoes. They are SEXY.

Because Becca is going on as the Iowa Housewife after this gig and they don't have the time to train her in, the cast gets to run the show with her today. They aren't paying us for it and the run is almost over. Legally, it falls under the category of "rehearsal time." I've said it before, and I'll say again, when push comes to shove, the performers are the ones who have to suck it up and compromise. Performers are **always** at the mercy of the powers that be. This is an Equity gig and we really should have been paid for this extra rehearsal at the end of the run. But if I say anything, I'm the bad guy for pointing this out, I'm the troublemaker.

July 6, 2013

So, I ran into the touched caretaker, Jim, in the elevator that stinks to high heaven. He's standing there in his white athletic socks on the dingy, stained carpet, holding a bottle of pepper. He seems to feel guilty as if he's been caught.

"Oh, hi, Holly," he says. "I figured out a way to deal with the stink in this elevator. I'm going to put pepper on the carpet so those dogs won't pee in here anymore." He was very pleased with his cleverness.

FOUR HOURS LATER

I ran into Jim in the elevator again.

"You probably think I'm an evil guy," he said. "I felt so guilty about sprinkling the pepper that I came in here and vacuumed. Between the pee and the pepper, it smelled so bad, I gagged."

July 6, 2013

So, the touched caretaker Jim meticulously cleans the pool every day, but it is never used because they haven't opened it. Not up to code, they say.

"Next week we'll open it!" It was 104 degrees for four days in a row. The only ones who have used the pool are the mallard ducks.

July 12, 2013

The show is closing in a few days. I told my mom about the hippie cowboy, Andy. She asked if he had any children and I said, "No."

Her response was, "So, then you'd get everything."

I told her about how we have an amazing connection.

"Do you think he'll want to get married?"

"Well, he's tried it three times before. Can't imagine he wouldn't try again."

"Good. Because you're going to need a new car."

July 15, 2013

I realized today that I have only gambled two dollars at the casino in three months! Being a performer is enough of a gamble. I'm thankful I got to experience this part of the country and empower the thousands of women who saw the show.

July 16, 2013, Chicago, Illinois

I came back from the wild, wild west to my dusty, humid Lincoln Square apartment full of historical documents, antiques, and oddities. The city, as always, has its own charm and relevance. As I walked in, I heard a Mexican man standing next to the dumpster, singing "Oye Cómo Va."

My mother is glad I'm home safe and sound. Today she told me I'll inherit all the same medical issues she's suffering from right now.

"All that family gave me was their bad parts," she said. "We have bad veins!"

November 24, 2013

Hippie Cowboy Andy Robinson is visiting from Nevada while the Holly Hotel is full to capacity. It is Thanksgiving week, so I have eight dogs. To avoid all these pups being seen by my neighbors, who may report me to the landlord, Andy and I sneak out the back door with them, in shifts. But because I'm the pack leader, they won't go very far unless I'm with them. Its adorable how they make Andy wait in the alley until I'm downstairs. It's never a dull moment around here, especially when Frank E. Schwartz and Bruno are at the hotel. It doesn't matter if I have two dogs or eight. They adapt to our energy and all get along.

Christmas 2013

I had a good pack for Christmas that included a toothless Chihuahua named Francois Jean-Claude Gradle. His tongue hangs out of his mouth because he has no teeth to keep it in. And he is on Prozac. He bit me several times when his owner Stephanie was here because he was protecting her. As soon as she left, he was my best friend. That's quite often the way. Stephanie is darling and has a long-haired Chihuahua named Roz as well. Stephanie's note about Francois:

> *"Francois has a severe heart murmur that often makes him gag, so don't be alarmed when he seems like he is choking. His arthritis makes cold weather uncomfortable for him. It is also part of why he can't do stairs. More, his bad history is why he has so many fears—stairs, gangways, big dogs, being alone, strangers, etc."*

I told Francois as we drove to my mother's house, "Francois, you and I are not that different. We both have a heart murmur and mine never shuts up. Can I be honest here? I have more fears than you. They include snakes, a bad marriage, parking garages, and dying alone like Dorothy Parker." He listened and thought about this. And then he licked my hand.

Winter 2013

Right now, I have six dogs cooped up at the Holly Hotel as snow-storms rage outside. It's probably not a good idea to take care of dogs in an apartment with Persian rugs. It's my own fault for trying to surround myself with luxury.

March 1, 2014

It's a week of bad luck. I lost my only set of car and house keys. They literally vanished. I retraced my steps back to the fountain in Lincoln Square in front of Café Selmarie and still can't figure it out. Thank God for my roommate Sandeep, who took a cab with me to a Honda dealership to get a copy made. It cost me roughly $100 for my error. Now I have to call my landlord for another apartment key.

So, Mother calls and could tell I was upset. Apparently, she's still angry I didn't continue dating a man 25 years older than me who I was involved with in Minneapolis. I didn't want to tell her that I lost my keys, but she got it out of me. Her response was absurd.

"If you had married Mr. Opitz, none of this would have happened. You would not be looking for your lost keys."

May 19, 2014

FYI, I have a new client who is the love child of two shelter dogs—a Chihuahua and a Pomeranian. His name is Moose. His owner Natalie and I call him Moose Man. He is extremely precocious and plays constantly. We made another video called "The Cuban Conga" and Moose is the star. The other dogs are jealous of him because he's so adorable. Charlie White does not like sharing me with him.

Moose was neutered on May 16. I was expecting him to be calmer. No dice. He hasn't missed a beat and still hurls himself at life with wild abandon. It will take a few months before the testosterone surging in him subsides.

When his owner Natalie drops him off, she opens the car door and he races to the door of my building, jumping up and down to come in. He is such a light in my life. Last time she picked him up, we stood outside talking about him as he squinted at us.

Natalie said, "When he's tired, he gives me the Chihuahua squint." She said they got in the elevator yesterday in her building and stood next to a neighbor who was wearing flip flops and Moose peed on the man's foot.

"Is it harder to potty train small dogs?" she asked. "Because my black lab never did any of this. I have to put screens around my houseplants because he'll play in the dirt," she said. Then she looked down at him and said, "When are you going to stop peeing on everything Moose? This is why we can't have nice things."

I love Moose like I gave birth to him.

May 20, 2014

I've been seeing a therapist. She told me, "You HAVE to detach from your mother. Your own survival depends on it." I can't seem to do it. The best I can do is attempt to set boundaries, which is very difficult because everything is on her terms. I'm clearly co-dependent. She wants me to visit but won't let me bring my canine clients.

"Can't you get someone else to take care of them" she asked. All those years I took care of her dogs and trained them and now I can't bring a few small dogs to her house, which has been overrun by no less than 70 dogs since 1972? It's about control. She even controls the garbage now. When I throw anything away, "What'd you throw away?" she'll ask and double check the trash. It. Is. Insanity.

Andy and I went to an A.C.O.A. (Adult Children of Alcoholic and Dysfunctional Families) meeting. I put Moose and Bijou in the bedroom because it was thundering. We were gone an hour and a half. I walked into my boudoir after the meeting and knew immediately. I looked everywhere on the floor and found nothing. Then I looked at the bed where I'd left the clothes I'd worn earlier. Moose had pooped in my bra. He'd aimed it so perfectly into one cup, it follows the curve of the underwire. He's so talented.

June 12, 2014

I'm sitting on a sunny deck, hand feeding raw meet to a 16-year-old, blind dog named Conan. We are listening to a passing ice cream truck out front play, "She'll be comin' round the mountain when she comes. She'll be comin' round the mountain when she comes. She'll be comin' round the mountain, comin' round the mountain, she'll be comin' round the mountain when she comes."

Conan's eyes are sunk into his head, as he's been blind since he was five. He walks in circles and often bumps into furniture. When dogs get this old, they resemble cartoon characters. Conan reminds me of the cartoon fox in *The Fabulous Mr. Fox*. What is so astonishing is how fearless he is. He fell down a few stairs one day and I was horrified he'd been hurt. He popped right back up like he was made of springs.

July 23, 2014

At this point in my life, I've been the struggling writer, the starving artist, the student and the teacher, the other woman, the down and out, the drama queen and the cliché. So, this is a nice change but there is a lot of work in running a pet hotel. This morning, none of us wanted to get up, so we lolled on my Tempurpedic, marshmallow bed, even past the song of the black-capped chickadee calling from the bird clock in the kitchen.

Rufus, the official goodwill Ambassador of the Holly Hotel, is splayed right next to me and keeps contorting, stomach skyward, so I can pat his stomach. Every time he stretches, he waves his paws right in my face for dramatic effect. When I open my eyes, he's staring at me lovingly from the fringe of his wiry black face. Then he licks my mouth. Daisy the Chihuahua is on the other side of me, plastered to my left kidney. Malka is snoring in the center of the bed, and Max is in a side splat, guarding the door. Sweet slumber engulfs us. What seems like minutes later, the Northern Cardinal shares its song, which means its nine o'clock. How did THAT happen?

What I love about these dogs is they adjust to my schedule. Malka is not a morning dog. When she stays at the hotel, she requests a Do Not Disturb sign on the door. Every day begins with stomach rubs. When I'm ready to face the world, the fellas race to the door and wait to be leashed. Then, I snap the blue sports harness onto Daisy, who needs the bulk because she's no bigger than a loaf of French bread.

We wander down Campbell Street to sniff, pee, and say hello to Lilly, the mutt at the end of the block. Lilly had a bad experience at the dog park. Then, we wag our tails at the three-legged boxer who does his business on the lawn in front of 5424.

Breakfast is then served. When the White Throated Sparrow chirps from the kitchen, we know its 10 o'clock and time for Dog Church. We listen to the Mormon Tabernacle Choir on the radio and read out loud from Eckardt Tolle's book the *Power of Now*. When Dog Church is over, we walk to Rosehill Cemetery. Choco, the three-legged apricot poodle is always at the head of the pack.

We often walk to Rosehill Cemetery to visit the dead and study tombstones. The cemetery always puts life into perspective. Bruder, Choco, and Bella led me to a stone statue of a dog. I explained Doggy Heaven and the Rainbow Bridge to them. And they listened.

January 2015

I feel a lot of empathy for the people in my ACOA group. Or maybe it's the pain killer I took an hour ago. No, it's the people. We are all in the same boat (life) together, frantically bailing water (pain/trauma) to stay afloat.

Last night, one of my favorite members, who is a doctor and people-pleaser who grew up in Minnesota, talked about how he was always such a good boy growing up. He learned that if he kept doing and accomplishing things, he wouldn't get beat. He was always a model student. I relate. He told us today that at the hospital he works in, there was an unlit menorah, and even though he's not Jewish he said, "Let's light it!" The nurses said, "Noooo, we can't because of the fire regulations." He said, "Oh come on, get me some matches. I'm lighting the menorah!" We all applauded him.

THERE'S NEVER ENOUGH TIME BETWEEN TRAGEDIES

January 26, 2015

Everything is changed. The moment I've dreaded my whole life has come. I can hardly even *say* it. My mother is dead. Everything has changed.

My fierce, complicated, controlling, damaged, emotionally unavailable, hilarious mother is gone. When I was a child, the mere thought of it reduced me to tears because she was everything to me. I used to lie in bed at night and wonder how I'd ever survive it.

As soon as I answered the phone and heard the words, "This is the coroner in La Porte County," my heart skipped a beat, my head turned upside down, and I couldn't breathe. It couldn't be. Then, she said the words.

"I'm sorry to inform you, but your mother has passed away." Shock, disbelief, guilt, and fear gripped me. Maybe they made a mistake? Maybe if I get in my car and drive to the house, it won't be true?

"Do you have a funeral home that you want to work with?" the coroner asked. I picture Larry, who handled all our family funerals at Haverstock's. I see him sitting with my father, mother, and me in his office when Danny died.

Barb, my mom's cleaning lady, filled me in on what happened. Barb had arrived at the house to clean about 10 a.m., and because my mom didn't answer the door, she assumed my mom was at a doctor's appointment. She cleaned for an hour and went into the bedroom to vacuum. That's when she found my mother, curled up on her side. She called 911, and the coroner found my number on my mom's cell phone to call me. I feel bad for Barb that she had to be the one to find my mother but thank God it wasn't me. I'd never get over it.

I had just turned in an invoice for a freelance job in which I was writing teachers' guides using the common core standards, the most over complicated writing project I've ever had. My mother had asked me to come visit, and I had literally just left her a message on her answering machine saying I could come visit now.

But "now" is too late. Just like death to make me realize time is a thief and the inevitable always comes. Three of five family members are gone. But this death is a bit different than my brother and my father's deaths. My body is so heavy right now, I can't climb the stairs.

I tried to look at it differently, and to my surprise, I found some relief. The last six years were physically brutal for my mother and hard on my sister and me too. The doctors said there was nothing more they could do for the veins in my mother's legs. Now, her pain is over. Phyllis feels the same. Mae Schroeder could never have survived life as an amputee.

To hear the words, "Your mother has passed away," from the coroner instead of a family member or friend is the pits. I flash back to when her granddaughters were little and asked her on the phone how she was.

"Not good," said my mother. "I could die at any moment."

I found relief knowing my mother's last day was pleasant enough. She went with her neighbor Ellie to a matinee, and then Mother cooked pork chops for them. Later that evening, after watching *Downton Abbey*, my mother, feeling more exhausted than usual, climbed into bed, curled up on her side, and died. I always thought she'd live long past 80. My parents died in the same room, 16 years apart.

When I called my sister to tell her our mother had died, her response was, "Oh!" She is stunned. Then, I called Tighe Publishing and explained that my mother died, and I'm planning a funeral. Knowing there were plenty of other writers to take over my pages, I quit the project. If writing teachers' guides was difficult *before* my mom died, it would surely be impossible now.

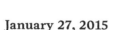

January 27, 2015

I'm tired of having to be so strong all the time. I'm hanging by a friz-zled thread. If only I could talk to Mother right now. I feel horrible that I wasn't with her when she died. I'll bet she's angry about that. This is such a shock and so final. My dear friend Michael Altobello followed me to LaPorte. My mom's dog Ruby was at the front door staring out the window when I pulled up. She was so relieved to see me, she clung to me and gave me love bites. A small pot of tomato soup sat on the stove. The house was silent, cold and eerie.

Barb said that Ruby followed the men out of the house when they took my mother away and chased after the truck. Then she smelled the tracks in the driveway and stood there, like little girl lost. The image of this breaks my heart. She knew. Only the animals were with my mother when she passed, which, to be honest, is fitting. From the time she was a little girl, my mother loved animals more than people. That love and commitment to their well-being was her greatest gift to me, as was her sense of humor.

Michael and I drove to Haverstock's Funeral Home. And, as it turns out, Larry, whom I was hoping to greet, died years ago. I really wanted to go through this process with Larry, but he's dead too. I ask the undertaker if he knows what killed my mother.

"A heart attack most likely. Her legs are full of blood clots. They're like cement." I know how much her legs hurt her and feel terrible she suffered.

My sister Susie got to the funeral home a little later, as she had a three-hour drive. She broke a bone in her foot recently, so she hobbled in wearing a cast and acted upbeat. The undertakers were eager to begin the process and showed us the brochures and prices. Susie seemed upset that a friend of mine came along for moral support. He's been through this process before when his own mother died. After two hours of discussion, the undertaker said, "We don't usually spend three hours on this process and need to finish up, now."

My sister and I couldn't be more different. She has not cried and is always passive aggressive towards me. She wants to host a gathering at the house after the funeral and I told her I don't think it's a good idea.

"People expect food and beverages," I said. "AND a clean house, and this house is not ready for company." I don't understand how she doesn't realize that. She wanted dog show people to come and fought me on it. "Let's just get through the funeral," I suggested. "We can have a gathering later when the weather is better." I know it's not good timing to have a gathering. I've hosted enough to know that we can't pull it off. We have no one to help us either. Most families going through the process of death have family, friends, and neighbors who bring food over. Ellie, my mom's neighbor, is the only one who brought over any food. As per normal, we are entirely alone.

Then, Susie tells me her daughter Alyssia, who has been estranged from her for five years now, won't be coming to the funeral because she has to work for her dad taking pictures at McCormick Place in Chicago for the Chicago Dog Show. Alyssia lives three hours away but is actually going to be an hour away the day of the funeral. Her grandmother has passed away suddenly and instead of attending her grandmother's funeral, she insists she has to work, for her dad, who said she could go to the funeral. I'm crumbling inside. Where is the respect? I can't imagine how devastated my mother would be, knowing one of her two granddaughters is choosing to NOT attend her funeral. For 49 years I've known and witnessed the pain my mother has endured. And yes, she was a very complex individual who took her anger out on people around her, especially Susie and Dad. She was very demanding and controlling, but she still deserves to have family at her funeral. And we need Alyssia's support. We need her. What I don't understand is how anyone wouldn't feel that sense of decency and duty to pay respects. It's what we do as human beings. It's tribal! Too bad my mom didn't raise elephants. They would be at her funeral.

My mother isn't even in the ground yet, so she's rolling over on the slab at Haverstock's. My mother whispers in my ear.

"All those times Alyssia was nearby and didn't visit me and now she's not coming to my funeral? You've GOT to be kidding?!"

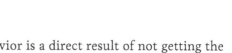

I wonder if Alyssia's behavior is a direct result of not getting the love she needed from my sister, who didn't get it from *our* mother, who didn't get it from hers. The anger and hostility has been passed down three generations. Why am I the only person who sees this?

I try to be understanding and let the pain go. I've got to find pictures for the funeral slide show in an extremely cluttered, disorganized house. Alyssia hasn't spoken to her mother (my sister) for five years and Susie won't call her. I should've let my sister handle it. She is her mother, after all, but my sister ignores the whole situation. And Millennial Alyssia won't talk, she'll only text, the worse form of communication. At one point she tells me I'm being "insensitive." When I begged her to come to her grandmother's funeral she responded with,

> *"Quit texting me until you pull your head out of your ass. Running and owning businesses are different than 9-5 jobs and dog walking things. Rob isn't available and the job has changed so much in the last few years that our back-up photographer won't know how. The other people I know are all booked too. I'm sorry if my life is inconvenient for you, I really want to be there. I'd have been totally happy with a closed casket on Monday, especially since there is a wake on Friday."*

The distance between her generation and mine is wider than I thought. I explain that her grandmother was gone 15 hours before she was found by her housekeeper and that the undertaker said Monday would be "pushing it." Must I go into detail about how blood pools in the body when someone dies lying on their side, and that skin color changes, and the body gets stiff?

Then there was this one:

> *"And I can grieve however I damn well please. If I want my memories of Grandma Mae being all short and goofy bopping around her kitchen with cats and birds and green bean casserole to remain untarnished by the cold pale image of her after death then I am totally and completely entitled to not attend, entirely because it's an open casket."*

I don't have the energy for her anger. I write the eulogy.

My mother, Mae Schroeder was many things: an animal lover, a fan of the theater, a bargain shopper, a movie critic, a clipper of coupons and recipes, as well as a devoted reader of the LaPorte Herald Argus *and* Reader's Digest, *a collector of anything that is cute, makes noise, or is on sale, and most of all, a dear friend and confidante to many people, who relied on her for advice, laughter, and her opinion on the latest* Downton Abbey *episode.*

My mother was FUNNY and that's because she spoke her truth. I learned the power of words from her. She cut through the fluff and got right to the point. To say she was one of a kind doesn't do her justice. In many ways, she was an enigma, an unforgettable character in a novel, a rule breaker. And, according to her doctors, an energizer bunny that just kept going.

And boy, did she go. To church events, Christian Women's Club outings, dog shows, potluck dinners, VFW fish fries, musicals, plays and movies— lots of movies. When Gene Siskel died, I told her she should join Roger Ebert as a movie critic.

Growing up as the baby of the family, I was my mother's keeper and went everywhere with her. Errands before kindergarten included a withdrawal from the First Federal Savings Bank, a visit to Barbara Links on Lincolnway, and then a wash and set at Juanita's, a smoky beauty shop in the center of town, where my mother was a regular.

Every week, Phyllis Roach defied gravity and transformed my mother's hair with a tease comb and a shield of Aqua Net. At night, my mother swathed her hair in toilet paper and slept on a silk pillow. My mother has not done her own hair in 50 years.

Some of my favorite memories of my mom are her taking me to the LaPorte County Fair in a stroller when I had stitches in my foot and couldn't walk. I was 13 and she plunked me into a child's stroller, put a plastic bag around my bandaged foot, and rolled me around the fairgrounds. She always won playing the mouse game.

I love my memories of going to Rose's Hatchery in South Bend, Indiana with her. The first time we went it was for cedar shavings for my guinea pigs. Overcome by the sound of peeping hatchlings, we forgot the cedar shavings and returned home with six goslings. And that was the beginning of the Schroeder menagerie, which grew and grew to include dogs, ducks, geese, chickens, rabbits, parakeets, hamsters, guinea pigs, and a Moluccan Cockatoo, Porsche.

Animals were a great solace to my mom. And we rarely counted them because her attitude was, "We already have seven, what's one more?" It was in the 1970's that a basset hound named Jason changed her life and introduced her to the world of dog shows. I am grateful for that world because she found her tribe. In the later years, these folks helped get her through emotional and physical pain. Losing her only son Daniel when he was 31 was tragic beyond belief.

But if there's one thing she never lost, it was her faith in God. She always held onto her faith. She said that God reached down and plucked my brother Danny off the earth for himself. My mother also believed in angels and that we should talk to them. I have no doubt she'll be one of mine. Now, she gets to do what she's always wanted to do. Pick out the perfect man for me.

Rest in peace, Mother. I promise to take excellent care of Ruby.

February 1, 2015

I think my mother would have approved of her funeral, but I'm kind of relieved she can't give me feedback. I'm exhausted. One of her three siblings attended. The youngest, her sister Carol, was the only one who came because Judy is housebound due to her health, and Tom said he couldn't fly in from Florida due to bad weather. So, Carol's family attended, Aunt Bobbi, my cousin Janice, and my mother's closest friends. I was grateful for their attendance. One of my mother's two grandchildren, Krissy, also came. She was late but at least she showed up. Alyssia came to the wake, thankfully. She wouldn't speak to me or her mother but at least she showed.

"Doesn't your grandma look wonderful?" I asked. Alyssia rolled her eyes and walked away.

Knowing the importance of appearance to my mother, I was pleased she looked so good, and the second I saw her, I knew her body was now just a shell. As I touched her hands and cheek, I could see her soul had moved on. Where would she want to be? Heaven's version of the Westminster Kennel Club Dog Show, where she'd win Best in Show.

Mom's friend Phyllis had her daughter Beth deliver her eulogy, and Paul Marsh from Nationwide Insurance also spoke. I wish I'd had it filmed, as it was the most personal part of the service. I delivered the infamous line my mother said to me when I dated a Jewish film producer. "I think you'd make a great Jew. God knows you were never a good Lutheran." The pastor sitting onstage across from me at the podium turned and looked at me. It dawned on me what I had just said. I looked at him, took a beat and said, "It's not true. I'm a pretty good Lutheran."

At the luncheon, I encouraged everyone to celebrate my mother by having desert first. It was comforting to be at St. John's Lutheran Church. Members of that congregation give of themselves without question. When we drove from St. John's to the cemetery, all oncoming traffic stopped to wait for us to pass. I imagined my mother with a tickled expression, sitting on the hood, waving to everyone as her parade passed by.

Standing graveside, the flakes of the predicted snowstorm swirled around us and onto the casket. I heard my mother's voice clear as a bell followed by one of her dramatic sighs.

"Holly, how's your weather? It's snowing here. Again." Solemn and weary, we stood by. I'm grateful Amy Burris and Michael Altobello—the tried and true, stayed till the bitter end. The plot of three for my brother, father, and mother is now complete. Within hours, a record-breaking snowstorm blanketed Indiana and Illinois with a blinding white, dead silence. If we'd had the funeral on Monday, no one would have made it.

Mom, siblings Judy, Carol, and Tom,
with their Uncle Matt

THE TRUTH COMES OUT

February 3, 2015

My warrior spirit is working overtime. Phyllis came over with a bottle of wine to tell me what she learned 30 years ago. I'm the product of a 20-year affair—and everyone knew but me.

"Make no mistake, Holly, you were conceived in love," said Phyllis. "They had a spark, and she never stopped loving him. You're a love child."

It sure would have been nice to know the truth, but the truth was hidden to protect everyone else. I could've gotten to know my real father before he died in 1984, not to mention half-sisters and brothers.

Some memories filter through the fog in my brain. I remember my biological father Walter visiting my mother when I was a child. He had charm, and the three of us sat in the front seat of his truck. I remember the year I was 18, when my mother heard of his passing on the radio and came into my bedroom crying. I had just passed out S.A.D.D. (Students Against Drunk Driving) flyers at the mall.

"Holly, Walter is dead!" She rarely showed that kind of emotion. I had no idea what the hell was going on. I didn't know that he left the hospital after kidney surgery, got drunk, and drove into a telephone pole that sprung his stitches. He went into a coma and died at the hospital.

Then, I have a flashback to the year I was 29, when I asked my parents for their blood types. My doctor asked me to get them as we were trying to figure out what was wrong with my stomach. My mother asked suspiciously,

"What do you need our blood types for?" A week later, my father called, when Mom was out of town.

"The reason mother doesn't want you to have our blood types is because I'm not sure if you're mine or not. Back in '65, your mother became good friends with the house painter. He wanted to marry your mother at one point. If I'd known then what a pain in the ass she was going to be, I would've personally delivered her to him in a wheelbarrow."

This was a chaotic time in my life and because there's only so much trauma a person can process at one time, I buried it. A year or two later, Mom visited me in Minneapolis, and I took her to the Minnesota State Fair.

"I want to park right up front," she said.

"Are you aware of the size of the Minnesota State Fair, Mother? There's no parking right up front. This is the second largest fair in the country, with two million visitors each year. People take shuttles from all over hill and dale to get here."

"Well, I don't care. I can only walk so much."

"Then you'll have to make allowances and pace yourself. This fair is hard core and pulls out all the stops. You won't even believe the food. Compared to the Minnesota State Fair, LaPorte's county fair is a mere *attempt* at a fair."

While we were in traffic and she couldn't escape, I told her about Dad's confession. She wouldn't admit a thing.

"Oh, your father's nuts. He always has been a loony tune."

Who is the loony tune here? Projection, twisting the truth, and living a lie was her modus operandi. If I didn't love her, I could never have endured her personality disorder. We did have a marvelous time at the fair. By the end of the day, my mother's shirt held so many food spills and splotches from pronto pups, a pork chop, a Rueben, fried green tomatoes, corn on the cob, and custard that we could have made soup out of it.

But I digress. After Phyllis delivered the news and left, I told my sister what Phyllis said.

"Susie, I just found out why you and I are so different. We don't have the same biological father." My sister didn't stop what she was doing or even look at me. She just sighed.

"You always were skinnier than me." That was it. I picked up Ruby, went to bed, and cried into my pillow. Ruby gave me love bites and we looked into each other's eyes.

"Ruby, I'd be lost without you. Thank God you're here. If only you could talk." And then she licked the tears off my face.

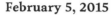

February 5, 2015

In my mom's car was a small plastic bag holding an Aldi receipt and a sausage with a bite out of it. Apparently, she was returning the sausage which cost $1.78. Then I found her last grocery list. She listed AA and AAA batteries, Tide ($5.49), and White Castle cheese-burgers. My words of warning about her diabetes were always in vain. I remember the day at lunch when she squeezed a lemon and an entire packet of sugar into her water.

"Why would you pour sugar in your water, Mom? You're a diabetic."

"Because it is too boring otherwise," she said. "Now I have lemonade!"

February 6, 2015

The minute the coroner said, "Your mother has passed away," I felt like I'd fallen off a cliff. It's too late, I thought, for speaking to her from my heart. In January, I had tried to have a heart-to-heart talk with her.

"Mom, I want to talk to you about some things that mean a lot to me."

"Go get the paper in," she said. It just wasn't in her to speak of emotions. I spoke to my friend Michele Davis, who has an emotion-ally vacant mother.

"All you wanted was her approval," said Michele. "And now you'll never get it."

Looking at my mom's medical reports, her life, extended by doctors and surgeries, was more fragile than she admitted. Timing is everything. At 74, she went in for a physical and found out she had a corroded artery and would've been dead in a week had it not been discovered. She got the corroded artery fixed first and then she had a quadruple bypass. A year or two later, her circulation was so bad, she had an artificial vein inserted from her groin to her ankle. In between all this, she fell and broke her arm. It was one thing after another. A year before she died, she had her second knee replacement surgery. It is a blessing she passed before things got even worse. But that doesn't change the pain of losing her.

February 14, 2015

This was my first Valentine's Day without receiving or sending a card to my mother, who was an expert card and package sender. Thank goodness I've saved so many of her letters.

Dear Holly,

Nice day and going to see the Tuna play with Mary Tobar. Scott was over to weed and then back later to trim bushes. I loved the Mexican restaurant Phyllis and I went to called Abuelo. Krissy's boyfriend broke up with her and took the kitten to his mother so she could not have it. Too bad for her. Gotta close.

Love, Mom

February 20, 2015

My friend Perrin came to visit and offer her help, and my sister came to town for a day for the reading of the will. The lawyer said if our mother wasn't dead already, he'd kill her himself.

"I called her several times and said Mae, get your daughters names on your house!" Because Mom was too busy going to lunch and movies to put our names on it, the house will now go into probate, which means more expense.

Perrin was helping clean out a drawer so full we could barely shut it and threw away a 30-year-old, yellowed, cracked piece of Tupperware missing its lid. Susie grabbed it out of the trash and yelled at me.

"You're throwing away our mother with glee!" Perrin grabbed it out of her hand.

"This isn't your mother. This is garbage and it should have been thrown out years ago."

Next, Susie wanted to know if she's *allowed* to keep Mother's rubber bands because she uses rubber bands. To demonstrate, she pulled out a small jumble of coupons, her check book, and receipts, all held in place with two rubber bands on each end. I'm looking at the task of cleaning and making livable a neglected, four-bedroom, three-bath house, stuck in the 1970s and '80s, crammed full of 44

years of living and extremely disorganized, and my sister wants to discuss rubber bands?

She goes through the trash in the garage because she doesn't trust me. There was a decrepit, yellowed plastic water bowl for the dogs that had been chewed all the way around the bottom. There are no less than 30 metal and ceramic dog bowls in the house. I threw the mutilated plastic one away. My sister pulled it out. I threw it away again, she pulled it out. Then she hung on the clothesline a small rag with more holes in it than a piece of Swiss cheese. It is worthless and can't even be used as a *rag*. She not only washed it, but she hung it on the line to dry. She inherited that inability to throw anything away from our mother.

I find a photo of my mom on the phone, in our 1970s style kitchen, showing the countertops, which were always crowded with antiquated mixers, a crockpot holding fish gravel, and expired spices. In the cupboards are pots and pans that should be in a museum. My mother's favorite skillet is a cast iron artifact whose wooden handle is still held together with a thick rubber band. I smile to myself, remembering the wonderful pancakes she made in this 50-year-old skillet.

March 1, 2015

I may go mad trying to corral clutter and sort through my parents' possessions, my brother's things, and remnants of grandparents, aunts, and uncles. There's no rhyme or reason as to how things are stored or put away, which reflects her clouded state of mind. I found a pistol, with bullets, in a Santa tin in my mother's nightstand, next to her diabetic cream and Bible. Every check and bill since 1972 have been kept in a kitchen cupboard above the phone. Jewelry is in the bathroom vanity, toxic cleaning supplies stored next to perishable food, prescription drugs in the spice rack, shoes in short wastebaskets, and bird food in the liquor cabinet. And the basement and garage are full of tools and contraptions from the days of yore.

Two large kitchen drawers are crammed full of nothing but free return address labels. I remember trying to get her to throw away some of them.

"Mother, you'd have to live three lifetimes to use all of these. Why are you saving all of them? You can barely close the drawer."

"Don't touch my labels," she'd say.

Every single drawer in the kitchen is broken. Open one and it falls. Without my dad, such things never got fixed. I'm sure she was just sick of the minutia of life and overwhelmed by the maintenance required to keep this house and property going. But why was there never a conversation with her daughters about what happens when she dies?

The closet in my childhood bedroom is full of fur coats and stoles. The basement has piles of rugs whose rubber backings have disintegrated. In an upstairs hallway closet are towering stacks of my mother's beloved dog publications, *Tally Ho* and *The Bugler*, dating back to the 1980s and '90's. Many people *tried* to help her organize, discard, and donate shabby, timeworn and depleted items from her closets, cupboards, and cabinets, but no one succeeded. When asked why she wouldn't donate to worthy causes, her response was, "I want to know who is getting my things."

I realize that this house is a gift, and I'm thankful for the valuable antiques, jewelry, guns, coins, and silver, but what is maddening is the volume of Beanie Babies, stuffed toys, collectibles, tools, tote bags and stationery from the World Wildlife Fund, the Humane Society of the United States, and the ASPCA. Some people would just fill a dumpster with this stuff but I can't bring myself to do that. Our whole family had that annoying attachment to objects, which brought us a false sense of security. It's as if my father's nutcrackers are infused with him, so I feel guilty for getting rid of any of them, but I can't cart 12 nutcrackers with me for the rest of my life, or 53 pocket knives, or photo albums of people I don't know who died a century ago. I'm completely overwhelmed.

How on earth will I be able to go through every single item? So far, I'm doing a lot of donating. Years ago, when I asked my sister what she and I would do when it was time to take apart this house, she said,

"We'll just burn it."

Here is a short list of curiosities found this week in this house:

1. 15 fly swatters
2. 33 dog bowls (ceramic, metal, and plastic)
3. 14 German nutcrackers
4. 6 scales of various sizes and age
5. 12 dormant orchid plants
6. 414 Beanie Babies
7. 45 decorative plates
8. 54 *Bugler* magazines
9. 160 *Tally Ho* magazines
10. 53 tablecloths
11. 18 plug-in air fresheners
12. 21 liquid hand soaps
13. 12 Christmas sweaters
14. 14 snoods for basset hound ears
15. 23 tote bags
16. 13 plastic rain bonnets for my mother's bouffant

My mother's generation kept everything. When you grow up with scarcity, you prepare for it, for the rest of your life. Over half the pantry is full of dented cans marked down in price.

March 10, 2015

Death sucks the life out of people . . . both living and dead. The one thing I've rarely done in my mom's house is sit still. Well, I am now because as far as energy goes, I've got zip. My sister and I are the only ones left. She says she has painful memories of growing up in the house and has her own house and property, so she won't be helping. Doesn't seem fair to me. I can't live in Chicago 90 minutes away and deal with this house too. It's too much.

March 11, 2015

So, I was in Chicago, over at my neighbor John Fogel's apartment, gathering up some of my cigar boxes from his basement. We ran into John's older, bizarre brother near the washer and dryer. He started out with his attitude right off the bat, but I cut him off.

"Gary, my mother died . . . in her sleep." His response?

"Well, so did ours. But ours shot herself first. Guns trump sleep. We win."

March 15, 2015

Mornings are hardest. Ruby is grieving as well. Thank God we have each other. I was going through all my mom's eyeglasses because she saved every pair since the 1950s, when a ring fell out of one. It was Danny's gold band with a diamond. Being in this house alone where there's been so much pain is crippling. I decide to focus on a pleasant memory instead.

THE CRIPPLING
PUPPET SHOW

One of my favorite memories of my mother was when she took me at 11 years of age to the LaPorte County Fair—in a stroller. It was July of 1977, after another freak accident at the Gebhardt house. My pal Beth and I were in the middle of performing a puppet show for Marilou Gebhardt. During the *Planet of the Apes* number (I was Cornelius), I jumped into the air and landed on a prop—a drinking glass, which shattered under my foot. It felt like pins and needles, right in the arch, and the blood gushed out. Beth's older brother Mark carried me into the kitchen and put a dishtowel around it. Everyone looked very concerned so I knew a band-aid wouldn't be enough.

At the hospital, I got stitches in the bottom of my foot and a pair of crutches. It was SO painful.

When I got home and hobbled inside with my crutches, all I could think about were my plans to go to the LaPorte County Fair with the three Amy's: Amy Burris, Amy Lawrence, and Amy Odell. I was devastated at the thought of missing the fair with the three Amy's. I begged and pleaded with my mother to take me. Then I wrote a suicide note that said, "I'll die if I can't go. I WILL DIE."

July 22, 1977
I've been moping and complaining so she'll take me to the fair. If we don't go and see the chickens and have elephant ears, I don't know what I'll do.

July 24, 1977
Mother took me to the fair! We covered my stitched foot with a plastic bag and rubber band, and then I squeezed into a toddler stroller, so my legs dangled over the front.

Mom pushed me down the midway. We visited the draft horses, saw prize-winning pies, the swine weigh-in, the scarecrow exhibit in my favorite building of small projects, and the chicken flying contest. I love chickens!

We heard the jug band and went to the building that smells like water. It's the conservation building, with the real fish in flowing water and stuffed animals on display. Real stuffed animals, not the ones you have to win. And then we ate elephant ears, corn dogs, and frozen bananas.

We entered sweepstakes, got free fly swatters and pamphlets on water softeners. My mom won a stuffed dog at the mouse game. I held her prizes in my lap as she pushed me through the gravel. We rolled past the horse race game, water balloon game, the dart game, and ring toss. We passed greasy carneys with jack-o'-lantern smiles that whooped and hollered at us, their horse faces leering at us as we strolled by.

"Step right up and win a prize, little lady," they said. "You can't lose at this game! What'd ya do there, little Missy? A little too old to be in stroller, wouldn't ya say?"

I told them I cut open my foot and got stitches. And that I'm 11. All four mocked deep concern as they sucked their Salem's and blew smoke in the air.

They asked me what the heck I did to need stitches.

My mother said in a disappointed voice that I crippled myself during a puppet show, and I chimed in.

"I'm accident prone!"

This was too much. They guffawed with my mother. Then, one of them reached into a secret box behind the booth and pulled out a stock carnival prize—a cheap, pink plastic poodle so thin it dented if held too tightly. He presented it to me as if it was made of gold. I reached up from my stroller and gently took the precious poodle. What a day!

Apr. 15, 2015

I am in my mother's chair as I type this. To my right is her 1958 Smith Corona—the typewriter that linked us for most of my adult life. I can't get over the fact that I've come full circle, living back in the town I couldn't wait to leave 31 years ago. After all the moves to "better" places, jobs, and relationships, how the hell did I end up back here in Indiana? Is it tragic or meant to be? It is a lot to process.

April 27, 2015

It's a good thing I'm not squeamish over rodents. Here at the ranch, Fanny Frou Frou is picking up the slack as the only cat (out of four) that actually hunts. She caught a mouse (I hope it wasn't Francois) and then proudly carried it to my bedroom, jumped up on my bed with it, and dropped it on top of my pajama bottoms. It then ran up the leg of my pajamas. I caught him at my waist band. I took the mouse outside and released him.

April 28, 2015

So, I pulled my big bottle of olive oil out of the lazy Susan to refill my smaller, cuter bottle that's on the counter. Then, I realized there was a piece of garlic, or shallot, in the oil. I look closer. Then, I see that the garlic has a mouth with tiny teeth and whiskers. I hope it's not Francois. Clearly, he scampered up the bottle, peeked inside it as the lid was off, fell in and drowned in olive oil—extra virgin.

April 29, 2015

Today was hard. At three months, the finality of it all hit me hard. I slept on the wicker love seat in front of the house and lost the whole day. I just didn't have the energy to do a thing.

May 21, 2015

From the mundane to the miraculous, there's much to process here at the ol' homestead. Is four decades of personal effects, clothes, tools, bric-a-brac, collectibles, junk, and basset hound paraphernalia the legacy I've returned home to claim? Or is this about coming full circle? I'm now calling the house The Ranch.

June 3, 2015

The house is full of ghosts. Sometimes I swear I can hear my mother call my name.

"Holly! Let the dogs in, will you? Holly! Make some tea. Holly! Elaine Stritch is on TV!"

In the past week, two trees fell in the woods, shifting and cracking and falling hard onto the forest floor. The apple tree, which is still producing, is now 40 years old. I'll never forget my dad perched in it and pruning as my mother shrieked at him from the deck. Must have been about 1979. He'd been in a hit and run accident and his nose was broken and bandaged. He was supposed to take it easy, but no one could keep him down, so he was up in that apple tree pruning.

"Bob, what the hell are you doing now? Get out of that tree!"

"Just a cotton-pickin' minute, Mae!" he shouted back. Right then, a twig snapped back and struck him square on the nose. He flinched, and from his expression you could tell he knew what was coming because no matter your pain, my mother couldn't help herself.

"I told you so!" she shouted.

June 4, 2015

I reached out to my old beau Rick Carlson on Facebook. It was 1985 when I last saw him. He is a house painter and devoted to his church and trumpet. His ex-wife calls him "Trumpet Boy."

Here's his backstory. My senior year of high school, Rick and I met in the symphony orchestra. I flirted with him from second chair of the violin section. On our first date, his tie fell in his soup, twice. He ranked high on the adorability scale and drove a red '59 Chevy made for stargazing. But he was 32, and I was 18. We had a wonderful summer together, but he was ready for marriage, and I was bound for college.

June 5, 2015

What a week at The Ranch. The full story is that a fawn was left next to the Honda I'm selling, which is parked in the weeds. A doe often plants her baby close to humans because predators will be less likely to go after the baby. I waited for the mother and she didn't return.

This fawn is precious. What a magnificent gift to find peacefully resting in the grass. I got milk and a bottle at Tractor Supply and nursed her on the first day. Then, I had her spend the night with me, Ruby, Malka, Galileo, and Fanny.

Ruby is over the moon about the fawn. It can take a few days to get them to nurse from a bottle and it worked the first time I tried, but then the second day it was a no go. She wanted to suckle my chin, not the bottle. She is less than three weeks old, so I contacted the Moraine Ridge Wildlife Rehab Center and they encouraged me to bring her to them. Just like other young animals, it is better for her to be with other fawns her age.

June 7, 2015

I've been slowed down by bronchitis. Two days of prednisone and antibiotics and I'm a force to be reckoned with. Rick Carlson was here briefly to check in on the fawn, who was walking around the kitchen with me. She won't take the bottle and I know she's hungry. If I put her in the bedroom momentarily, she'll bleat loudly. She can't walk on smooth floors or she ends up like Bambi on the ice, her legs all splayed out. Ruby is beside herself with joy over the fawn. I tried to attract the mother with the fawn but she's a no show. The fawn wandered down the hill in the backyard and I went to retrieve her. Ruby tucked her crippled feet under her and shot down the hill like a torpedo.

I was sweating behind the neck and wheezy when I put her in the car with me. Three nights with no sleep and this gurgling, welling bronchial dirge coming out of me, I look and sound like Fontaine in *Les Misérables*. I can't sleep until I've done the right thing, and because I can't give this little miracle of life what she deserves, no matter how hard I try, I call the DNR and confess how I tried to give her back to the wild, but the mother didn't come for her.

The young girls at the center are very nice and one of them will take my fawn home with her and get her to eat. I didn't want to part with her, but I did. She was paired up with another fawn about the same age. I cried all the way home.

I talked to the girls and, as it turns out, *she* is a *he*. Bucks are rarer. He will be released on a 100-acre forest when the time comes, which is better than the woods behind me. What a blessing to have shared a few days with him. Ruby keeps looking for him every time she goes outside.

June 9, 2015

On a musical note, I had a great rehearsal with David Llahm at Nancy's B&B in Harbert Michigan. She sold a successful catering business in Chicago before buying the house and spending eight months remodeling it. There are five bedrooms, and she is booked every weekend in the summer with guests.

What a fascinating page of my life. I started a B&B for dogs in the city, and now, as fate would have it, I have a house on 4 acres in the country. Instead of spending money on things like rent, I'm spending it on a new roof, furnace, air conditioner, stove, flooring, paint, light fixtures, and contractors. There is a staggering amount of work to be done. My mother really let it go to hell. Every single day I confront remnants of the past as I rip out carpeting, clean out and paint closets, walls, and cabinets. My cousin Janice came one weekend to help me carry out an ancient TV that weighs about 200 pounds and make a fire pit. Then we got the salt delivery man to help us haul dog houses off the back deck.

In the basement family room, generations of mice have a hoedown every night, racing across the ceiling tiles when I enter the room. My brother's basement bedroom is now a junk room, and I hate it. The linoleum floor is bare in spots, old birdcages and dog crates litter the room, and the aroma of male cats lingers. Mother used to breed Scottish Fold cats in this room, and I'm not sure it was ever properly cleaned. Eww de toilette. I plan to replace the 43-year-old ceiling tiles and as I start to remove them, mouse turds rain on my head and into my ears. After I put on a mask and my father's pith helmet, I discover just how many mice have made this country house their home. It takes hours to clean up the debris of shreds of insulation, lint, poop, seeds, and two petrified mice.

June 19, 2015

One of my mom's skittish, spooky cats, morose Tuxedo, has a permanent expression of ennui and at twelve years and 25 pounds, slinks and dashes his way through the house, unwilling to be touched. He scrambles like a mad cat to get away from everyone. He's bigger than a raccoon and when he scales the downstairs gate to avoid me, I can see the girth of his feet. Rick Carlson said when I firmly swaddled him,

"You've got guts. I wouldn't pick up that cat. He's crazy!"

In the basement, he sleeps on piles of rugs, and today he tried to hide from me by daintily climbing into a pre-decorated, 4-foot Christmas tree shrouded in a bed sheet. I've been patiently wooing Tuxedo but he is stuck in fear mode. I cherish the times I was able to pin him, pet him, kiss him, and whisper in his ear. Rarely was I able to catch him so I could trim his nails and brush his dander-ridden fur. I need to have a relationship with the animals around me. And he didn't want one.

I remember when Susie and I took a mother cat and her kittens to the Humane Society when my mom had to have her heart surgery. These cats had been living in a room in the basement and they hissed at everyone because my mother never touched them. Because there were just too many animals in the house to care for, we reached out to the Humane Society in LaPorte. When we brought them in, one of the employees, who knew my mother, said, "Your mother's cats aren't socialized and friendly. They are basically feral cats. No one is going to adopt them, so they'll be put to sleep." Those poor kittens. It's not their fault.

June 25, 2015

The borer bees have made the beams on the deck look like bead board. They hover right in front of me, challenging me, like they own the place. One afternoon, while standing on the back deck looking at the yard, sawdust floated down into my hair. I looked up and there was one of these bastards, drilling gaily through the wood.

Pests like these are aplenty out here in the sticks. But I don't kill productive spiders, natural pest catchers, that pull their weight around here. I need all the help I can get. I am very fond of the wolf spider. Talk about pulling something out of your ass. I have a lot of respect for an insect that pulls a string out of her own body to masterfully weave a web on which she lives and catches dinner. I wish I could do that. Imagine all the money I'd save on rent.

When I come back and see her web dashed and limp because of wind and rain, I whisper to her,

"Charlotte, you are an inspiration to us all. Keep working your magic." The next day she's bopping on an even more intricate web, trapping a *smorgasbord* of gnats and mayflies.

July 15, 2015

I'm trying to sell my Honda and several people have expressed interest. Selling my chariot is personal. I want the right person to end up with my wheels. Dan Keane is interested. Years ago, I was close to his mother, Joyce Keane, an accomplished artist whom I adored. Joyce was like an aunt to me. She passed away in 2003. Ever since her funeral, I've kept her memorial card in my glove box, along with the owner's manual, a folder of receipts, and an ice scraper. For some unknown reason, I left Joyce in my glove compartment for twelve years.

Imagine Dan's surprise when I sold him the car and he opened the glove box to find his mom staring at him. I can hear Joyce chuckling.

July 24, 2015

Progress is slow, though my head leaps forward to the day when I can feel contentment. I keep reminding myself that it took forty some years for it to get to this point. It's impossible to fix it in one. I realize now how our family tried to find happiness in objects: collector plates, Toby mugs, Lladros, German Nutcrackers, antique dolls, and holiday décor for Christmas, Halloween, Thanksgiving, Easter, Valentine's Day, St. Patrick's Day, and the Fourth of July. Combined with my Dept. 56 treasures acquired when I worked there editing their magazine, it is just too much. I'm drowning in it all. I've said it before, and I'll say it again. I am done, done, done with all this *stuff*.

And then there's the property, which has been neglected for so long, gnarly, thick vines have wrapped themselves around so many trees, choking them to death. Paths are overrun with barbed vines

and rotting trees. Decades of fallen leaves have clogged the creek which used to flow each spring. These woods were full of wonder when I was growing up.

My sister was here recently on her way to a dog show. I took care of her basset hounds for her. I had put the stacks of *Tally-Ho* magazine published by the Basset Hound Club of America and *The Bugler*, also a magazine about bassets, into the garage for recycling.

"You're not getting rid of those, are you?" she asked, horrified.

"Yes, I'm recycling them," I said. "You are more than welcome to take them home. They're from the 1980s and I won't be reading them."

"I don't have room for them in my car," she said. "Otherwise, I'd take them." She also made a passive aggressive comment I tried to bury.

"I wish Mom had left you the house and me all the money." Nice.

August 1, 2015

I'm watching one of my precious hummingbirds right now hover at eye level, three feet away. We make eye contact every day as I spy on him from my 1960s glider. Fresh sugar water is cooling inside, and I'm watching a storm roll in.

While I do miss Lincoln Square, my Thai restaurants, Mertz Apothecary, and the vibe at the Grind on Lincoln at Wilson, I don't miss the speed bumps in the middle of every block, the cluster fuck of traffic on Western Avenue, the construction zones where no one is working, red light cameras, parking nonsense, and the creepy Armenian who stands on the corner of Campbell and Bryn Mawr waiting for something to happen.

Aug. 11, 2015

I feel like I've unplugged from the world. It's like I'm consumed by this house and all that's in it. The other day, I went through my brother's desk, which has been collecting spider webs in the basement since 1991.

I found his Holiday Inn nametag, Boy Scout and Eagle Scout badges, bullets, a coin collection, and ALL of his report cards, starting in kindergarten and going through his college years at Purdue University. With every picture of him, especially his baby pictures, there's an ache of sadness. A life cut short is pure sorrow.

I came upstairs tear stained, and Daisy, one of my favorite canine clients, had a red flower in the middle of her forehead, like a Bindi, which signifies in some parts of India, a spiritual and religious meaning. The third eye can see that which can't be seen and represents secret wisdom. My dog clients always send me subtle messages.

August 15, 2016
Charlie and Emma, two of my canine clients, were just here from Chicago. Charlie had to wear a diaper the first day because he kept marking the vinyl floor samples from Von Tobel. Phyllis and Rick helped sand, polish, and paint kitchen cabinets and brass hinges. Toby and Bailey, my mother's basset hounds (who normally live with my sister) are here for a few days. Ruby is lounging on one of my latest purchases from Hoity Toity—a 1960's retro aluminum and vinyl glider. It is marvelous!

Sept. 2, 2015
I opened a very old frame, which I believe belonged to my great grandparents. Inside the frame I found a time capsule—four pages of the Sears Roebuck and Co. catalog from 1911. In those days, you could order a tombstone from the catalog as well as radio goods, raincoats, rifles, rivets, union suits, and valves! Clothes for large size men and women are called "Stout Sizes."

September 10, 2015
Phyllis and Rick helped me take down all the kitchen cabinet doors to sand and repaint them Navaho White. Goodbye dark brown cupboards with ugly 1970's handles. I'm replacing the yellow countertops, circa 1972, as well. Lighting is next, and the bedroom vinyl floor planks will be installed on Monday. I can't believe these vinyl floors. Who knew floor shopping could be so fun? Contractor Rich Mormon has been an enormous help, and he's a smart ass. The other day he said,

"My youngest hasn't got the brains God gave a chicken."

The new quartz counters were bought from Lowes, as were the paint, light switch covers, cabinet knobs, transition strips, and vents. Backsplash tiles came from The Tile Outlet in Chicago. I purchased new trim and ¾" base shoe from the Molding Outlet in LaPorte and painted it all myself. I'm a full-service gal—stripping, painting, sanding, and nailing. But no matter how much I accomplish, there's still so much more to do.

I'm looking forward to painting the bathrooms. Rich Mormon advised,

"No pink. The only thing in the bathroom that should be pink is nipples."

Oct. 2, 2015

On Friday, I drove to Kentucky with Jules Wallschlager for a family reunion at her sister's house and pole barn. We ate great food, laughed, sampled bourbon, and went on a madcap hayride with moonshine made by Jules' nephew and brother-in-law.

Jules and I went to Burnheim Forest, where we saw an impressive collection of holly species and wandered the streets of historic Bardstown to check out the Talbot Tavern, Jailers Inn, antique shops, and Mammy's. We had heard from Jules' sister and niece about a medium by the name of Tulip Moon, who is the real deal. On Friday, we just so happened to find ourselves in front of her shop. It can take two years to get an appointment, so when we heard there were two cancellations for Monday morning, we decided to stay another day. Sunday night, we stayed at her sister's house, which is the most charming Kentucky Home way out in the sticks at the end of a winding dirt road. Years ago, it was used for drying tobacco. As we departed Monday morning to meet with Tulip, a huge prehistoric looking bird with a twelve-foot wingspan slowly led us down the dirt road and out of the woods to the main road.

We were both emotionally ready for something extraordinary. Each appointment is a half hour. Her daughter schedules appointments and takes only your first name. There are no cards, crystal balls, or hocus-pocus. Tulip (whose real name is Beth) and I sat at a card table and she drew my aura during the session with pastels.

Right away she knew I meditate. We talked about my highly creative, intuitive nature and then we discussed how my fear and doubt holds me back. And then the spirits started coming.

Honest to God, the first spirit to come through was my mother.

Tulip said, "Mabel, no wait, Mae is here. Yes, its Mae. Wow, she's really direct!" I couldn't believe it. "Mother," I said, "I'm sorry for the hurtful things I've said."

Tulip cut me off and spoke for my mother: "NO! I'm a stubborn woman, and you are a stubborn woman. You are your mother's daughter."

"Why didn't you tell me about Walter?" I asked.

"I don't know who that is," said Tulip, "but your mother said, 'I couldn't speak of it.'"

Then Tulip said, "Daniel, is here. Who is Daniel? Did he die suddenly? I see something with his lungs."

I was stunned.

"Yes, he drowned."

"Don't worry, it didn't hurt," said Tulip. Then she smiled at me and said, "Danny says it didn't hurt." Clearly, my brother told her we always called him Danny.

"Who is David?" she asked.

"I almost married a David and often thought I'd made a mistake by leaving him."

"No, Danny says you did the right thing by not marrying him. NO REGRETS."

Then she said, "Ann or Anna is here, bringing lots of love." I was so glad to hear this. Aunty Ann was a big part of our life and died at 100. In fact, my mother was with Aunty Ann when she took her last breath.

"Do you know an Earl? Oh, wait. I'm sorry. Oril is here," said Tulip.

Talk about specific. There are quite a few photos of Oril in the house and I'd just sent a package of photos of him and Lucille and his

daughter to Barbara Manwaring, who lives in Florida. He thanked me for that because it was "for the greater good."

"Who is Susan?" Tulip asked.

"My sister," I answered.

"Your family says *accept*. Just accept."

"Who is Karen?" Tulip asked. Two spirits are calling you Karen. Is it George? Who is that?"

And then I remembered; my grandparents called me Karen when I was very young.

"My first name is legally Karen. George is my grandfather."

"Can Robert come through?" she asked

"Of course!" I said. "Dad, I'm trying to honor you with what I'm doing in the house."

"You are," he said.

As a group it was suggested I slow down, breathe, stop being such a worrier and don't doubt myself. BELIEVE and finish what I started. Follow through and I'll be glad I did.

"Finish the book?" I asked.

"Yes! Finish it. You are where you're supposed to be. You were supposed to go back to your childhood town and home. And you will marry."

Jules' reading was also powerful, and she's going to get hitched too. We drove back to Indiana with renewed faith in the unknown.

October 16, 2015

I have a new protégé. Her name is Chloe, she's eight and lives three doors down. She stops over every day for chitchat. Today we took feed corn from the field across the street for the squirrels.

Chloe told me that two weeks ago, she and her mother and grandmother saw something unusual. A hawk flew up to the front door of my house, The Ranch, and looked in the window at Ruby. Ruby barked and the hawk flew away. Then the hawk went back one more time to look at Ruby.

"Are you serious?" I asked because I'm aware of the significance. "When did this happen?"

"I meant to tell you before and forgot. It happened two weeks ago when you were away. Oh, and after he left the front door, the hawk flew around your backyard several times." Well, two weeks ago, I was in Kentucky touching base with the familial spirits through Tulip Moon. On the way to the appointment, a huge bird led Jules and I out of the boondocks, down a skinny, winding dirt road.

I have a history with animal spirits. Months before my mother died, I was in the city walking in an alley when a hawk swooped down in front of me and sat on my neighbors' garage. He was close enough to touch. I knew in that moment a big change was coming.

The hawk holds the key to higher consciousness. It is time for me to free myself of thoughts and beliefs that limit my ability. I need to soar above my life and get a greater perspective. Just like the hawk can see in great detail at great distances, I may be able to perceive what others do not. Extra sensory abilities and intuition are supported by the power of the hawk, which is strongly connected to spiritual realms.

March 20, 2016

I am sitting on my couch in the middle of my mother's living room with tears dribbling down my cheeks onto my lap. I knew moving back home to go through the entire house and all its contents would be painful, but I really had no idea just how much. The worst part of it all? No one cares. Really and truly. No. One. Cares.

My mother went to lunch, the movies, and had a team of people that took care of cleaning, mowing, and dog and cat washing. She didn't even do her own hair. Me? I do everything myself. Always have. And because she couldn't bear to throw anything away and kept compulsively squirreling away more random stuff, and my sister won't help in any way, I'm the one left "holding the bag." My mother never had any intention of dealing with all the stuff in this house. I'm convinced of that. I'm the one picking up the pieces and cleaning up the mess she left behind. Feeling so angry about this.

LET GO OR BE DRAGGED

Sometimes renovating the house was a labor of love, at other times, I wanted to take myself out with Dad's Smith and Wesson 686. I labored over every object. I couldn't throw away ancient history like WWII medals, my grandfathers' WWI uniform, my father's engineering certificates, and my brother's Boy Scout patches. It was emotionally draining and not one person went through these items with me. Not one.

It was time to find my tribe in the area. I heard about an open mic at the Acorn Theater in Three Oaks, Michigan, and went. The theater is charming and close to Three Oaks, which is quaint, and I met David Lahm, the piano player for the open mic. Turns out David, who can transpose on the spot and play just about anything, is the real deal. He also is the son of Dorothy Fields. THE Dorothy Fields, the librettist and lyricist who wrote over 400 songs for Broadway and Hollywood films. Musical theater royalty is right here in my midst. This is blowing my mind.

His mother Dorothy Fields has had quite the career collaborating with American musical theater greats like Jerome Kern, Ethel Merman, Cy Coleman, Irving Berlin, Arthur Schwartz, and Jimmy McHugh. She worked with Arthur Schwartz on "Stars in Your Eyes" and "A Tree Grows in Brooklyn." In 1936, she and Jerome Kern won an Academy Award for writing "The Way You Look Tonight." In the 1950s, she won five Tony Awards, including Best Musical for writing the musical *Redhead*. Her story goes on and on. Dorothy and her brother Herbert Fields wrote the book for Irving Berlin's *Annie Get Your Gun*, while Irving Berlin wrote the music. She was best friends with Ethel Merman, and in the 1960s, worked with Cy Coleman to write songs like "Big Spender", "If My Friends Could See Me Now, and "There's Gotta Be Something Better Than This" for the musical *Sweet Charity*. All of this music has resonated with me throughout my career.

What are the odds of meeting someone like David Lahm in Michigan? David has always lived in New York City but visits here a lot as his girlfriend Chef Nancy Watson owns and runs the Harbert House Bed and Breakfast in Harbert, Michigan. Life is full of delightful surprises!

April 14, 2016
Been working on forgiving my mother, my sister, and myself. Without forgiveness, I won't be able to embrace success in life and have loving relationships. I chose the bad boys and bright lights, so here I am, alone on the fringes.

May 27, 2016
I just took care of a Great Dane named Hudson who has Wobbler Syndrome. Ruby was very kind and patient with him. His owners said he preferred to be on the couch or on his bed all day. I took him in the yard for a short walk and he wobbled all over the place for three hours! He was so thankful he gave me love bites.

His owner came to pick him up and put Hudson in the car. When we were inside getting his food, Hudson climbed out of the car, on his own, and went all the way around the house to the back-yard and into the pen, by himself. He didn't want to leave. I am thrilled to have the space for big dogs now. What I would give to have my own Great Dane or Bernese Mountain Dog. The Twins Coco and Charlie have been staying here at The Ranch quite a bit, and this week, Tabitha the Bernese mountain dog was here. Would you believe I painted the hallway with five dogs in my midst? My next task is power washing the enormous deck and staining it.

June 15, 2016
Had an epiphany this week. This house and everything in it, reflects my parents limiting beliefs, emotional stiltedness, fear of not having enough, and secrecy. I always tried to respect them, but so many of their actions and advice negatively impacted me. They were always raining on my parade. I fought tooth and nail to become who I am today. Who would I be if I'd lived the life they wanted for me?

Even if you have struggled with the cumulative effects of family cycles that were an expression of established modes of living and a reflection of the strife your ancestors were forced to endure, you can still liberate yourself from the effects of your family history. The will to divest yourself of old, dark forms of familial energy and carry forth a new loving energy may come in the form of an epiphany. You may one day simply realize that certain aspects of your early life have negatively affected your health, happiness, and ability to evolve as an individual. Or you may find that in order to transcend long-standing patterns of limiting beliefs, irrational behavior, and emotional stiltedness, you have to question your values and earnestly examine how your family has impacted your personality. Only when you understand how family cycles have influenced you can you gain freedom from those cycles.

To truly change, you must give yourself permission to change. Breaking family patterns is in no way an act of defiance or betrayal. It is important that you trust yourself implicitly when determining the behaviors and beliefs that will help you overwrite the generation-based cyclical value system that limited your individual potential. Many people are on the earth at this time to break family cycles, for all of you are true pioneers. In breaking negative family cycles, you will discover that your ability to express your feelings and needs grows exponentially and that you will embark upon a journey toward greater well-being.
—Madisyn Taylor

June 16, 2016

When I was in Minneapolis last week visiting friends, I drove by my old house. The porch is no longer screened in and the garden is overgrown and gnarly. So many elm trees marked for removal on the street. It's sad, but it doesn't disturb me as much as it did when I lost that house. I spent so much time fixing it up. I should've been doing other things with my time because in the end, I didn't make a dime on it—couldn't sell it. Nothing was selling at that time. It took living in a mediocre condo first for three years on Pleasant Avenue (aka

Peasant Avenue) that I fixed up to sell to be able to buy the house in the first place. To think I worked so hard to get it, fix it up, and then lost my little, gingerbread house.

But if I dwell on any of that I'll go mad. I can't dwell on the fact that I lost it. Join the club. So many people got caught up in that mortgage industry fiasco. The house was for eight years exactly what it was meant to be—a starter house.

July 21, 2016

Ruby isn't doing well. She has sickness in her eyes and isn't eating much. I took her to the vet, and he pushed her hernia back in. He said it was harmless for many years but may be causing problems now. Something isn't right inside of her. She's been such a wonderful companion, but I must do what's best for her. I took her to the beach the other day and carried her through the sand to the water and a little girl befriended her. Ruby loved every minute of it.

The vet is coming to the house to help her cross over the Rainbow Bridge, and I just want to die along with her. My mother's wounded warrior, Ruby has been a source of love and support for 13 years. I love the sound of her little feet clicking up and down the hallway, her beautiful nose, and soulful eyes. Honest to God, I never would've survived the last two years without Ruby. Jules, Ellie, Dan, and Amy came by to say goodbye. For me, nothing will relieve the pain of missing her.

October 15, 2016

I had new vinyl floors put into the basement and new carpeting in two of the bedrooms upstairs. The three Romanian workers from Empire were really great. $4900 for all the flooring, tax, and installation included. I had to supervise and then sent them on their way with caramel apples.

The latest plan is that I'm turning The Ranch into a dog-friendly Airbnb. It would be a way to meet people and make money for The Ranch!

November 1, 2016

Ray, who came to my mother's rescue and worked as a handy man for her, stopped by today with corn for the squirrels. His son Nick had also worked for my mom. Ray said,

"Yes, she was certainly tight with her money. I used to tell people, 'I'm paid in pie.' Your mother was very demanding and loved to be waited on."

Phyllis admitted to me that in the past a few people had said to her,

"How can you be friends with that woman?"

Even Donna Burris said this week,

"Your mother used people, but I loved her."

And so it is. I hated how my mother judged people, so I don't want to do the same and judge her. I'll never get the time back I spent feeling wounded from her criticism and verbal abuse, but I also can't harbor resentment. She did teach me self-reliance, how to care for animals, and that my sense of humor would be my saving grace.

Thanksgiving 2016

A tuxedo cat showed up today at the front door. First, it looked in the window at me as I prepared the turkey and said, "Help me." I opened the front door, and it walked in. I explained that I'm preparing a turkey. The cat grabbed the gizzard and ran off with it.

"Hey, you little Mooch!" And the name stuck.

I cooked a 20-pound turkey and all the fixings for my sister and Dan Keane. Did the bake-it-in-a-bag route and it turned out marvelous. Dan arrived with enough liquor for a party of 10, including a homemade punch made with several different types of booze. He admits he's a "booze hound" and has a tumor on his neck he named "Poncho."

I'm grateful to be where I am right now. I'm still manic and hard on myself, but I've let go of a lot. My purpose now is bringing the best of myself to the world any way I can. So, what if I'm not doing theater or writing projects at this moment? I can live each day artfully, instead. I can create all kinds of art. No more packing up and leaving town because it's greener over there. It is only greener in patches. Be. Here. Now.

June 2017

A client of mine has requested I take their dog Buddy, who has horrible separation anxiety. This dog doesn't play or bark. They have two boys, a struggling business, and they don't have time to give Buddy what he needs. They can't confine him in a crate because he's busted several and his own teeth in the process, just like our shepherd Major did years ago. Buddy is part shepherd and collie and the saddest dog I've ever met. I hope I don't regret taking him in but I have to. The husband showed up with Buddy and handed him over. The wife was too distraught and didn't come. I'm his third owner and, I've decided, his last. Buddy is very thin and when I asked the husband what kind of food they fed him, he said, "Food from the dollar store." Oy vey gevault.

The first thing I did was buy him quality dog food. In his first week with me, he ate an entire stick of butter and then threw it up in the car. The next week, he took half an Entemann's coffee cake off the counter. But I got there in time. He has a thing for carbs. On the rare occasion that I leave him alone in the house, he will pull a loaf of bread off the counter and carry it to his bed without opening it, saving it for later.

Buddy is terrified of water and has separation anxiety so severe he is always within a few feet of me. He is tolerant of other dogs and submissive. When Fionn, Maybelline, and Domino come to The Ranch, they all run around together. Buddy also protects me and the house. I have no doubt that, since I've rescued him, he will rescue me.

September 7, 2017

I'm turning the house into a dog friendly Airbnb so I can still run my dog business. People in Chicago are willing to pay more to board their dogs than people in LaPorte. I have also taught acting and improv for Lubeznik Art Center. None of these things on their own make much money, but I've been juggling numerous part time jobs for years.

Summer 2018

I have been consumed by this house, and now I'm focused on the four acres surrounding it. I hired a guy who calls himself "Hillbilly" and his tall assistant "Lurch." They're going to cut down and prune dead and overgrown trees. He wears those boots with the spikes and, wielding a chainsaw, shimmies up the trees, a cigarette dangling out of his mouth the whole time. He works with two fellas and they carried away six truckloads of branches taken from the trees in the front yard. Now I can see the field across the street!

I've planted perennials, created a raised bed for a small garden, replaced the rusty fencing and poles in the dog pen, and power-washed the 60-foot deck three times. It had never been washed or stained since the 1980s. Mom's friend Christine Graham has been my savior and helped me stain it. WHAT. A. JOB. She also helped me remove wallpaper and paint my bedroom and the basement.

The other day, the kitchen flooded with dirty water because the pipes under the basement floor have crumbled and broken down. I was supposed to head into Chicago to take care of a senior Jack Russell Terrier and had to rearrange things. I hired a guy to install new pipes that run across the ceiling of the basement. This fella also replaced the aluminum vent pipe that carries lint out of the back of the dryer.

"You are so lucky you didn't have a fire," he said. He pulled out two huge clogs in the pipe, each the size of a human head, made of compacted lint, seeds, and mouse feces. It was gross. The negligence of her letting this house go to shit infuriates me. She had the money to pay people to help, but she refused. A house is a living thing that cannot be ignored. And this one speaks to me. "Thank you for lovingly restoring me to my former glory."

July 5, 2019

Went to my 35th high school class reunion on June 29. Classmates who organized it did a bang-up job. Now that we've all been clobbered by life, most of the posturing is in the past. Chatted with a classmate named Will Link. His smile and eyes triggered a memory. He is so familiar to me, but I can't remember why. It's easy being with him. We went to dinner and spent time together on July 4.

He is unlike anyone I've dated. He's modest, smart, upbeat, positive, kind, and very tall. He's six-five. We grew up three miles from each other, and he said he thought I was unattainable. HA! He went to grade school at St. John's Lutheran School, which is the church I grew up in. He was a Delta Tau Delta like my brother, and he goes by his middle name, like me. His legal first name is Frank, one of my favorite names.

His dad Bill Link was an engineer like mine, and his mother Nancy has three degrees and is an amazing artist. He's lived and worked all over the country, so he has the perspective and life experience I find attractive. The best part? He appreciates and supports me and all the wacky things I am. And as accomplished and smart as he is, he isn't the slightest bit arrogant. I can't stand arrogance in a man.

He doesn't complain about my dog clients either. He sees that all these dogs touch my heart in different ways, just by being who they are. Dixie and Lily are often here. The first time they stayed at The Ranch, Lily slept in the front closet. She just hunkered down on top of all my shoes and boots. Dixie is a lightbulb short of a chandelier and doesn't understand the concept of walking at the end of a leash. All the other dogs walk together effortlessly, but not Dixie. She plants herself, leans away from the direction we're heading, and won't budge until she thinks about it for four minutes. Then, she lurches forward a few feet and stops again. She prefers eating to walking. One day I made a batch of chili and foolishly left it on the counter to cool. I went to run an errand, thinking I'd pushed it far enough away. I came home and thought, "Wow, I'd really love some of that chili right now." The container was gone. Instead, I found it on the floor so clean, it looked like it'd been through the dishwasher. All those beans, I thought, my God, the diarrhea I'm going to have to clean up. I looked at them, beached on the kitchen floor. It didn't take long for me to find out who ate most of the chili. It was Dixie.

Dixie loves to push her tongue hard against the glass of the sliding door and drag it. Between my dog and people clients, there is never a dull moment. Haps is the house clown and had no social skills when owners Connie and Don rescued him. He marched into

The Ranch with attitude, strolled into the master bedroom, and peed on the drapes. After a lecture, he never did it again.

August 15, 2019

Will came to visit and brought his Cavalier King Charles Spaniel Bebe, who's lost a few teeth, so her tongue hangs out. She's adorable and all the dogs get along. Will and I make a great team. We attack the minutiae of life with great aplomb and have big ideas for future adventures. He helps me with things around the house, and we take short excursions with the dogs to the Indiana Dunes. He is easy to be with, loves music, and I adore his family. I prayed for a sign that he has the character, strength, and stability to be my guy. And lo and behold, my childhood diary opened to the following page, written 40 years ago.

August 1979

Carla Strom is moving away to Florida. I've known her since kindergarten. She invited me and Amy Burris to her going away party. A boy my age and his friend came over to Carla's at 9:00 that night. I'd met him on my school bus before and I truly like him. He supposedly likes me, but I knew he was going with another girl. I could tell Amy liked him too because she never stopped talking to him. I wanted to be with him alone, but Amy never left us two alone. About 10:00 the boys went home. Will, the one I liked, wanted me to go to his house, but Carla wouldn't let me leave. That night, I pictured Will and I together, and I so wanted to go to this house to spend time with him.

IF YOU BUILD IT, THEY WILL COME

Turning my childhood home into an Airbnb introduced me to people I wouldn't otherwise have met. My profile attracted a diverse population of straight, gay, and transgender people of all ages from all over the United States, as well as Poland, Singapore, Ireland, Germany, and Canada. And all the while, I could have my doggy pals there too.

One of my favorite guests was Fred, who stayed with me on his way across the country. His truck was loaded with construction supplies, so the first time he stayed, he helped me repaint some of the kitchen and remove an unsightly handicap bar from the bathroom. Then, he made a delicious goulash and an almond tart. He shared stories about his children and his Swedish mother, who taught him to cook and bake.

The second time Fred stayed, he fixed the garage door, which sprung a giant bolt, making it impossible to open the door. Then, he met Frank, my possum, who lived in my garage for two months in the dead of winter. I opened the kitchen door that leads to the garage, and there was Frank, standing in the garbage can enjoying leftover cake from Ann Sathers.

"Oh, my God he's huge!" said Fred. "And I didn't expect him to be right on the other side of the door!" I told Fred that I visit my marsupial to pet him and talk about the rent. But when I realized Mercury is in retrograde (Mercury rules communication and expression), I advised Frank to stay for another three weeks to avoid misfortune. Frank was grateful and curled up in the warm blanket I provided.

I had personable, comical guests, like the couple from Chicago who look like Mr. and Mrs. Claus. The husband accidentally locked the bathroom door and didn't want to bother me, so he peed outdoors for a night.

In the morning, they sheepishly admitted they'd locked the bathroom door and the wife had spent time looking for a solution on the Internet. She'd written out instructions on how to unlock the door.

"You should've just knocked on my door!" I said. "I wouldn't have been upset. There's another bathroom downstairs, and all we need to unlock the door is a bobby pin." I poked one in the hole and it unlocked. We all laughed ourselves silly and went to breakfast in LaPorte.

Many people admitted to feeling drawn to The Ranch. People prayed with me, brought me gifts, and left plants, gems, stones, and notes of gratitude. One woman had just lost her father and sister and felt their spirits were following her across the country. Every picture we took had an orb in it. She and I listened to Judy Garland on her record player and danced around the kitchen with our dogs.

Two transgender fellas stayed one night on their way somewhere else. Ever eager to please, I thought they were at dinner, and opened the door to draw the curtains and put mints on pillows. They both sat up, startled. I apologized profusely for rudely walking in on them, but they weren't all that concerned.

An empowered warrior woman named Antonia admitted she was leaving her husband and on a spiritual journey. She smudged my house with sage and did a reading. When she stood in front of my mother's 1950's Smith Corona typewriter she said,

"There's a lot of energy coming off this typewriter. Put it in the basement for a while."

My mother wrote a lot of letters to me on that typewriter, so it was hard for me to do it, but I did. Antonia and I went on a boat ride with energetic, resourceful Steve Doig, another guest, who lived with me for months when he first moved to LaPorte. Before Antonia left, she gave me a beautiful turquoise bracelet, which I still wear because it reminds me of her.

Mary, from Ireland, stayed for five days and nights because a film crew was shooting a horror film in her Chicago home. When she wasn't reading or smoking on the deck, Mary cracked jokes and commiserated with me about the state of Chicago and the self-absorbed, fixated-on-money nature of American culture. I'll never forget her Irish accent, phrases, and eye rolls. At one point, we made her bed together, and she said,

"You've got to turn the pillow this way or your dreams will escape, or some such rubbish."

During my last summer, an easy-on-the-eyes, arborist resembling Tarzan stayed numerous times when in town for work. He and I went to the pine trees to retrieve bags of pine needles to help nourish the struggling ornamental cherry in my front yard. When an ailing tree came down in the front yard during a storm, I paid him to cut it up and stack it. I made him muffins, and he taught me about trees. His calm energy was marvelous.

Traveling nurses stayed with me, and one guest named Corey stayed on three different occasions for two months at a time. I'll never forget the night Dan Keane popped by for a cocktail and didn't realize Corey was living at The Ranch. The hallway was dark, and Corey, six-one, with dreadlocks to his waist, came strolling down the hallway into the kitchen.

"Whoa!" said a startled Dan upon seeing Corey. I introduced them, and all three of us laughed at Dan's reaction. Corey looks intimidating but is anything but. He's smart, works hard, checks in with his mother regularly, and travels to Europe every chance he gets.

One of my favorite repeat guests is Arielle, who was 4 the first time she stayed. She and her mother Stephanie come from Chicago for bike rides and festivals. There were no closed doors when Arielle visited. She'd just stroll right in and start talking. They stayed in the green room so she could look out the window at the lights in the tree and because that's the room with the Fisher Price farmhouse in the closet.

Wild about Mooch and Buddy, she tucked them into their beds and talked sweetly to them. We went apple picking at Garwood's Orchards and blueberry picking at The Blueberry Patch in Sawyer, Michigan. During one stay, after we scoured the lawn for pinecones and shiny stones, she sat in my lap and I zipped around the yard on my ride-around tractor. She squealed with delight. It is the smallest things that bring her the greatest joy. And that is a life lesson I embraced at The Ranch. My joy came from helping people have a calm, joyful experience and be one with nature.

I loved being an Airbnb host, and for four years, it **was** fun juggling it all. And then it wasn't.

Will and I had gotten serious, the threat of Covid became very real, the real estate market was going gangbusters, I was tired of being a cleaning lady, and my father's coin collection disappeared. A guest had stolen from me.

I *needed* to sell The Ranch. I asked my sister Susie, since she's a professional photographer, if she'd take photos for the real estate listing. She can't. She's off to a dog show, so I hired someone through my realtor.

October 31, 2020

The house was on the market for three days and I have a buyer. The showings were fast and furious. Thanks to my hard work, they offered a little more than asking price, $300K, which is pretty good for a small town. My efforts over 5.5 years doubled the value of the house.

TO HELL AND BACK

Nine days after I found a buyer, on an unseasonably warm November 9, Will and I took a walk down the country road I've walked and biked since the second grade. As always, we walked off the road, in the gravel. Just as I was about to turn around and head home, a car coming up from behind us struck me hard with a sickening *thud*. The car had brushed Will's arm and he reached out for me, but I was airborne, like a rag doll, and thrown ten feet through the air into a ditch.

From head to toe, I vibrated like a giant tuning fork. In shock, I looked at my left leg, which resembled a Picasso painting because it was broken in two places. I immediately thought of French gymnast Samir Ait Said, who broke the same bones—tibia and fibula in 2016 while vaulting during the men's team qualifications. My zig zagged leg looked like it was made of rubber.

"Holly can you talk? Oh, my God, I can't lose you. Talk to me!" said Will. I couldn't speak because I had five broken ribs. I just looked into his eyes, confused. Buddy ran to the Huber household to get help, and Chloe, my 13-year-old neighbor, came running outside in her bare feet. What went through my head was not *I just got hit by a car and my leg is broken*, it was, *Chloe really needs to start wearing shoes outdoors. It's November.*

Will called 911 for the ambulance.

"Don't worry, it's going to be okay. The ambulance is on its way. Can you talk?" I whispered four shameful words whose subtext is: I'm an idiot for flying by the seat of my pants and deserve to be in this predicament.

"I don't have insurance."

Then I heard a shaky voice from the opposite direction.

"Oh, my God, I'm so sorry, I didn't see her!"

"You hit her," said Will to the driver. "Don't go anywhere."

The ambulance arrived in eight minutes as well as four deputies. My leg was stabilized, they put me on the gurney and loaded me in. Will assured me he'd follow me to the hospital. I whispered to him,

"Call Bob Swan and cancel the dinner party."

"I'll call him," said Will, "and see you at the hospital."

As we made our way to the Franciscan Hospital in Michigan City, the voice in my head said loudly,

"After all the shit you've been through, you cannot die like this. You can't be taken out by a moron on his cell phone. That's a lame ending. It would be much better to die onstage, like actress Irene Ryan singing, "I've got a whole lot of livin' to do."

The team of people at the Franciscan Hospital were amazing. A CT scan surveyed the damage and a nurse applied on my behalf for Medicaid. What a blessing **she** was!

"Karen, we're going to have to remove your spleen," said a voice.

"Don't call me Karen," I said. "Call me Holly. And don't I need my spleen?"

"Your injuries are too severe to do these surgeries here," she said. "So, we're flying you to University of Chicago Medical." I was zipped up in a big blue bag, loaded into a helicopter, and ear plugs pushed into my ears. I imagined Bob Fosse dancing with a zig-zag leg.

"I used to be a dancer!" I shouted. *SLAM!* went the door of the helicopter. And then I puked into a paper cone.

My traumatic collision with a car resulted in a "pleural effusion, splenic laceration, and fracture of distal end of left tibia and unspecified fracture morphology." In other words, a lot of damage. Within 24 hours, I had two major surgeries. Orthopedic doctor Nicholas Maassen, M.D. inserted a titanium rod and screws into my left leg, and I had a splenectomy. From my abdomen to my chest, they slit my stomach like a fish.

The surgeries were extremely intrusive, and five broken ribs made sitting up or moving excruciating. I hardly noticed the road rash on the back of my left leg or the stitches in various parts of my body. But the nurses who cared for me and Physician Assistant Dr. Rebecca Friedlander provided the compassion and professionalism that saved me. They were my lifeline. Humbled and grateful doesn't begin to describe how I felt in their presence. These people give so much back, and what have I been giving back? Was it too late to become a nurse?

I used to be terrified of needles, but I got over that. Gabapentin, Oxycodone, Naloxone, Ondansetron, and Pantoprazole managed my pain. While the fear of having no spleen and catching Covid never left me, staff entered wearing Hazmat suits and meticulously changed gloves. I thanked every nurse that pricked and poked me, as well as the x-ray technicians for procedures done at all hours of the night, and the trauma doctors for their visits, no matter how brief. Weekends in the trauma department are chaotic at University of Chicago, where 60% of the trauma patients are gunshot victims.

After four days in the ICU, I was moved to a different floor. Will worked from the hospital as best he could and emptied my bed pan when I allowed it. He was a saint and stayed with me before he was sent home due to Covid restrictions. When he told me Medicaid had accepted me, I wept.

Nine days later, I went home on a walker with a lot of drugs, but I felt terrible. When I bent over and talked, I sounded like I was underwater. I had shortness of breath, chest heaviness, couldn't lie flat and had a dry cough—symptoms of a pleural effusion. On December 2, I was readmitted when an x-ray revealed that the left chamber around my lung was half full of fluid, threatening to collapse my lung. Because of Covid, Will wasn't even allowed to escort me to my room. We said goodbye at the double doors.

A steel tower of power held IV's, oxygen, and ticking metal boxes that monitored my every move. First, 1.2 liters of fluid were removed from around my lung with a needle, the doctor explaining the procedure to a group of medical students. I posted a picture on Facebook of what that much fluid looks like in a bag, and my sorority sister Stephanie Gesse Paradine said, "Is that merlot?"

I laughed so hard I peed in the bed.

There was too much fluid remaining, so a pigtail tube (chest port) was inserted in my back near my broken ribs. Dreadful. Within two days, it was decided I needed a bigger tube. The dread of these procedures as I waited for doctors to show up was horrible. The area was numbed, but I was wide awake as they placed another chest port inside. Burning, throbbing, and searing was the pain as tears rolled down my face. A nurse by the name of China held my hand and got me through. Now, I had two plastic suitcases by my side that measured expelled lung fluid.

My whole world was room 3038. To distract myself from pain and self-pity, I thought about my best friends, possum rescue, and going to Ireland with Will. I thought about how hard I'd worked on the house, doing things like unhooking a chair lift from the basement stairs, pulling the pink carpeting off the basement steps, sanding the stairs and staining them. I remember how I spent weeks shopping for the right front door, paint colors, flooring, backsplash, light fixtures, window treatments, and landscaping. I thought about how I let my mom's handy man move into the basement for over two years when his father died and his girl-friend kicked him out. My "cellar dweller" helped me as much as he could when he wasn't drinking. I had fixed up my brother's bedroom and basement family room for him and tried to feed him because he was so skinny, he looked like he might blow away. He lost his son and brother while he was living with me, and then he got cancer. I recalled all the projects we had going on—the dog pen fence, posts and gate, the bushes in the front of the house, removing a dilapidated chicken house, the mowing, the weed whacking, the plowing, the painting. All during this, he was fighting his own demons.

I felt gratitude for my friends Stephanie and Gordon Medlock, who would be taking care of me when I got out of the hospital. I thought fondly of all the concerts I'd done with Bob Swan and his opera company at the Acorn Theater. I thought about how much I loved doing *Love Letters* with Bob, of how I'd played Madam Arcati in *Blithe Spirit* at the haunted Valpo Memorial Opera House and Dotty/Mrs. Clackett in *Noises Off* at the Dunes Summer Theater. With such gratitude, I thought about the generous cast and crew at Fourth Street Theater, where I played Marge in a stunning production of *Bridges of Madison County*. Several of us from the production won NIETF (Northern Indiana Excellence in Theater Foundation) awards. And I teared up thinking about the caba-rets I'd done with an eclectic group of locals longing to be heard at the Harbert House Bed & Breakfast with David Lahm and Nancy Watson.

Being back in LaPorte, a place I couldn't wait to leave, had been a gift with lots of blessings. I'd found my way back home and was able to be myself in a way I couldn't as a child. My hometown had become dear to my heart, and I'd made peace with pain from the past.

All this swirled around in my brain, and then I got more bad news. The doctors aren't satisfied with the results, so I was put under again, an arc carved into my back so they could explore the area around my left lung. When I awoke from this surgery, I couldn't move. Lifting my arm wasn't an option because any movement tugged on the tubes in my back near my broken ribs. I lay plastered to my hospital bed. I prayed and cried. A male nurse entered my room one night and said, "Why are you crying? Don't you know? Everything happens for a reason." I glared at him. There was one reason why I was hit by a car—negligence on the part of the driver.

Without a spleen and the damage around my left lung, I'm immunocompromised and would endure lots of vaccinations and warnings to stay away from people. Catching Covid could be disastrous. At night, I looked out the window at the icy, pale sky, thinking about my years living near Wrigley Field and Lincoln Square. I'd had some grand adventures and made some wonderful friends in Chicago but, of **all** the things I wanted to leave behind, my spleen wasn't one of them.

Visitors weren't allowed, but the nurses and Rebecca kept me going as I fought thoughts of revenge against the idiot who struck and diminished me. I was determined to rise above my injuries.

While I'm in the hospital, Will, his brother John, and good friend Jon Ulmer move everything out of the house to the garage and prepare for the moving van. Will spackles and cleans the house for the new buyer. I'm still in the hospital when the moving van comes and loads my life into the truck.

As for the driver, he passed the breathalyzer test. Later we'd learn he has no assets and a rap sheet of reckless driving, speeding, and a DUI. He would suffer no consequences.

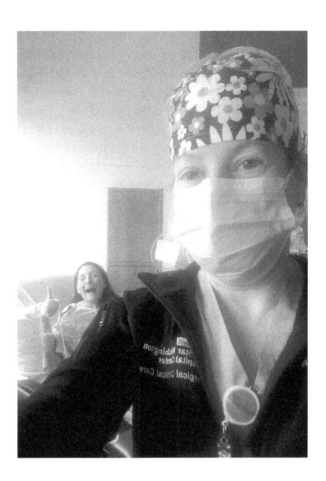

BETTER, NOT BITTER

"You do not get to choose the crisis that transforms you."

Thank God for that! Who would choose getting hit by a car? Of all the trauma I'd survived in my life, this one changed me the most. Suddenly, I wasn't the same person. What was once important to me—acting and singing—now seemed selfish and trite. Priorities shifted. My emotional and physical health became a priority, as did my purpose. What contribution to the world would I leave behind? I'd already screwed up procreation.

My need to be liked and appreciated by everyone came to an abrupt halt. I couldn't give energy anymore to people who don't care about me. My sister's daughters, my two nieces, hadn't communicated in any way with me since their grandmother's death five years ago. They didn't even call me after I'd been hit by a car. I have made some mistakes with them and lived far away from them when they were growing up, but I didn't deserve this. They had time to post things on Instagram and Facebook but didn't have five minutes to call their aunt who almost died? It was time to face facts. I mean nothing to them.

I would learn later that while I was in the hospital, my sister got herself a lawyer. She'd send an email to the title company and everyone involved in the closing except me, telling them to split the proceeds of the house in half. Her reasoning?

"Well, you're getting married to someone who will pay your expenses, and you're moving to a warmer climate, and you're going to get a big settlement from the accident." I don't even know how to respond to her distorted thinking. There was never a mention of how much work I did to renovate and sell the house. She would show up to load some things into her van, and then she'd lead a smear campaign against me, telling people I "stole her inheritance," which wasn't true. I owed her $43,000 dollars. I should have paid her the entire buyout amount in the beginning, but because she got $200K from our mother I thought she'd be okay with waiting till I sold the house. She's my sister, after all, and I invested half my inheritance to update the house. But I made a mistake, and she would make me pay for it. In the end I paid for everything and did ALL the work. I would have to hire a lawyer to settle it all, another expense I didn't need. To be done with it, I did pay her more money, and yet, I'd still be depicted as the bad guy. I would get back the money I put into the house and not much more for 5.5 years of blood, sweat and tears.

It became crystal clear that going forward, I had to let go of toxic relationships with people who don't care about me. No more defending myself to people who are determined to misunderstand me. No more reacting to barbs from people who are unaware, consumed with their own pain or jealousy. It was time to let them all go. If someone wants to throw a stone, I won't throw it back. I'll collect them all and build a bridge to somewhere better.

Let go the people who are not prepared to love you. This is the hardest thing you will have to do in your life, and it will also be the most important thing. Stop having hard conversations with people who don't want change.

Stop showing up for people who have no interest in your presence. I know your instinct is to do everything to earn the appreciation of those around you, but it's a boost that steals your time, energy, mental and physical health.

When you begin to fight for a life with joy, interest, and commitment, not everyone will be ready to follow you in this place. This doesn't mean you need to change what you are; it means you should let go of the people who aren't ready to accompany you. If you are excluded, insulted, forgotten, or ignored by the people you give your time to, you don't do yourself a favor by continuing to offer your energy and your life. The truth is that you are not for everyone, and not everyone is for you.

That's what makes it so special when you meet people who reciprocate love. You will know how precious you are. The more time you spend trying to make yourself loved by someone who is unable to do so, the more time you waste depriving yourself of the possibility of making this connection to someone else.

There are billions of people on this planet and many of them will meet with you at your level of interest and commitment. The more you stay involved with people who use you as a pillow, a background option, or a therapist for emotional healing, the longer you stay away from the community you want.

Maybe if you stop showing up, you won't be wanted. Maybe if you stop trying, the relationship will end. Maybe if you stop texting, your phone will stay dark for weeks. That doesn't mean you ruined the relationship; it means the only thing holding it back was the energy that only you gave to keep it. This is not love, it's attachment. It's wanting to give a chance to those who don't deserve it. You deserve so much, there are people who should not be in your life.

The most valuable thing you have in your life is your time and energy, and both are limited. When you give your time and energy, it will define your existence. When you realize this, you begin to understand why you are so anxious when you spend time with people, in activities, places, or situations that don't suit you and shouldn't be around you, your energy is stolen.

You will begin to realize that the most important thing you can do for yourself and for everyone around you is to protect your energy more fiercely than anything else. Make your life a safe haven, in which only "compatible" people are allowed.

You are not responsible for saving anyone. You are not responsible for convincing them to improve. It's not your work to exist for people and give your life to them! If you feel bad, if you feel compelled, you will be the root of all your problems, fearing that they will not return the favors you have granted. It's your only obligation to realize that you are the love of your destiny and accept the love you deserve.

Decide that you deserve true friendship, commitment, true and complete love, with healthy and prosperous people. Then wait and see how much everything begins to change. Don't waste time with people who are not worth it. Change will give you the love, the esteem, happiness, and the protection you deserve."

—Anthony Hopkins

THE COMEBACK

Physically and emotionally, it was not an easy time after the accident, but I shouldered on. Just as I expected, my rescue dog Buddy became my therapy dog. In eight months, I was hit by a car, spent a month in the hospital during a global pandemic, sold my childhood home, moved to Nashville, Tennessee, got engaged, got married, and met new family of my biological father who found me through MyHeritage. The universe brought my true ancestry to light and, as it turns out, half of me hails from Switzerland! I'm going to start yodeling.

True to form, as I write this, I'm grieving the loss of The Ranch. It didn't matter that it was too much house and property for one neurotic, middle-aged broad with ADHD. Selling it felt like a betrayal. Would the new owners take care of the trees and hummingbirds and possums that relied on us? I cried like a baby when I locked the door for the last time. I remembered the trees as saplings when my sister, brother, and I stood in front of them for a photo before a new school year. I could see my mother standing on the front porch waving goodbye to me like she always did. I could see my Father walking to the end of the driveway with a shovel in his hand, my brother Danny washing his car, and my sister Susie weeding the flower bed. Time stood still. It was impossibly hard to drive away.

I asked myself, *wasn't it time, after so many disappointments, to build a life and a future with a good man?* Will proved himself seaworthy before we even talked about marriage, doing the "in sickness" part before the "in health." He stayed by my side at the hospital and through my recovery. He has been the rock I never had. Yet, I was afraid because of the failures that had come before.

I would spend the next year recovering from the accident and staying away from people per doctors' orders. I would learn that my dear friend Jeanne Fowerbaugh Chandler died of cancer the same day I left the hospital, a devastating blow I can't accept. My brilliant friend

Frank Lortscher died of glioblastoma after 18 months of suffering, a beloved man I called my spiritual advisor, Wes Cline, died of Covid, and my cousin Steve Manwaring lost his battle with diabetes. I grieved the loss of so many people I loved. I grieved the loss of The Ranch and the loss of who I used to be because I am not the same.

On the other side of so much trauma and the fact that I couldn't stand long or physically handle a traditional wedding and reception, Will and I decided to not make a big noise about our nuptials. We didn't need a wedding party, an audience, or a band. Our wedding was about us. On July 11, 2021, my dear friend Scott Carter gallantly walked me down the candle-lit aisle of the historic Little Church of the West in Las Vegas, to stand by Frank William Link. It was 114 degrees outside. Music played, and vows were exchanged. Then, we strolled down the aisle, my left leg (broken just 8 months ago), leading the way out the door into a bright future, full of promise.

A QUIET THING

When it all comes true, just the way you'd planned
It's funny, but the bells don't ring.
It's a quiet thing.

When you hold the world, in your trembling hand
You'd think you'd hear a choir sing!
It's a quiet thing.

There are no exploding fireworks, where's the roaring of the
crowd?
Maybe it's the strange new atmosphere
Way up here among the clouds.

But I don't hear the drums, and I don't hear the band
The sounds I'm told, such moments bring
Happiness comes in on tiptoe
Well what'd'ya know?
It's a quiet thing
A very quiet thing.

—John Kander and Fred Ebb, lyrics from *Flora The Red
Menace*

ACKNOWLEDGEMENTS

Without the encouragement and expertise of the following people, this book would never have been published. Thank you from the bottom of my heart: Mary Dean Cason, Kathi Davis, Phyllis Roach, Kate Ryan, Roger Nygard, Michael Altobello, Debra Ganshaw, Perrin Post, Vera Mariner, Pamela Hill Nettleton, and Frank Will Link. I am forever in your debt. Seriously.

ABOUT THE AUTHOR

Holly Schroeder Link is an accomplished actress, singer, and writer who works professionally in theater, cabaret, the voiceover industry and publishing. Holly lives in Nashville Tennessee with her husband Will and fur babies Buddy and Mooch.

ABOUT THE PUBLISHER

The Sager Group was founded in 1984. In 2012, it was chartered as a multimedia content brand, with the intention of empowering those who create art—an umbrella beneath which makers can pursue, and profit from, their craft directly, without gatekeepers. TSG publishes books; ministers to artists and provides modest grants; designs logos, products and packaging, and produces documentary, feature, and commercial films. By harnessing the means of production, The Sager Group helps artists help themselves. For more information, visit TheSagerGroup.net

MORE BOOKS FROM
THE SAGER GROUP

Artifex Te Adiuva

CPSIA information can be obtained
at www.ICGtesting.com
Printed in the USA
BVHW031325150122
626361BV00005B/131